**Duncan Mackenzie**
**Andy Baron**
**Erik Porter**
**Joel Semeniuk**

W9-BRS-294

# Microsoft® Visual Basic® .NET 2003

## KICK START

**SAMS**

800 East 96th Street, Indianapolis, Indiana 46240

# Microsoft® Visual Basic® .NET 2003 Kick Start

International Standard Book Number: 0-672-32549-7

Library of Congress Catalog Card Number: 2003092629

Printed in the United States of America

First Printing: November 2003

06   05   04   03          4   3   2   1

## Trademarks

## Warning and Disclaimer

## Bulk Sales

Sams Publishing offers excellent discounts on this book when ordered in quantity for bulk purchases or special sales. For more information, please contact

**U.S. Corporate and Government Sales**
**1-800-382-3419**
**corpsales@pearsontechgroup.com**

For sales outside of the U.S., please contact

**International Sales**
**1-317-428-3341**
**international@pearsontechgroup.com**

**Associate Publisher**
*Michael Stephens*

**Executive Editor**
*Candy Hall*

**Acquisitions Editor**
*Todd Green*

**Development Editor**
*Mark Renfrow*

**Managing Editor**
*Charlotte Clapp*

**Project Editor**
*Andy Beaster*

**Copy Editor**
*Kezia Endsley*

**Indexer**
*Erika Millen*

**Proofreader**
*Tracy Donhardt*

**Technical Editors**
*Andy Baron*
*Erik Porter*
*Joel Semeniuk*

**Team Coordinator**
*Cindy Teeters*

**Interior Designer**
*Gary Adair*

**Cover Designer**
*Gary Adair*

**Page Layout**
*Point n' Click Publishing, LLC*

# Contents at a Glance

# Table of Contents

# About the Author

**Duncan Mackenzie** is the Visual Basic Content Strategist for Microsoft's developer Web site, and as such, he chooses topics, acquires content, and writes material for the Visual Basic developer center on MSDN (http://msdn.microsoft.com/vbasic). Duncan writes the monthly MSDN programming column "Coding 4 Fun" and has authored a variety of other articles on MSDN. He has been the author or co-author of several books on Visual Basic (and related Microsoft technologies), including *Sams Teach Yourself Visual Basic .NET in 21 Days*, *Platinum Edition Using Visual Basic 6.0*, *Word 2000 VBA Programmer's Reference*, and more. In addition to writing, Duncan has also been active as a Visual Basic trainer and has taught many courses ranging from intermediate to advanced VB programming.

# About the Contributors

**Andy Baron** is a Senior Consultant and project manager at MCW Technologies (http://www.mcwtech.com), a Microsoft Certified Partner. Andy also creates training materials for AppDev (http://www.appdev.com), and he has been awarded Microsoft's MVP designation since 1995.

**Erik Porter** is a Microsoft .NET MVP and Lead Software Architect at Aptera Software. He has been developing enterprise .NET applications since Beta 2. He also gives presentations on Windows Forms, ASP.NET, and ADO.NET, as well as other .NET subjects across the Midwest. He can be contacted at erik@apterasoftware.com.

**Joel Semeniuk** is a MSDN regional director and vice president of software development, heading up all new development projects for ImagiNET Resources Corp., a highly specialized Microsoft Gold Partner in ECommerce and Enterprise Systems based in Canada. Reach him by email at JoelS@ImagiNETs.com.

# Dedication

*Writing a technical book is a rather time-intensive undertaking, which often leads to some late nights as I try to juggle my writing, my work, and my family. I would like to dedicate this book to my wife Laura, and my son Connor, who were very understanding when I needed to work, and even understood when I needed to relax after a long week of working all day and writing all night. Thanks to them, I get to write technical books; books that I hope will be useful to many developers; developers who need to get their own work done so they can go home to their own families.*

# Acknowledgments

I would like to take this opportunity to acknowledge all of the great work by my co-author and technical editor, Erik Porter. Erik not only did a great job checking my code and my facts, but also rose to the challenge of writing several chapters himself. I would also like to thank Joel Semeniuk and Andy Baron, the other two co-authors who provided me with great content for this book. Finally, I would like to thank the great editing team that made sure this book was published even when deadlines were tight and material was a little (or more than a little) late in arriving; Mark Renfrow, Todd Green, Andy Beaster, and Candy Hall—all of whom worked quite hard to create this book.

# We Want to Hear from You!

As the reader of this book, *you* are our most important critic and commentator. We value your opinion and want to know what we're doing right, what we could do better, what areas you'd like to see us publish in, and any other words of wisdom you're willing to pass our way.

As an associate publisher for Sams Publishing, I welcome your comments. You can email or write me directly to let me know what you did or didn't like about this book—as well as what we can do to make our books better.

*Please note that I cannot help you with technical problems related to the topic of this book. We do have a User Services group, however, where I will forward specific technical questions related to the book.*

When you write, please be sure to include this book's title and author as well as your name, email address, and phone number. I will carefully review your comments and share them with the author and editors who worked on the book.

Email:      feedback@samspublishing.com

Mail:       Michael Stephens
Associate Publisher
Sams Publishing
800 East 96th Street
Indianapolis, IN 46240 USA

For more information about this book or another Sams title, visit our Web site at www.samspublishing.com. Type the ISBN (excluding hyphens) or the title of the book in the Search field to find the page you're looking for.

# Introduction

Visual Basic has slowly evolved over the years, incorporating a variety of features and moving itself into the world of "enterprise" development, but everything was being built on top of an already existing foundation. This is not unusual; most development tools progress in this way, but it has the unfortunate side effect of garbage accumulation. New versions of the tool try to stay compatible with, and therefore have to keep all the less-than-perfect aspects of, the previous versions. To rewrite the language from scratch is almost unthinkable. The work required would be enormous and breaking compatibility with the user's existing code is bound to make you unpopular. The benefit of such a move would be a completely clean and new implementation that can keep the good and throw away the bad parts of the existing language.

That is exactly what Microsoft has done in the move from Visual Basic 6.0 to Visual Basic .NET. They have rewritten the language to create a clean version that does away with the garbage built up over a decade of successive language improvements. That means a hard learning curve for people who were experienced in the previous version of the language, but the end result is worth the effort. This radical shift makes this a great time to get up to speed on Visual Basic .NET, as the concepts taught in this book will have a much longer lifespan than material covering the previous version.

There are many benefits to this change, all of which were motivators for this decision, but the most significant motivation was the need to conform to the new .NET environment. As a necessary bit of background before you can jump into the specific changes that occurred between Visual Basic 6 and Visual Basic .NET, you'll learn more about .NET, including what it is and how Visual Basic fits into it.

# What Is .NET?

At first glance, .NET might seem to be just a marketing concept, a way of avoiding yet another number at the end of Visual Basic, but it is much more than that. .NET represents an entire platform on which you can develop applications. Just as the operating system provides a level of base functionality to applications (such as the capability to read files from a hard drive or floppy disk), .NET is a layer that exists beneath your programs and provides a set of base services and functions. The .NET environment can be broken into these three key elements:

- The Common Language Runtime (CLR)
- The Common Type System (CTS)
- The Microsoft Windows .NET Framework (no real acronym for this one)

## .NET BRINGS LANGUAGE INDEPENDENCE

The fact that your Visual Basic .NET code is compiled into IL, as is J# or C# code, means that once you have compiled your program it is no different than the output from the equivalent program written in another .NET language. The language a program was written in ceases to be relevant once it is compiled, a fact that is very important when you are dealing with multiple groups of developers using different languages. Although I would certainly suggest as much standardization as is feasible in your organization, a compiled .NET component, regardless of the language it was written in, can be used from another .NET project.

The Common Language Runtime is the underlying system that takes the code you have written in Visual Basic .NET (or any other .NET language) and executes it within a controlled environment. The Common Type System enforces a set of types across any .NET compatible language, which allows easy interoperability between programs written in different languages (such as C# and Visual Basic .NET). The Framework includes a set of class libraries available to any .NET compatible programming language. These class libraries provide all of the base functionality that you need to write your applications (including data access, file IO, network communication, and so on). Code that is created to be executed by the CLR is also known as *managed code,* because it executes within a controlled environment whereby security, memory usage, and other aspects of the code's behavior can be monitored and constrained.

The CLR itself does not deal directly with Visual Basic .NET code. Instead, your code is first compiled into an Intermediate Language (IL). That IL is compiled into native machine code by the CLR when it needs to execute your program. IL sounds a lot like Java's bytecode concept, and there are many similarities between .NET's concept of managed code and Java's Virtual Machine technology (generally referred to as the JVM). There is no doubt that those similarities exist, but there is also a key difference. .NET code is actually compiled down to machine level instructions (assembly code) and then executed within a controlled environment, whereas Java bytecode is an interpreted language whereby each programming instruction is evaluated and executed by the JVM. The process whereby the IL for your program is turned into machine code right when it needs to be executed is known as *just-in-time* compiling and is often referred to as *JIT*.

# What has Changed from Visual Basic 6 to Visual Basic .NET?

The single most important change in Visual Basic .NET is that it now targets the Common Language Runtime, meaning that you cannot create anything but managed code using this programming language. That is certainly not the only difference between Visual Basic .NET and Visual Basic 6.0 though. There are several key areas of change:

- Enhanced OO programming capabilities

- Data types and type safety changes

- Other language changes (changes to the For/For Each loops, new conditionals, new operators)

- COM is no longer the underlying object technology in Visual Basic

- New types of applications (Windows Services and Console Applications)

- New error-handling model

- New data access model

- New Windows development model

- New event-handling model

- Built-in Web development

# What This Book Covers

We will cover each of these areas as we go through this book, but we won't be covering them one at a time in isolation. Instead, we will be combining various topics (such as Windows development and event handling) so that you can see all of the changes in a useful and practical context. The breakdown of chapters in this book is as follows:

- Chapter 1, "Introducing Visual Basic .NET 2003," covers installing Visual Studio .NET and includes a detailed walkthrough of the new IDE.

- Chapter 2, "Visual Basic .NET Language Changes," covers the changes in language syntax and behavior from VB6, new language features, changes from VB6's data types, and data type conversion.

- Chapter 3, "Building Windows Applications," is a meaty one. Chapter 3 covers the new Windows Forms model for developing Windows interfaces, and the techniques for working with more than one form at a time in Visual Basic .NET.

- Chapter 4, "Working with Files," uses a simple Windows application to illustrate three key concepts; how to work with files (read/write), how to manipulate strings in .NET, and the new .NET way of error handling.

- Chapter 5, "DataBinding," covers the basics of the new .NET data access technology (ADO.NET), as well as how to set up data binding with a Windows Forms application. Once the basics are completed, the next section of this chapter introduces more complex topics in data-binding, including creating a Master/Detail form, doing data binding without the drag/drop controls from VS.NET, and correctly processing updates to the database through your application.

- Chapter 6, "Data without the Binding," covers the final set of topics around data access, including calling a stored procedure, directly executing SQL, and other data tasks outside of a Windows interface.

- Chapter 7, "Object-Oriented Programming in Visual Basic .NET," introduces the set of OO functionality now available in Visual Basic .NET and explains how each feature can be used to create your own classes. At the same time, it covers a new type of application in VB .NET, the Console application, as we read and write values from the command line.

- Chapter 8, "Building Custom Controls," digs into a very important VB topic—developing custom controls/components, the equivalent of ActiveX controls in the .NET world.

- Chapter 9, "Integrating with COM," covers how .NET applications can work with COM objects (such as DLLs created in VB6) and how COM clients such as VB6 can access .NET objects. Throughout this chapter we will cover strategies for gradually migrating existing VB6/VBScript/ASP applications into the .NET model. The use of ADO 2.6 in a .NET application (through this interoperability layer with COM) is also covered in this chapter.

- Chapter 10, "Advanced Topics," digs into a few of the less common Visual Basic development topics including the basics of developing Web Forms in VB .NET, creating COM+ applications, working with XML, and ending with coverage of developing and consuming Web Services.

- Appendix A, "The Upgrade Challenge," covers two of the key tools for moving your code from Visual Basic 6.0 to Visual Basic .NET; the Upgrade Wizard and the Visual Basic 6.0 Code Advisor.

For every chapter, there are related resources available on MSDN and other Web sites, but it is hard to provide useful links inside a book. You can't click on a book so I've created a "Related Resources" set of pages on my personal site at www.duncanmackenzie.net. Check it out for some great additional reading.

# Introducing Visual Basic .NET 2003

## Getting Ready to Code

Before you can do any work with Visual Basic .NET, you have to install it, and this section walks you through the process and the important notes about installing it onto your system.

### Choosing an SKU/Edition

If you have not purchased Visual Basic .NET 2003 yet, you need to determine which edition is right for you. Visual Basic .NET can be obtained on its own as Visual Basic .NET Standard, but it is also included as part of any of the editions of Visual Studio (Professional, Enterprise Developer or Enterprise Architect). With all of the extra features included in Visual Studio .NET, it's probably best to purchase it rather than buy a standalone copy of Visual Basic .NET Standard. The other option is to buy a copy of Visual Studio on its own, or purchase an MSDN subscription instead, which includes Visual Studio in addition to many other Microsoft software products for developers. You can go to the Web and check out the options at http://msdn.microsoft.com/vstudio/howtobuy/choosing.aspx, but I can certainly give you my blunt opinion. I am biased of course, because I work for MSDN at Microsoft, but when you look at the prices yourself you will quickly see that the MSDN subscription is the best way to get Visual Studio Professional or higher. The cost difference at the time Visual Studio .NET 2003 was released was roughly $120 U.S. more for a Professional level MSDN subscription than for buying Visual Studio .NET on its own. MSDN was offering a rebate if you choose to have your subscription delivered on DVD, which reduces the difference to almost nothing. Regardless of whether you obtain it with or without the MSDN subscription, the second part of my blunt opinion is that you should purchase Visual Studio Professional or higher. The lower edition, Visual Basic .NET Standard, is cheaper but it is limited in several key ways, including the inability to create custom user controls or library projects, making Professional the minimum level you should obtain.

## Installing and Configuring Visual Basic .NET

You should have several CDs or a DVD (depending on where you obtained the product) from which you can install. You can also install from a network location, but the process is the same in each of the three cases, with the major difference being a bit of CD switching if you happen to have the multiple-CD version.

The first screen you see when you insert Disc 1, or run setup from the DVD or network, is a dialog box that lists four separate steps (see Figure 1.1).

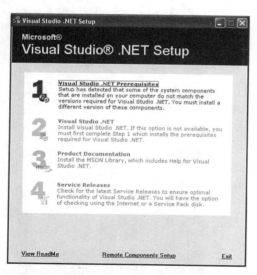

**FIGURE 1.1**   The process of installing Visual Studio .NET is broken into four main steps.

Step 1 is the "Windows Component Update" (WCU), which updates the operating system components of your machine to the level that .NET requires. You will likely need to run this step before any of the other items become available, so click the first option on the setup dialog box to start the update. If you are using a multiple-disc install, the system will prompt for the WCU disc. After you provide that disc, the installation will begin. I will not go into the exact details of the WCU setup, because the setup process is dependent on the current state of your machine. Some of the possible installs include service packs for Windows, MDAC 2.7 (updated data access components), and Internet Explorer 6.0. One item that will be installed for most systems is the .NET Framework (version 1.1) itself, which does not include the Visual Studio .NET IDE, but provides the Framework classes and support-ing files required to run .NET applications. It is worth noting that you need to have already installed IIS onto your machine (along with the Front Page Server Extensions) before running this first step if you want to have ASP.NET functionality. You should not worry if the setup tells you that nothing required updating; through Windows Update and other mechanisms, it is quite possible that you have updated the required components yourself. Depending on which components are required, the install program might also need to reboot your computer one or more times.

When this installation completes, you will go back to the original setup dialog box, as shown in Figure 1.1.

To install Visual Studio .NET itself, click Step 2 to start the next part of the installation. You will be required to enter your product key and to accept or reject an End User License Agreement (EULA) before the main installation can start. After you supply the required information and agree to the EULA, you will see many options where you can choose which elements of Visual Studio .NET you want to install (see Figure 1.2).

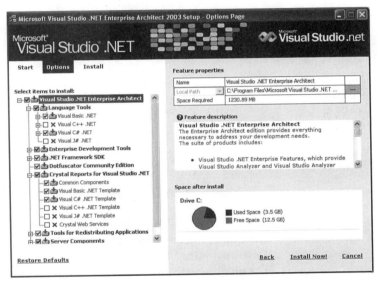

**FIGURE 1.2**   You can choose which Visual Studio .NET components you want to install.

Figure 1.2 shows the install options screen of Visual Studio .NET Enterprise Architect, so a few of the options will be missing if you are installing a lower edition, but overall you should see the same list. If you plan on programming mostly in Visual Basic .NET, I suggest selecting the same options as you can see in Figure 1. 2. The first selection worth noting is the choice of Visual Basic and Visual C# in the Language Tools options. Visual C# is not required, but you will find that many code samples will be available in this language, and it is more likely that you will experiment with C# than C++. You can also select Visual C++, but it's best do so only if you reasonably expect to use it because it takes up a larger amount of disk space than Visual Basic or C#. Next, make sure that you select all the options available under Enterprise Development Tools, Server Components, and Tools for Redistributing Apps. I will not go into each of these options, but by selecting all of them you ensure you have all the features available in your version of Visual Studio.

After you make all your selections, click the Install Now! link at the bottom of the dialog box to start the installation. Various bits of text describing the features of .NET are displayed as the install progresses, finally ending with a completion screen (see Figure 1.3). If anything goes wrong during the installation, it will appear on this screen.

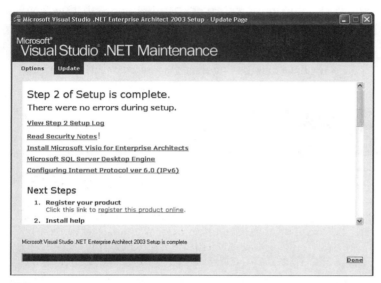

**FIGURE 1.3**    If anything goes wrong during installation, you are informed of the problem at this screen.

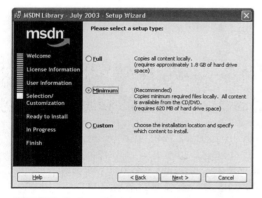

**FIGURE 1.4**    The MSDN libraries, containing a great deal of useful documentation, articles, and samples, can be installed locally for increased speed.

When you return to the initial setup screen, the third choice is available, Product Documentation. The Product Documentation option installs MSDN in one of three ways, Full, Minimum or Custom. Leave it at the default setting of Minimum, which requires access to your CD, DVD, or Network install location, or if you have enough drive space, switch it to Full (see Figure 1.4). Running MSDN from the install location is slower than installing it to your local machine, but the decision is usually based on available disk space instead of speed.

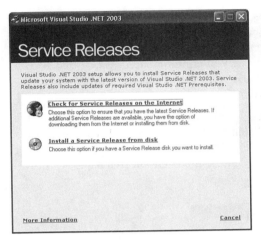

**FIGURE 1.5** The Visual Studio .NET install program can download and install updates from the Internet.

Once the main install is finished, you will be returned to the starting screen where the fourth choice is waiting. Clicking this option, Service Releases, takes you to another dialog box (see Figure 1.5), where you can choose to install updates from the Web or from disk. If you have Internet connectivity, I recommend choosing the first option to ensure that you have the most recent list of updates. Once that update completes, I also suggest visiting windowsupdate.microsoft.com and applying any recommended fixes.

Visual Studio .NET is now installed, and should be ready to run, so you can move to the next section where you will get started writing a bit of code.

# Introducing the New IDE

If your main programming experience has been in Visual Basic 6.0 or earlier, the new Visual Studio .NET IDE will seem a little alien to you. As an evolution from the previous version of Visual Studio, the interface has more in common with Visual C++ 6.0 than with Visual Basic, but all of the features you need (and more) are there. When you first fire it up, Visual Studio will attempt to customize itself based on your background and preferences by asking you to select the appropriate "profile." The choices include several that may be useful for a Visual Basic developer, such as the aptly named "Visual Basic Developer" profile or even the "Visual InterDev Developer" profile. The real trick is to make sure you choose the Keyboard Scheme for Visual Basic 6, otherwise all of your memorized keyboard functions won't work inside Visual Studio .NET.

*SHOP TALK*

**SETTLING INTO VISUAL STUDIO**

Personally, I never leave any of these settings at the default. I pick the Keyboard Scheme for Visual Basic, and then when I am back in the IDE I start off by clicking Auto Hide All from the Window menu. This causes all of my various tool windows to automatically retract/minimize to the sides of the IDE when I am not using them and leaves me with the largest possible area for my code. Then, from that starting point, I eventually turn the auto-hide feature off on a few tool windows and play with the sizing until I get it exactly right. Changing the keyboard scheme alone is enough to confuse another developer sitting down at your machine, especially if they are more keyboard than mouse focused. The right configuration for you is dependent on your screen size and the type of development you do, but Visual Studio .NET offers many options to ensure that you are able to set everything up exactly how you want.

For now, choose the Visual Basic Developer profile, and you can come back to this page later to change these settings if you want. Click the Projects tab (along the top of the Web page) to leave the profile settings page. What you are currently looking at is the main work area of the Visual Studio IDE, a general location that holds a variety of content, such as code that you are editing or Web pages that you are designing. It also includes a built-in Web browser, which is used to display help and other HTML content.

On the home page (see Figure 1.6), you have several useful options. The first tab, Projects, is the page that will be shown whenever you open Visual Studio. Designed as a launching pad for your work, this page provides both a list of recently opened projects and a link to create a new project, enabling you to get going with a single click somewhere on this page. For now, choose the Online Resources tab at the top of this page.

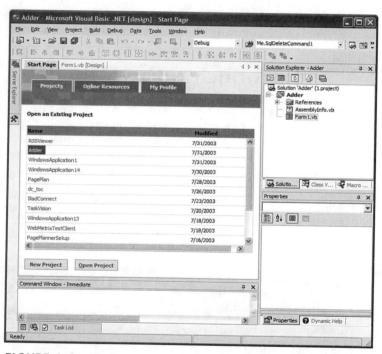

**FIGURE 1.6**    The home page provided by Visual Studio gives a functional view of projects you have recently opened.

Once you get to the Online Resources page, navigational options appear along the left side of the page. These options include the following:

- The ability to search for code samples by keyword or type (from the Getting Started page; see Figure 1.7).

- Details about the new features of Visual Studio .NET. What's New links to various online resources such as newsgroups (Online Community).

- A live news page about Visual Studio and other developer-related topics.

- A direct link to doing a Web search (Search Online).

- A link back to the profile selection page you were shown by default on the first run of the IDE (My Profile).

All these are valuable resources for a Visual Studio developer, making this home page a good starting point for many people. However, if you feel like adding to these options or totally replacing the entire set of pages, the complete source of the default page is made available for you under \Program Files\Microsoft Visual Studio .NET 2003\Common7\IDE\HTML. A note of warning though—the default pages are not simple, and it would be easy to damage them beyond repair. Make a copy of the directory as a backup before you start to customize!

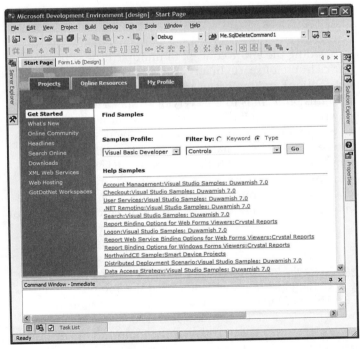

**FIGURE 1.7**  The Getting Started Page lets you search for code samples right from within Visual Studio .NET.

## The Main Windows of the Visual Studio IDE

As useful as this home page is, it is only one of the many windows available as part of Visual Studio and you are going to walk through most of them in this chapter. With the Visual Basic Developer's profile chosen, you have several windows visible already: the built-in Web browser, the Solution Explorer, the Properties, and the Toolbox, along the left side. The other windows, which I will discuss in today's lesson, but which are not visible by default in the current profile, are as follows:

- Object Browser

- Command/Immediate

- Task List

- Class View

- Server Explorer

Later chapters cover a few other windows as they become relevant.

### Common Window Features

All the features of these windows, including the entire concept of multiple little windows, revolve around making the most efficient use of space. In any IDE, and especially in Visual Studio. NET, the number of available options and tools is nearly limitless, but the area of your monitor is not. One solution to this problem is to get every developer a 21-inch (or larger!) monitor. For some strange reason, that still has not caught on, so other methods have been developed. One such method is to divide the options available to the developer into different windows, which is the approach taken by Visual Studio. NET. Now, the goal is to make the placement of these windows both easy and flexible enough for developers to create their ideal work environment. Each of these individual windows is referred to as a *tool window*. The members of a tool window all share some common features, such as the capability to be docked/undocked, hidden, and combined into tabbed groups of windows. They also can be resized in various ways.

### Docking/Undocking

With the Visual Basic Developer's profile selected, the Solution Explorer and Properties are both flush with the right side of the encompassing Visual Studio, and the Toolbox window is flush to the left side (see Figure 1.8). The placement of a window flush to another boundary is described as *docking* that window. While docked, the window is locked to that boundary along one or two sides (two sides if docked into a corner). Any of the tool windows in Visual Studio .NET can be docked, and there is no limitation as to which edges of the application they can be docked to.

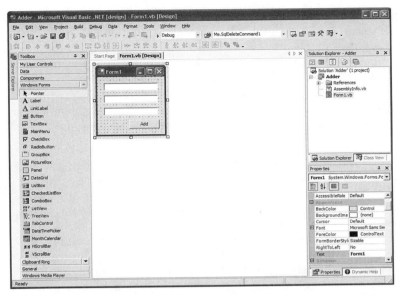

**FIGURE 1.8** When Visual Studio.NET is set to the Visual Basic developer's profile, it arranges its windows in a close approximation to Visual Basic 6.0's IDE.

To move a docked window to another area of the screen, you can click and hold the mouse on the title bar of the tool window, and then drag the window to the new position. While you are dragging the window, an outline will appear on the screen to show where the window would be placed if you were to release the mouse button. To dock the window to another side of the IDE, simply drag the window, continuing to hold down the mouse button, to a border of the IDE and release the mouse button when the window's outline shows the desired result. On the way, you might have noticed that the outline can look as if it was not docked to any portion of the IDE. If you were to release at this point, the tool window would become *undocked*, also known as a *floating* window, at which point it is no longer attached to any of the IDE's borders. When you are undocked, you can re-dock a window by following the same procedure that you just used.

It can be tricky to get a docked window back into the exact place from which you moved it, so here is a little tip: Instead of dragging a window to dock and undock it, double-click the title bar. This will undock a docked tool window, or take a floating window and put it back into its original place.

### Hide
Docked or undocked, the windows still take up space on your screen, but it is possible to hide or close individual windows that you do not want to have visible. Each tool window has an X button on it, similar to the regular close icon on other windows. Clicking this button

closes the tool window, removing it from the screen. To get the window back, you will need to use a menu option. For instance, if you click the X button on the Solution Explorer, it will disappear from view. To get it back, you need to select Solution Explorer from the View menu (or press Ctrl+R). Not too difficult, especially for a window that you don't use often, but what about those windows that you might not be using right at this moment, but do use frequently? The Visual Studio.NET IDE provides a way to recover the screen space used by those windows, while still making them easily accessible—the auto-hide feature. Each docked tool window has an icon on its title bar that looks like a small pushpin (see Figure 1.9).

**FIGURE 1.9** Every tool window has a small pushpin that enables you to lock the window in an open position.

This is a toggle button that controls whether the window should be automatically hidden when not in use. By default, the Server Explorer window is set to use this feature and therefore shows up simply as a gray tab or button along the left side of the IDE. Hovering over this tab with the mouse pointer will cause the full Server Explorer to become visible, sliding out into view. Any tool window with the auto-hide option turned on will automatically be minimized into a tab along the side of the IDE on which it is docked. The hidden window will be brought into view whenever the user moves the mouse over that tab, meaning that the window will only take up space when it is needed. This feature, along with the menu option Window, Auto Hide All, is what I use to configure Visual Studio to my desired appearance. This leaves maximum space for the main window, where code will appear when you have work open. Such an extreme interface might be unnecessary when working on a large monitor, but, as a laptop user, I find it perfect.

### Tabs

Another space-saving feature, multiple tool windows, can be combined into a single area of the screen, where they will automatically become individual tabs in a multi-tab window (see Figure 1.10). In the Visual Basic Developer's profile, several windows have already been combined (the Solution Explorer shares space with the Class View window, and the Properties and Dynamic Help windows are similarly configured), but any combination of tool windows is possible.

**FIGURE 1.10** Tabs enable you to have many tool windows open while using up the same amount of precious screen space.

To add a window to a group of tabs, or to create a tabbed window, simply drag one tool window (by clicking its title and dragging) onto another, releasing the mouse button when the outline changes to indicate a tabbed window, displaying a small tab extension at the bottom of the outline. Removing a window is done in a similar fashion. Simply drag one of the tabs away from the group until the outline loses the tab indicator, and then drag to the desired new location and release. Once a window has been added to a tab group, you can change the order of the tabs by dragging them left or right. Note that when you drag a window within a tab group, you will not see any helpful outline to indicate where you are moving the window.

### Resizing

Any tool window can be resized, but, if the window is docked, it can only be resized along its undocked borders. To resize a window, move the mouse pointer over the edge of the window, until the pointer turns into a resizing indicator, which shows the direction of resizing allowed. When the pointer indicates that you have the mouse in the right position, click and drag to extend or retract the window's border to the desired size. Note that resizing between two docked windows is really changing both windows because one must shrink to allow the other to expand.

### Toolbox

One of the more commonly used windows, the Toolbox, provides a listing of various text snippets, user interface elements, and other items that are provided for you to add into your projects. The Toolbox in Visual Studio .NET isn't all that different than what you would have been used to from Visual Basic 6.0, but it has a few extra features. First, the selection of items shown depends on what is being edited in the main window of the IDE. For instance, if nothing, or just the Web browser, is selected in the main window, the only available item in the Toolbox is the Pointer icon. This icon, which is always present, is provided as a way to deselect any other item in the Toolbox window. If you were editing something, such as the HTML of the Visual Studio home page (right-click in the Web browser and select View Source), additional tabs will be added to the Toolbox window. In the case of HTML editing, an HTML tab has been added (see Figure 1.11); it contains a variety of items representing different HTML tags.

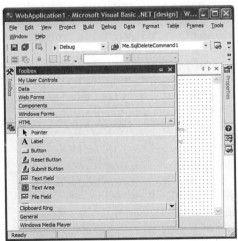

**FIGURE 1.11** When editing HTML, all of the common HTML UI elements are available through the Toolbox.

Any item, with the exception of the special Pointer item, can be used in one of two ways:

- Click and drag the item into the editing window (releasing when you have moved the mouse to the desired location).

- Double-click the item, which results in the item being added to the editing window at the currently selected insertion point (wherever the cursor was positioned in the editing window when the item was double-clicked).

Both these methods of using items are available for any type of document being edited, but if a graphic user interface (any visual, non-text document such as a Windows Form) is the current document, the preceding two options behave slightly differently and a third option also is available:

- Clicking and dragging the item onto the visual document works the same as with text, but instead of a cursor insertion-point, you see an actual outline of the item as you move your mouse over the document.

- Double-clicking also works, but, because a visual document does not always have a currently selected insertion point, the new item will be created in the upper-left corner of the document.

- A third option, not available with text editing, is to select the item by clicking it once, highlighting it in the Toolbox, and then clicking and dragging on the visual document. This outlines the size and location at which you want the item to be added to the document and the new item is created accordingly.

## THE NATURE OF THE VISUAL STUDIO IDE

There is a bit of vagueness to the preceding descriptions, which might make you wonder whether the Toolbox is more difficult to use than it seems. Well, the vagueness is a result of the nature of the Visual Studio IDE, because it can service a wide variety of programming languages, not all of which are even available today. With this in mind, the exact behavior of the IDE (or any part of it, such as the Toolbox) is difficult to describe. However, you can be confident that it will always work in the general fashion described previously, regardless of the language that uses it.

I will walk through an example of using the Toolbox with a visual document later in today's lesson, as you create a Windows form as part of your first application using the IDE. The Toolbox is capable of holding any arbitrary snippet of text, in addition to the provided parts for HTML editing, forms development, and many other types of work, which means that you can create your own items that represent sections of text. This feature is a useful way to take some piece of text (which can be, and likely will be, code) that you expect to use often, and make it easily available.

To accomplish this amazing feat of productivity, select the desired text in the editing window (which might involve typing the text first), and drag this selection onto the Toolbox window. Whichever tab you drag, its text will determine where your newly created item will appear. As shown in Figure 1.12, the item will display some boring and meaningless default name, such as "Text: Dim x as …", but you can right-click it and select Rename Item to provide a proper description. Voilà! You now have a new, custom item in the Toolbox, which you can use whenever you want simply by dragging it into the editing window.

**FIGURE 1.12** Code, HTML, or other text snippets can be placed on the Toolbox and then used (dragged into code and HTML editing windows) just like any other Toolbox control.

The Toolbox, as with the rest of the IDE, has many additional options that I won't be covering, such as the capability to add more tabs (tabs are those sliding sections of the Toolbox window), rename tabs, and change your view of any section's icon list. These other features are accessible through the Toolbox's context menu (the right-click menu), and also are documented in the IDE help files. If you want to add controls to the toolbox, such as existing .NET or COM/ActiveX components, you can right-click and select Add/Remove Items.

### Command/Immediate Windows

Do you ever find yourself running the command console (or *DOS window*, as some like to call it) to accomplish a task? For many people, some tasks can just be done faster using the keyboard and a command-line interface than using the mouse to navigate icons, menus, and dialog boxes. Because programmer productivity is the ultimate goal, any method that might be quicker is worth trying. Visual Studio .NET includes a window that provides two console-based ways to interact with the IDE. One has been part of Visual Basic for some time, the Immediate window, and one has been present in Fox Pro for many years and has finally been added to Visual Studio, the Command window.

In terms of usage, these are really two windows, but they have been combined to make things a little bit more confusing. You can think of them as two windows (I know I am going to), after you have learned two key things: how to switch the mode of the window (from Command to Immediate and back again) and how to determine which mode the window is currently in. First things first—let's make this window visible; select View, Other Windows, Command Window from the menu, bringing up this new window.

This window, now titled Command Window, should contain only a blank line proceeded by a > prompt (almost exactly like the command console, or DOS prompt that you are used to). This window is now in Command mode, and you can enter any command you want and execute it by pressing Return. To switch this window into Immediate mode, you can just type the command **immed** (and press Return or Enter) at the provided prompt. Now, the window will have switched into Immediate mode, distinguishable from the previous state by the addition of - Immediate to the window's title bar and the removal of the > prompt from the actual window text. To return to Command mode, type **>cmd** and press Return (yes you have to include the > prompt yourself). Now that you know how to switch back and forth between these two modes, you can look at the purpose and use of each mode.

The Command mode of this window allows you to control the IDE using typed commands— for example, typing **File.NewProject** to accomplish the same task as selecting the File, New, Project menu item. A console interface can often be faster than a graphical user interface. This duplication of functionality is provided as a potential way to speed up your work inside the IDE. A large number of commands are available, but the quickest way to find many of them is to go through the names of the visible menus. After you have typed a name (such as Edit, or File), add a period, and you will be given a drop-down list of available commands for that menu name. Here's a short list of commands worth knowing:

```
File.NewProject
File.SaveAll
Window.AutoHideAll
```

The Immediate window provides the capability to evaluate code statements directly (immediately!). This enables you to enter a single line of code, and see the results without having to create an entire sample project. This feature is usable when you are in Break mode, which is when you have stopped the execution of a program in progress. Let's create a quick sample project, in which you will use a breakpoint to cause program execution to stop on a certain line of code.

You will use the Command window to start this example, just to get a feel for how it might be useful to you in the future. Make sure that the Command window is visible and in Command mode by selecting View, Other Windows, Command Window from the menu bar. The Command window should now be visible, and have a > prompt showing that is it in Command mode. Type the following command **File.NewProject** and press Enter. A dialog box appears, prompting you to create a new project. Select the folder named Visual Basic Projects from the list on the left and the individual project type labeled Windows Application from the box on the right. Click OK to close the dialog box, creating a new blank project.

The project you have created contains only a single Windows form, and you have yet to add any code of your own. Under the covers though, Visual Basic has placed a small amount of code into your form already, the little bit of work that is required to create and initialize the new blank form. You can see that code by right-clicking the new form (in the center window of the IDE) and selecting View Code. This will add and select a new tab in the center window, a code window that displays the code associated with this form. Because you have added nothing to this form, the code is limited, but it is enough for the example.

Find the area of the code marked with "Windows Form Designer generated code" and expand it (it should be displayed as a box, with a plus symbol next to it, this is known as a Region). Find the line InitializeComponent(), and then select the line End Sub below it. Now, you want to mark this line as having a breakpoint, so that code execution will pause or "break" when it hits this line. There are three ways to mark the line. One is to click in the margin (the light gray area on the left side of the code window), another is to right-click the code line and choose Insert Breakpoint, and the third is to use the keyboard shortcut for this function by pressing F9. Using whichever method you want, add the breakpoint, and you will see a red dot appear in the margin next to the line. This dot indicates the presence of a breakpoint.

With this breakpoint in place, you can run the project, and the execution will pause when it hits this line. As with the breakpoint, there are three main ways to start a project: One is to use the Toolbar button (which looks like the play button on a CD player or VCR); another is to use the menu option Debug, Start; and the third is to use the keyboard shortcut F5. Of course, which option you use is up to personal preference. Many programmers find that, in the long run, the keyboard shortcuts are the easiest way to access the more common functions.

When you start the program running, it will quickly stop and display the line of code that you marked with a breakpoint. Now, you are in Break mode, as indicated by the [break] in the Visual Studio IDE's title bar. The yellow arrow that you can see in the margin of the code window indicates the line that is about to be executed (run). At this point, you can switch the Command window into Immediate mode and try it.

If your Command window was visible before running the project, it should still be present, although the layout could be different as certain windows are automatically opened when you are in the midst of a running project. If the Command window is not visible, open it by using the menu option View, Other Windows, Command Window. Click the window to select it (making it the active window in the IDE) and type `immed` (followed by the Enter key) to switch the window into Immediate mode. Now you can type in any Visual Basic statement, and it will be evaluated immediately (hence the name). Try the following statements:

```
? Me.Width
Me.Width = Me.Width * 2
? Me.Width
? 3 + 5
? 3 = 5
```

Using the up and down arrow keys while you are in the Command/Immediate window does not always move you to different lines within the window. Instead, if you have started entering some text already, you can cycle through commands you have already executed. If you do select a past line (in the window) and start to add text to it, a copy of that line with your new changes will be automatically created at the bottom of the window. This makes any text before the last line of the window effectively read-only.

Notice the ? in front of some of the preceding statements? This indicates "print" and, without it, Visual Basic does not know what to do with statements that return a value. For instance, 3 + 5 will evaluate to 8, but, without the print statement, 8 is not a valid Visual Basic command. On the other hand, Me.Width = Me.Width * 2 will work without the ?, because it is a valid assignment statement. Try that statement out before continuing.

Press F5 to make the code execution continue past the breakpoint, and the form will appear on the screen, wider than the original size if you executed the sample statements given previously. As you can see, it is possible to affect parts of your program from the Immediate window, making it an excellent tool for debugging.

It is worth noting at this point that Visual Basic .NET is missing an important feature of Visual Basic 6.0—Edit and Continue. In Visual Basic 6.0, you could stop your code at a breakpoint, change the code, and then have execution continue from that point. You cannot do this in Visual Basic .NET; to change code you need to stop debugging your program (by clicking the Stop Toolbar button), change the code, and then restart your application (by pressing F5 or the Play Toolbar icon). The Edit and Continue feature will be returning to Visual Basic in the next release (currently known by the code name Whidbey).

### Dynamic Help

This tool window is set up as a tab with the Properties window (if you are using the Visual Basic Developer's profile settings), and provides context-based documentation references to Visual Studio's help files. Instead of waiting for you to ask for help, this tool window acts proactively when you press the F1 key or select something from the Help menu. Based on your current selection or task, it displays a list of related topics.

In addition to the directly related help topics, this window will usually display a link to several more generic topics such as (in this case) the Coding Techniques and Programming Practices section of the documentation. This tool window also provides a quick link to the contents, index, and search sections of the help documentation through the three Toolbar icons provided.

### Server Explorer

This tool window (see Figure 1.13) provides a visual listing of two main resources, databases and servers. The first set of resources represents all the connections established between your project and various database servers, and enables you to explore those databases to see tables, stored procedures, and other useful information.

The second set of information, Servers, represents any machines that you can connect to and that provide a visual interface to the resources that those machines can make available to your program. These resources include performance counters, event logs, message queues, and more, all easily found through this tool window.

### Properties

The Visual Studio IDE enables you to work with many items, projects, solutions, forms, classes, and more, all of which possess attributes or properties. These properties are pieces of information that describe the item, such as a name for a project. Although properties are automatically populated with default values, you need a way to modify them. The Properties window provides this functionality. Whenever an item is selected in the IDE, the attributes of that object will be displayed in this tool window. Some of these attributes might be read-only (they cannot be modified), but for those that are not, you can click them in this Properties window and change them as needed.

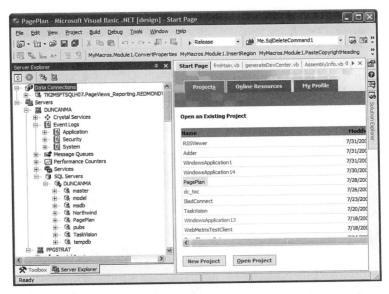

**FIGURE 1.13** The Server Explorer provides a visual way to view and use resources from both the local server and other machines.

### Solution Explorer

In many ways, the Solution Explorer is similar to the Project Explorer in Visual Basic 6.0. It is the file management interface within Visual Studio .NET. In Visual Studio .NET, the code you create can be organized using different layers of grouping: solutions (which replaces the idea of a project group from Visual Basic 6.0), projects, and files. The Solution Explorer window enables you to view a list of all of the available files in the current solution.

In addition to letting you view what is currently open, the Solution Explorer window gives you a variety of functionality. Through the window, you can

- Add new files to a project (right-click the project and select Add)

- Remove files (right-click an individual file and select Remove)

- Add and remove entire projects from a Solution group (right-click the solution to add a project, and right-click a project for the option to remove it from the current solution)

### Class View

As part of the discussion of the Solution Explorer, I explained that there can be many files involved in a single project or solution. Those files often correspond to the created classes (such as a Vehicle class or an Account class), but there is no requirement that the file organization must resemble the conceptual organization of the classes in the project. The Class View window is designed to let you view the object structure of your project and use that view to navigate within your code.

Within this window, you can collapse and expand the displayed objects to access the various properties and methods they expose. Double-clicking a particular item in the Class View will take you to that class, method, event, property, or procedure. If the item you double-clicked is not available as a part of your code, Class View takes you to the definition of that portion of the class within the Object Browser (see the next section). The Class View is useful as a way to look at your project through its defined classes, ignoring the physical details of the actual files.

### Object Browser

All programming in .NET is based on objects—objects provided for you as part of the .NET Framework, objects you create, even objects that other parts of your own team have created. All of these objects have properties and methods through which you can interact with them, but how do you know what is available? The Object Browser is designed to assist you in working with all of these objects, by enabling you to browse and search through a catalog of available objects. This catalog includes the objects (classes) exposed by any referenced class libraries, along with the classes contained within your own project. Similar in some respects to the Class View, the Object Browser goes beyond the functionality of that other window by including objects outside of your project. This window is most useful as a form of documentation or reference, enabling you to find classes within the .NET Framework or other class libraries and view the details of those classes, such as their properties and methods. Just like in Visual Basic 6.0, you can bring up the Object Browser by pressing F2.

### Task List

In any development project, even completed ones, there are likely to be a variety of outstanding tasks to be completed. Sections of the program might need performance tweaking. There might be known bugs or missing functionality that need to be remedied. When the outstanding tasks can be related to an actual area of the code, a common practice among programmers is to flag that area with comments. When the programmers consistently include certain words such as TODO or BUG in those comments, it is easier to scan through the code looking for those keywords to find the appropriate bits of code. Visual Studio .NET has formalized this process by providing an actual task list that is automatically filled with references to any section of your code that contains one of several keywords such as TODO (but, you can specify any keyword you want). Each comment found is then listed in an easy-to-use list, detailing not only the comment itself, but also the file and line at which it was found (see Figure 1.14).

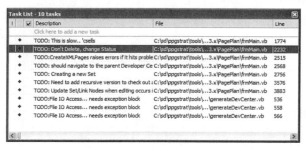

**FIGURE 1.14** Every comment flagged with a special keyword is shown in a nicely organized task list.

With a quick double-click a task, you are immediately taken to the code, where you can get to work on whatever the outstanding task indicates. In addition to this functionality—fairly useful on its own—the task list can hold a variety of other types of tasks. Visual Studio adds other tasks automatically, such as referring to compile errors and other notable items. It is also possible for you to add two types of tasks to this list: code shortcuts and user-defined tasks.

**ADDING YOUR OWN KEYWORDS TO THE LIST OF TOKENS**

You can add your own keywords to the list of recognized tokens by going through the Options dialog box. Under this dialog box's Environment\Task List section, you have the ability to add new tokens and to specify settings for the task created when this keyword is found. Keywords are considered a match only when they are found within comments in your code.

Code shortcuts are similar to comment-based tasks, but are a reference to any line of code. They do not require any special keyword. To add a code shortcut to the task list, click a line in the code-editing window and then select the Add Task List Shortcut menu item from the Edit, Bookmarks menu.

A new task will be added to your task list, with the description defaulting to the line of code selected (although you can, and probably should, change this to whatever description you want). Then, you can quickly return to that line just by double-clicking this task. When a shortcut has been created, a blue arrow will be placed in the left margin of the code window next to the appropriate line of code. You can remove the shortcut by clicking the line of code and then selecting Remove Task List Shortcut from the Edit | Bookmarks menu or selecting the new item in the task list and deleting it directly.

The other type of task that you can create is a *user task*, one that is not associated with any particular bit of code, similar to a standard task in Outlook. A user task is added by clicking the Click Here to Add a New Task section of the task list and filling in the details. Note that, unlike other tasks, these tasks do not have the file/line fields filled in, and therefore only have two fields available, the Description and the Priority (Low, Normal, or High). If you want to create a note about a particular area of code, you likely will find it more useful to create a code shortcut and change the priority and description to provide more detail on the actual issue.

## Solutions and Projects

As discussed in the "Solution Explorer" section, multiple levels exist for grouping your code together. The first level, the solution, represents the overall system being created, whereas the individual components within it are represented by separate projects. Before you can write any code inside the Visual Studio IDE, you must set up the solution and at least one project. In this section, you will go through the basics of organizing your code, creating new projects, and working with existing projects and files. The following is a quick overview of these topics, but, in the section immediately following this one, you will get to practice these skills by creating a complete sample application.

### Creating a New Project

A few ways exist to create a new project, but the most common method uses the menu option File, New, Project. This menu option brings up a dialog box showing all the different types of projects that the IDE is capable of creating (see Figure 1.15). Because the Visual Studio IDE works with a variety of languages, the dialog box shows options based on the languages you have installed, and might appear different from the one in Figure 1.15. For now, you will be creating projects based on the choices under the Visual Basic Projects folder.

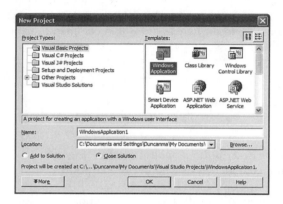

**FIGURE 1.15** Visual Studio has an expandable New Project dialog box, which allows for new project types to be added as you install additional templates or languages.

To create an application with a Windows-based user interface (with dialog boxes and other Windows UI elements), select Windows Application from the list of project types. To complete the creation process, enter a name for your new application and, if desired, modify the suggested path. Click OK, and Visual Studio creates your new project. It is a good idea to give your projects meaningful names, even when you are just experimenting; otherwise, you will quickly have a whole group of projects named WindowsApplication1 and WindowsApplication2, making it difficult to find anything that you have been working on.

### Opening an Existing Project

When you close Visual Studio, it will ask you whether you want to save what you are working on, and automatically close everything for you. When you want to get back to a previous project, you will need to open it into the IDE. Visual Studio provides a few easy ways to open past projects. One method is to use the menu through either File, Open, Project, or directly through the Most Recently Used (MRU) section near the bottom of the File menu. Another method is through the Get Started section of the Visual Studio home page, an HTML page that lists the projects you have recently worked with. There, you can click the particular project you want to open, or even create a new project through an additional link. Opening a new project closes any other project you currently have open (actually the currently open solution), unless you use the menu option File, Add Project, which adds a new or existing project into the currently open solution.

## Organizing Your Files

Solutions and projects exist almost purely for organizational purposes; the actual code resides in one or more individual files. When you create a new project, certain files are usually created for you, such as a new Windows Form (Form1.vb) when you create a Windows application and a new Module (Module1.vb) for a Console application. These files are created on disk and exist independently of their project, enabling a single file to be shared across multiple projects if desired.

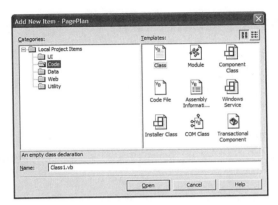

**FIGURE 1.16** Just like the New Project dialog box, the interface to add new project items is expandable.

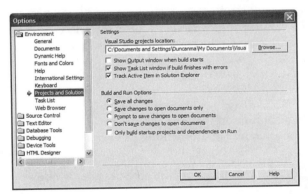

**FIGURE 1.17** Always check the "Save All Changes" setting when you use a new computer, to avoid losing a few hours of code.

### Adding Files to a Project

In addition to the files that are automatically created as part of your new project, you might also want to add additional modules, classes, forms, or other types of code files. Through either the Project menu, or the menu brought up by right-clicking the project in the Solution Explorer window, you can choose to add any one of a variety of files. Regardless of the specific menu option you choose, with the exception of Add Existing Item, all of the choices will bring you to the Add New Item dialog box (see Figure 1.16). If, instead of creating a new item, you want to add an existing file from disk, the menu option Add New Existing Item will bring up a standard file open dialog box for that purpose.

### Saving Everything

With all these different groups (solutions, projects, and files), it is important to know how to save any work you have done, even if it is located in more than one file. In the Visual Studio IDE, this is accomplished through two commands: Save and Save All. These commands, located on the File menu and on the Toolbar, enable you to either save just the currently selected file (selected in the Server Explorer window) using the Save command or to save all open files that have been modified using the Save All command.

If you are paranoid about losing work, as I am, you will be especially interested in one of the IDE's options. Under the Options dialog box (accessed through the Tools, Options menu item), you can expand the Environment group and select the Projects and Solutions item to see a set of three option buttons under a heading of Build and Run Options (see Figure 1.17). These options control whether the IDE saves any modified files before starting to execute a project. This is an important setting because, if the IDE is ever going to crash, it is most likely going to do it when you run your code. This option provides an easy way to ensure that all your changes are saved every time before you run your code.

# Creating Your First Windows Application

Now that you have learned some of the basics of using the Visual Studio IDE, you can put that information to use building an application without getting into very much code. This exercise focuses on using the IDE itself, which means that you are going to be creating a relatively simple application. For this example, you will make a Windows application (an application that uses the Windows user-interface and runs locally on your machine) that allows a user to enter two numbers. The application will then add the numbers, displaying the result.

## Create the Project

Using the menus, choose the File, New, Project command, bringing up the New Project dialog box. Under the Visual Basic category, select the Windows Application icon and change the project name from WindowsApplication(x)—the numbered default name—to Adder (unless you are bothered by snakes, in which case you can name the project whatever you want). The new project will already contain a form, which is all you need to get started on the application. Visual Studio automatically creates a Solution folder to hold your new project, naming it Adder as well. Click OK after you have entered the correct project and solution names.

## Develop the User Interface

You need to have three text boxes and a single button on the form. Positioning is not that important, but you might want to make your interface look something like Figure 1.18. Follow these steps to set up your form:

1. Double-click Form1 in the Solution Explorer, bringing it up into the designer window in the center of the IDE.

**FIGURE 1.18** Arrange the three text boxes and one button on your form to approximate this appearance.

2. Now, with the form in Design mode, select or open the Toolbox window. This window, which will show all the available objects that can be placed onto your form, contains a TextBox control and a Button control.

3. To place one of these controls onto your form, click and drag the control into position on the form.

4. When it is on the form, select the control and use its handles to resize it to the desired shape and size.

5. Play with resizing and moving these controls until you get all three text boxes and the single button onto the form and looking like the example (Figure 1.18). After everything is in place, you will change a few properties of these controls.

Select the first text box (the one closest to the top on the form) and display the Properties window (press F4 or select View, Properties Window from the menu, if the window is not already visible). Many properties are listed, but you are only going to change two of them:

- Text (under the Appearance group)—Represents the contents of the text box. Erase the contents of this property to make the text box blank when the program starts.

- (*Name*) (under the Design group)—In the code, you will refer to this text box using the name in this property, which defaults to a relatively meaningless name, such as Text2 or Text1. For the example, change this to txtFirstValue.

Continue with the other two text boxes, changing their Text property to blank and their names to txtSecondValue and txtResult, respectively.

Now select the button to display its attributes in the Properties window. For this object, you will also be changing only two values, (*Name*) to btnAdd and Text to Add.

Finally, just because you can, you will change one of the properties of the form itself. Select the form (click somewhere on the form that is not another object) and scroll through the list of properties to find the Text property in the Appearance group. For a form, this property represents its caption (the text displayed on the form's title bar), which you can set to Simple Adder for the example.

## Running the Project

Although you have entered no code, the project can be run just as it is now. When you run the application, Visual Studio compiles your code into an executable and then runs it. Unlike Visual Basic 6.0, there is very little difference (but there is some) between running the application inside or outside of the IDE. In both cases, the system is compiled and then run, but when you run within the IDE, it is possible to break the code execution at certain points and debug it as it runs. Creating an executable, or other type of output file from your project, is also known as *building*.

To run a project within the IDE, select Start from the Debug menu, press F5, or use the Toolbar button that looks like a right-facing arrow (or the play button on a VCR). Try this now, with the Adder project you already have open, and you will see the form that you have been designing appear in front of the Visual Studio IDE. Without your having written a single line of code, the form is functional. You can drag it around and minimize it, all because of the underlying .NET Framework and the IDE that allows you to visually create a user interface and that produces the code required to make it work. Although you have written no code, a great deal of code has been generated by the IDE, and that is what is being executed when the project is run.

# Building the Project

Building a project is the creation of an executable or other output files. For a Windows application like the example, this means compiling your code into an .EXE file, along with any other associated files. This is an essential step in running the application, so it occurs whenever you click the Start button inside of Visual Studio, but you can also just build it directly (without running the application) by selecting Build Solution or Build *<Project Name>* from the Build menu.

### Project Build Settings

To create the output files for your project, select Build from the Build menu (not a very creative menu name, but easy to understand). This command does not appear to do much, but the default Build settings have created an Adder.exe file for you, placing it within the bin subdirectory of your project folder. Unless you chose to customize the displayed path when you created this project, your project should be located at My Documents\Visual Studio Projects\Adder, and the executable at \bin\Adder.exe within that directory. To see the default settings, and perhaps to change them, right-click your project in the Solution Explorer window and select Properties from the context menu that appears. The property dialog box for your project contains a variety of settings, but the ones that are relevant to the build process are described here:

Under Common Properties\General:

- Assembly name—This value provides the first part of the filename for your output file. In the case of the example, it is Adder, so Adder.exe is created. Change it to MyAdder, and MyAdder.exe is created when you build.

- Output type—Tells the IDE what type of file is to be created from building this project, an .EXE if Windows Application or Console Application is selected, or a .DLL, if Class Library is selected.

- Startup object—Indicates the part of the project that should be run when the application is executed, by default. For the example, it should be Adder.Form1 to indicate that the form should be automatically run. Note that if you change, even temporarily, the Output Type from Windows Application to anything else, this property will also change and can end up set incorrectly.

Cancel the entire project property dialog box (by pressing the Cancel button along the bottom of the form) if you feel you have changed something that you do not know how to fix.

Common Properties\Build, despite the name, contains only a single property that is directly relevant to the build process. The Application Icon value determines the appearance of the final .EXE in Windows, and allows you to select any icon file (.ICO) you want.

Under the Common Properties\Build section, there is a Change button under Supported Runtimes. This button opens up a subject of discussion best left for advanced users, but I will briefly explain its purpose in case you ever have need of it. Underlying any .NET application is the .NET Framework and the Common Language Runtime (CLR). Just like any product, there are different versions of the CLR released at different times. Well, unlike Visual Basic 6.0 (which would only ever run against the Visual Basic 6.0 runtime files), a .NET application can use a different version of the Framework at runtime than it had available when it was originally compiled or built. As you might imagine, this is not a simple concept. Your code, which you tested against a specific version of the CLR (1.1 is what ships with Visual Studio .NET 2003), can end up being run against the older 1.0 version. If you leave the system set up as the default, your application will only run against the 1.1 version of the Framework, which is what is occurring when you are developing. The other two options are to allow it to run against either or to specify that it will only work with the 1.0 version of the Framework.

Although they are not the only other settings that affect the build, the last items I will mention are under Configuration Properties\Build. There you will find various debug-related settings as well as the Output Directory setting, which determines where the executable or other created files will be placed.

### Build Configurations

At the top of the Project property dialog box is a drop-down list marked Configuration. Solution Configurations are a useful feature of the Visual Studio IDE, allowing you to create more than one group of settings for the same project. By default, two configurations are provided (Release and Debug), designed to indicate whether you are building output for testing purposes (Debug) or for actual deployment (Release). The settings for these default configurations are a good example of the purpose of Solution Configurations, setting the status of a variety of debugging features and even setting a different output location for each.

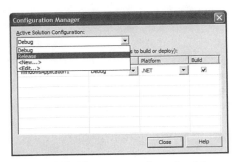

**FIGURE 1.19**  The Configuration Manager allows you to create different configurations for different purposes (testing, debugging, user acceptance, release, and so on), each of which can have different Build settings.

Using the Configuration Manager (see Figure 1.19), you can create as many different groups of settings as you want, or even remove an existing configuration. For now, you will likely want to leave the settings as they are, selecting the Release version of the output when you are deploying the project, and the Debug version when you are testing.

## Adding Your Own Code

Up to this point, the sample project you have been working on has contained only code generated by the Visual Studio IDE. As you might have guessed from the names and layout of the form, this application will add the values in the first and second text box and place the result into the third text box. To accomplish this, you need to add code to the project that will run when the user clicks the Add button.

Using the IDE makes this a very direct process, just like in Visual Basic 6.0: Double-click the form in the Solution Explorer to make sure its Design view is visible, and then double-click the Add button. This will take you into the form's Code view, and into a subroutine that has been added by the IDE. By default, the event procedure uses the control name, btnAdd, followed by the event, Click. It is possible to associate procedures with events, regardless of their name, but, in this case, the btnAdd_Click procedure will be executed if the user clicks the button. It is easy to try adding your own code by using the MsgBox function. The MsgBox function enables you to display a message in a dialog box with a single line of code, like this:

```
MsgBox("The Button has been clicked")
```

The simplicity of using this class makes it perfect for use as a testing or debugging tool. Add the preceding code line to the btnAdd_Click subroutine and then run the project by pressing F5. After the form appears, try clicking the button. Every click should cause the message box to appear, showing you that the code in btnAdd_Click gets executed whenever the button is pressed.

Now that you can see how to execute code in response to a button click, you can create the real code for your project. The code needs to add two values together to produce a result, which sounds easier than it really is. The values you want are the contents of your text boxes, available through the Text property of those controls, but before you can use them in a mathematical equation (adding them together), you have to convert them from strings (text) into numbers. The following code, if put in place of the MsgBox call you added earlier, accomplishes what you need:

```
txtResult.Text = CStr(CInt(txtFirstValue.Text) _
    + CInt(txtSecondValue.Text))
```

This code converts the contents of the two text boxes into numbers (integers, in this case), adds them together, and then coverts the result back into a string (text), so that it can be placed into the third text box. It takes quite a few steps for something that sounds easy enough when first described, but data type conversion is discussed in detail in the next chapter.

# In Brief

This chapter has provided a quick introduction to Visual Studio .NET, including:

- Choosing the right edition of VS.NET
- Getting it all installed
- Exploring the new IDE
- Creating a new project

# Visual Basic .NET Language Changes

**2**

## Key Changes

When Visual Basic .NET was released, there were some people who considered it so different from Visual Basic 6.0 that they dubbed it "Visual Basic .NOT," but don't let that give you an exaggerated view of the actual language changes. As a long-time Visual Basic programmer (starting with VB 3.0), I find the Visual Basic .NET language to be extremely close to Visual Basic 6.0, with a few exceptions.

The first big difference is in the use of variable types; Visual Basic .NET likes everything to be strongly typed, and although you can work around this restriction, you are better off facing the situation and going for a fully strongly typed world. Second, Visual Basic .NET is now sitting on top of the Windows .NET Framework and the Framework provides its own method for doing many of the things that VB6 already had built into its language (such as file IO). What this means is that in many cases, although the Visual Basic 6 method for accomplishing a specific task will still work, there is a new method available in the Framework.

Overall, aside from the data-typing issues, and the possible confusion between Windows .NET Framework functionality and actual Visual Basic language features, most of the changes between Visual Basic 6 and Visual Basic .NET are small details that can easily be learned. This chapter details the changes (big and small) in the language between Visual Basic .NET and Visual Basic 6, covering the new Option statements, new loop options, changes in numeric data types, and much more.

## IT IS ALL ABOUT THE FRAMEWORK

The real changes between previous versions of VB and VB.NET are not in the language but instead in many of the new Framework features. With the new models for Windows Forms, Web Development, Data Access, XML, and others, the Framework has replaced existing COM libraries (such as ADO and MSXML) or built-in features of Visual Basic 6.0. We will cover each of those areas in the following chapters.

# New and Changed "Option" Statements

Option statements are essentially compiler directives that are placed at the top of a code file (so a form, class, or module) to control how the compiler builds the code. In Visual Basic 6.0 there were four of these statements (Option Explicit, Option Compare, Option Private Module, and Option Base), but only two of those statements are included in Visual Basic .NET (Option Explicit and Option Compare). In addition to removing two of the existing statements, a completely new Option statement has been added, Option Strict.

## Forcing Variable Declaration with Option Explicit

Adding this statement to a code file in Visual Basic 6 forced you to declare all of your variables before they could be used, which helped you to avoid many confusing bugs due to mistyping a variable name. Without it, you could write code like Listing 2.1.

**LISTING 2.1**   Variable Declaration Is a Good Thing

```
Dim myName As String

Private Sub Form_Load()
    myNme = "Duncan Mackenzie"
End Sub

Private Sub Command1_Click()
    MsgBox myName
End Sub
```

You would not get a single error, at compile time or at runtime, but your MsgBox window would always be empty. This type of problem, hidden inside a much more complex project, can be very difficult to debug. With Option Explicit at the top of the file, the attempt to use a variable called myNme (because it was never declared) would result in a compile error and you would have to fix it before you could run your application.

In Visual Basic .NET, `Option Explicit` works in the exact same fashion, but with two improvements. First, the concept of choosing a default setting (it was always off by default in Visual Basic 6) is now available; you can pick whether `Option Explicit` should be on or off by default in the properties dialog box for your project (see Figure 2.1).

Whatever setting you choose in this dialog box will be used for any code files (in that project) that do not have an `Option Explicit` line at the top. Now that there is the concept of a default, the actual statement has been extended to require an additional parameter `On` or `Off`. Instead of just `Option Explicit`, you must now use either `Option Explicit On` or `Option Explicit Off`. Adding the `On/Off` parameter allows you to have a single code file that follows different rules from the project default.

## GOODBYE TO DEFTYPE

Visual Basic 6.0 provides a set of special statements to define the default data type for undeclared variables. These statements, which include `DefInt`, `DefDate`, and `DefDbl`, work by specifying a range of letters; any undeclared variable starting with a letter within that range is defined as the specified data type, instead of a variant. If you are using these statements in Visual Basic 6.0, you need to add explicit variable declaration when you move your code to Visual Basic .NET.

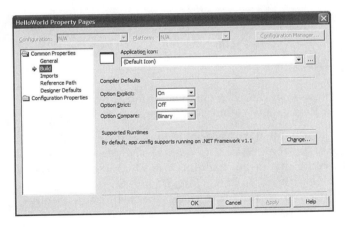

**FIGURE 2.1**   Default settings for each of the Option statements can be configured on a per-project basis.

## Understanding Option Strict and Data Type Conversions

A new setting in Visual Basic .NET, `Option Strict` reflects the new .NET preference for type safety across your code. With `Option Strict On`, a data type must be specified for all variable declarations (including in parameter lists for subs and functions) and "implicit" data type conversions are not allowed.

The first rule, requiring data types to be specified, is clear. For example, the code in Listing 2.2 is not allowed.

**LISTING 2.2**   All Variable Declarations, Including Parameters, Must Have a Data Type if Option Strict Is On

```
Sub Test()
    Dim x
End Sub


Private Function DoMath(ByVal myInt)
End Function
```

To allow the code from Listing 2.2 to compile with a setting of Option Strict On, it has to be converted to look like Listing 2.3.

**LISTING 2.3**   Adding Data Types to All Your Declarations Makes for Clearer Code

```
Sub Test()
    Dim x As String
End Sub

Private Function DoMath(ByVal myInt As Integer) As Integer
End Function
```

The variable x (line 2) needs a data type, as does the myInt parameter for DoMath (line 5). DoMath (being a function) needs to indicate a data type for its return value (also line 5).

The other effect of Option Strict On is that implicit conversions are not allowed. What does that mean? Visual Basic has a heritage of loosely typed code, where the language just tried to do its best to make everything work, even if that meant handling a few little details for you. In Visual Basic 6.0 or in Visual Basic .NET with Option Strict Off, if you assign a String to an Integer, Visual Basic will try to parse the text into a numeric value. That behind-the-scenes parsing is an implicit conversion, you never had to state that you wanted it to take place. Visual Basic just did it automatically. See whether you can spot all of the implicit conversions that occur in the Visual Basic 6 code shown in Listing 2.4.

**LISTING 2.4**   Implicit Conversions Are Not Always Clear, and That Can Lead to Hard-to-Spot Bugs

```
Private Sub Command1_Click()
    Dim myResult As Integer
    Dim myHighValue As Integer
    myHighValue = 5
    myResult = Text1 + Text2
    Text3 = myResult
```

**LISTING 2.4** Continued

```
    If Text3 >= myHighValue Then
        MsgBox "Result is >= " & myHighValue
    End If
End Sub
```

By my count, there are four implicit conversions occurring in this code:

- myResult = Text1 + Text2 (line 5) requires the conversion of each TextBox's contents from a String to a numeric value.

- Text3 = myResult (line 6) requires the conversion of an Integer (myResult) back into a String for placing into the TextBox.

- Text3 >= myHighValue (line 8) either requires a conversion of an Integer (myHighValue) into a String for comparing with the contents of the TextBox, or the conversion of String into an Integer. The fact that it could be either (actually depending on how you arrange your If statement) is one of the underlying uncertainties with implicit conversion!

- MsgBox "Result is >= " & myHighValue (line 9) requires another Integer to String conversion for myHighValue to be able to concatenate it with the rest of the message text.

If you choose to make Option Strict On the default for your project, or if you set it just for this code file, none of those implicit conversions are allowed. In each instance of an implicit conversion, you will need to explicitly perform the desired conversion yourself to allow this code to even compile. Listing 2.5 uses the familiar data type conversion functions from Visual Basic 6 to wrap each String value in CInt() when I needed to convert it to an Integer, and wrap each Integer in CStr() when I needed to convert them to Strings.

**LISTING 2.5** Just Like Adding Data Types to Your Variable declarations, Explicit Conversions Make for Clearer Code

```
Private Sub Command1_Click()
    Dim myResult As Integer
    Dim myHighValue As Integer
    myHighValue = 5
    myResult = CInt(Text1.Text) + CInt(Text2.Text)
    Text3.Text = CStr(myResult)

    If CInt(Text3.Text) >= myHighValue Then
        MsgBox("Result is >= " & CStr(myHighValue))
    End If
End Sub
```

Note that to convert the code from Listing 2.5 to Visual Basic .NET I had to change more than just the data type conversion elements, I also had to add the .Text after each TextBox reference. I will explain why that change was necessary in the "No More Default Properties" section later in this chapter.

The use of implicit conversions was not a configurable option in Visual Basic prior to .NET; implicit conversions occurred all the time, potentially causing problems without any warning at all. Now you can specify Option Strict On/Off at the top of a specific code file, and (as you can see in Figure 2.1) it can also be set at the project level just like Option Explicit.

## Option Compare and String Comparision

This statement, which toggles between two styles of string comparison (Text and Binary), works the same in Visual Basic .NET as it did in earlier versions. The only difference is that it is now a configurable project level option in addition to being configurable at the file level. Binary indicates that Strings should be compared based on their underlying ASCII/Unicode values, making A < Z < a < z (because the uppercase characters are located at lower positions in the character table than the lowercase characters). Text indicates that strings should be compared using a system that is independent of the underlying character codes and is therefore case insensitive (A=a, Z=z, and so on). Binary comparison is the default, but Text comparison is more understandable to a human user of your system. You should use the Text setting whenever you are sorting text for display.

## Default Settings and Enforcing Coding Standards

Given that each of these Option settings can be set at the project level and/or in the individual code file, what is the best way to ensure that your desired settings are always the default? Personally, I want to code with Option Explicit On and Option Strict On, but I often forget to include those lines in my code or to set the appropriate project level settings; so I needed a way to make these two settings the default for all the new projects I start or new code files I create. If you want to achieve the same thing, the key is to look at the template files used by Visual Studio .NET when it creates new projects or new code files. The individual file templates are located under C:\Program Files\Microsoft Visual Studio .NET\Vb7\VBWizards on my system, the exact location of yours will depend on where you installed VS .NET. Adding the desired Option lines to the top of each of the .VB code files will cause those lines to appear in each new file you create through the IDE's Add [Item] menu options. Templates for the project files are also available, under the same location in your VS .NET installation and you can modify those files if you want to set the default Option settings at the project level. See this book's Web site for more information on the details of setting up these defaults on your own system.

# Changes to Variable Declaration

In addition to `Option Strict`, which can require variable declarations to include data types, Visual Basic .NET includes a few other changes in the way that variables are declared, the way arrays work, and how objects can be initialized and assigned. As mentioned earlier, the `Def[Type]` statements (`DefInt`, `DefBool`, `DefStr`, and so on) no longer exist in Visual Basic .NET; it is not possible to create a default data type definition based on the name of the variable.

## Multiple Variables Declared Together

The first change is very minor, but has been a long time coming. In Visual Basic 6.0, if you declared multiple variables on a single line you could produce this very correct looking syntax:

```
Dim X, Y As Integer
```

Many people, for good reason, would say that this line of Visual Basic 6 code is declaring X and Y as Integer variables. In truth, it is declaring X as a Variant and Y as an Integer. Visual Basic 6 interprets this line of code as if X is being declared without any data type. In Visual Basic .NET, this code now behaves as it should; X and Y are declared as Integer variables. To achieve the same effect in VB6, you would need to include an `As Integer` clause after each variable name.

## Variable Initialization in Declaration

Variables can now be initialized as part of their declaration, which is not any better than having to do it on a separate line, but it certainly seems simpler (and it is a little less typing!).

```
Dim X As Integer = 5
```

## Object Initialization in Declaration

Just like non-object (or Value) data types, objects can be initialized in their declaration using one of two alternative forms. Either of these two lines will produce the same result:

```
Dim myForm As New Form()
Dim myForm As Form = New Form()
```

Obviously, the first version is shorter and simpler, but it carries with it a bit of a stigma from the pre-.NET days of Visual Basic and Visual Basic for Applications. If you declared an object As New in VB/VBA prior to Visual Basic .NET, the compiler would wrap every use of that object in code that would check if the object had been initialized, and would initialize it if it were equal to Nothing. The result was inefficient code and possibly worse as the extra bits of wrapper code could actually lead to bugs in your application. Do not worry though; there is absolutely no reason not to use this syntax in Visual Basic .NET.

# Arrays

The major change in arrays in Visual Basic .NET is in how an array's upper and lower bounds can be set. In Visual Basic 6.0, either you could specify just an upper value, in which case the Option Base setting for your code would determine whether the array had a lower bound of 0 or 1, or you could specify both the upper and lower bounds as a range. In Visual Basic .NET, all arrays have a lower bound of 0, which is why the Option Base statement no longer exists. Because of this explicit lower bound, specifying both the upper and lower bounds in an array declaration is no longer required or supported. In general, this change can cause a lot of confusion, and it can require quite a few changes in your code if you commonly specified the lower bound for arrays in your application. It is not uncommon to see a declaration like Dim years(1999 to 2003) As String in Visual Basic 6.0 code, but associating the actual array bounds with a real range of values cannot be done in Visual Basic .NET. Instead, you could declare your array using just an upper bound, and use a secondary variable to keep track of the starting point of the range.

```
Dim firstYear As Integer = 1999
Dim years(4) As String
```

In addition to being different from VB6, Visual Basic .NET array declarations differ from C#/C++/Java as well. In those other languages, declaring an array with a dimension of (4) would indicate an array with four elements, 0 to 3, in an array with a lower bound of 0. *In Visual Basic .NET this is not the case—an array declaration of (4) actually indicates an array with five elements (0 to 4).* This behavior, although it conflicts with some other languages, is designed to avoid upgrade issues from Visual Basic 6.0. Because the Option Base statement allowed the same array declaration (Dim years(4) As String) to either indicate 0-4 (five elements) or 1-4 (four elements), Visual Basic .NET's array declarations have to err on the side of caution. An array declaration with a dimension of four actually indicates an array with five elements (0 to 4), which is the best choice to avoid breaking VB6 code, as code written assuming either 0 to 4 or 1 to 4 will still work against a .NET array that goes from 0 to 4.

The other array-related change in Visual Basic .NET is that it is now possible to initialize a *dynamic* (no declared length) array when you declare it using a special syntax.

```
Dim myCats() As String = {"Sisko", "Kira"}
```

Even though I initialized the array with two elements, I end up with an array with upper and lower bounds 0 and 1.

# Data Type Changes

In the move to .NET, Visual Basic's data types were adjusted in a couple of ways. I will go into more detail on integers and variants, but here is a quick summary of the changes:

- The Currency data type has been removed completely, but you can use the Decimal data type instead.

- Date values in Visual Basic 6.0 were stored as Doubles, and programmers often manipulated them as such, but in Visual Basic .NET DateTime values are stored as 64-bit integers instead. If you need to convert a .NET DateTime value into or from a Double, you can use the System.DateTime.ToOADate or FromOADate methods.

- Integers were 16-bit values in VB6, they are now 32-bit. Longs have also moved from 32-bit to 64-bit, and a new data type (Short) has been added to Visual Basic to handle 16-bit numbers.

- Variants were special data types in VB6 that could hold anything from Integer or String values to object references. They no longer exist in Visual Basic .NET, but the Object data type is available and is, like a Variant, capable of holding any data type.

- The Framework provides a set of type-conversion functions, but the standard Visual Basic type-conversion functions are still available.

## Integers

Visual Basic has its roots as a 16-bit development language, not moving up into the 32-bit world until version 4.0, and that heritage resulted in a set of data types in Visual Basic 6.0 that did not line up well with other languages or the underlying operating system. As part of the move to .NET, Visual Basic's integer data types were redefined to make it easier for interoperability with other .NET languages. The following table shows various sizes of signed integers that are commonly used and the equivalent data type across Visual Basic 6.0, Visual Basic .NET, C#, and the underlying framework data type that corresponds to the language specific names.

| INTEGER SIZE (SIGNED) | VISUAL BASIC 6.0 | VISUAL BASIC .NET | C# | FRAMEWORK |
| --- | --- | --- | --- | --- |
| 16-bit (word) | Integer | Short | short | System.Int16 |
| 32-bit (dword) | Long | Integer | int | System.Int32 |
| 64-bit (qword) | (none) | Long | long | System.Int64 |

As you can see, the Framework equivalents are named to avoid any confusion about their size, and for that fact alone, it might be worth considering using them. Personally, I use the

Visual Basic data types, (such as Integer and Long), and I think the habit is too strong to break easily. Either way, it makes no difference to the compiler; the Visual Basic and C# data types are actually just aliases to the Framework types, so that you can continue to work using the terms you are comfortable with depending on your programming background.

## Variants and Objects

There are two main types of variables, value types and reference types. Reference types represent data types where the variable holds a pointer to the actual object, compared to a value type where the variable holds the actual data for the type in question. Integers, Doubles, and Bytes are all examples of value types, whereas Forms, Classes, and Strings are examples of reference types. In Visual Basic 6.0, any variable could be stored into a Variant, regardless of whether it was a reference or a value type, and the same is true with .NET's Object data type.

This is a little confusing because the Object data type is a reference type, it holds pointers to values, but yet it can be used to store both reference and value types. It would be an oversimplification to state, "Everything in .NET is an Object," but it certainly seems that way. In truth, what occurs is that value types are "boxed" or wrapped in a special reference type so that they can be stored in an Object variable. When you take these values out of an Object variable and back into a value type (an Integer, for example), the object is "unboxed" to extract only the actual value instead of a reference. This boxing/unboxing process means that using Object variables to store all of your values, instead of explicitly typing them (into Integers, Doubles, and so on), is inefficient and should be avoided.

## Converting Between Data Types

Visual Basic 6.0 includes support for converting from one data type to another, but with the addition of Option Strict, (if you choose to use it) you will need to explicitly convert from one data type to another more frequently. There are many ways to handle conversion in Visual Basic .NET, and it all depends on what you are doing, so I will first discuss the two types of data type conversion that occur.

- Parsing (actually interpreting the data and coming up with the equivalent in another data type)

- Type coercion (or casting, as it is commonly known in the C++/C# world)

Both types of conversion are often mistaken as exactly the same thing, and that confusion makes it difficult to pick the correct style of conversion. The following sections explain both of the types individually, with examples, to illustrate the difference.

**Parsing**

Say you have an application where the user can enter a number into one textbox and a date into another. Now, in your code you do not want to work with the two strings that are available through the .Text property of these textboxes, you want to work with an Integer and a Date variable. This is a classic example where parsing is required; a string is not a date or an integer, it is a collection of character codes, and the underlying numeric value of those codes isn't at all related to the date or numeric value the user typed. To take a text value like $12,500.00 and convert it to an integer, or to convert a string containing "October 5, 2003" into a date requires parsing. In VB .NET, there are three ways to parse a value into a different data type; using the Parse methods on the data type itself, using the methods of a Framework class called Convert, or using the built-in VB .NET functions. In the first case, you are taking advantage of the special function (Parse) available on each of the basic data types, as shown in Listing 2.6.

**LISTING 2.6**   Using the Parse Method on a Data Type

```
Private Sub btnParse_Click( _
        ByVal sender As System.Object, _
        ByVal e As System.EventArgs) _
            Handles btnParse.Click
    Dim myDate As Date
    Dim myInteger As Integer

    myDate = Date.Parse(Me.dateEntry.Text)
    myInteger = Integer.Parse(Me.numberEntry.Text)

    MsgBox(myDate)
    MsgBox(myInteger)
End Sub
```

For the second method, you are using the methods of a class within the Framework called System.Convert. This class provides methods for conversion to all of the standard types (ToInt32, ToInt64, ToString, ToDateTime, and so on) and a few less standard ones as well. You can pass any type of data into one of these conversion functions and it will attempt to parse it into the desired data type. Under the covers, Convert.To eventually calls the same Parse method I described in the first section, so the actual handling of strings is the same. The code in Listing 2.7 illustrates the same functionality as the previous listing, but using the System.Convert methods.

**LISTING 2.7**   Using System.Convert

```
Private Sub btnConvert_Click( _
        ByVal sender As System.Object, _
        ByVal e As System.EventArgs) _
            Handles btnConvert.Click
    Dim myDate As Date
    Dim myInteger As Integer

    myDate = System.Convert.ToDateTime(Me.dateEntry.Text)
    myInteger = System.Convert.ToInt32(Me.numberEntry.Text)

    MsgBox(myDate)
    MsgBox(myInteger)
End Sub
```

In Listing 2.8, you are using a more generalized solution. The Visual Basic .NET conversion functions (CDate, CInt, CDec, and so on) will convert values in any one of several ways, one of which is through parsing.

**LISTING 2.8**   Using the Visual Basic Conversion Functions

```
Private Sub btnVBConvert_Click( _
        ByVal sender As System.Object, _
        ByVal e As System.EventArgs) _
            Handles btnVBConvert.Click
    Dim myDate As Date
    Dim myInteger As Integer

    myDate = CDate(Me.dateEntry.Text)
    myInteger = CInt(Me.numberEntry.Text)

    MsgBox(myDate)
    MsgBox(myInteger)
End Sub
```

It is important to realize that these Visual Basic specific conversion functions are more powerful than the basic Parse and Convert.To methods described previously. For example, look at how each of these routines handles converting a selection of sample strings into integers.

| String | Integer.Parse | Convert.ToInt32 | CInt |
|---|---|---|---|
| "12,500" | Error | Error | 12500 |
| "12" | 12 | 12 | 12 |
| "12500" | 12500 | 12500 | 12500 |
| "12500.00" | Error | Error | 12500 |
| "$12,500.00" | Error | Error | 12500 |
| "$12,500.10" | Error | Error | 12500 |
| "&HFF" | (VB syntax for the hex value FF) 255 | Error | Error |

As the table clearly indicates, CInt is capable of successfully parsing a much wider range of acceptable text values into integers. You will obtain similar results if you compare the corresponding functions for other data types. Another standard Visual Basic function available in Visual Basic .NET, IsNumeric, correctly recognizes the same strings as CInt() as being numeric values. If you need to convert into a type other than the ones covered by CInt, CStr, and the other pre-existing conversion methods, you can use CType. CType takes two arguments, the variable or value to be converted and the desired type. The following line of code shows how you can use CType to convert a variable into an uncommon type.

```
Dim myClass As Class1 = CType(myObj, Class1)
```

### Type Coercion (Casting)

Both of these methods are performing conversions, but I consider a true data type conversion to be when you view the information in the variable as another data type. It is the same data, different view. As an example, consider this routine that accepts one of its parameters into a variable typed as an object. The Object type is essentially the same as stating no type information at all, so before you can use the value passed into this routine you will likely want to convert it into a strongly typed variable such as an integer (see Listing 2.9).

**LISTING 2.9** Sometimes You Have an Object When You Want a Strongly Typed Variable Such as an Integer

```
Sub ShowMyName(ByVal numberOfTimes As Object)



End Sub
```

Now, if the variable passed in was actually an integer, you are really just casting it back to that data type; you are not converting/changing it. To perform a conversion of this type in Visual Basic .NET you could use the CInt, CDate, CDouble, and so on functions, but you can also perform a true cast (just changing the data type of the value without interpreting or changing the information) by using the DirectCast function.

`DirectCast` is new to VB .NET, and it is a more efficient way to coerce a variable from one type to another, but it will work only if the object you are trying to cast is truly of the destination type. In general, the `CInt`, `CDec`, and `CDbl` functions are more flexible and will work in a wider range of situations. In many situations where I would consider using `DirectCast`, I first check the value to ensure that it truly is of the correct type for a `DirectCast` to succeed. To check a value's type, you can use the `TypeOf` keyword, as shown on line 2 of Listing 2.10.

**LISTING 2.10**   If You Know the Underlying Type of a Variable You Can Use `DirectCast` to Coerce it from Object to a Strongly Typed Value

```
Sub ShowMyName(ByVal numberOfTimes As Object)
    If TypeOf numberOfTimes Is Integer Then
        Dim idx, repeatCount As Integer
        repeatCount = _
            DirectCast(numberOfTimes, Integer)
        For idx = 1 To repeatCount
            Debug.WriteLine("Duncanma")
        Next
    End If
End Sub
```

## No More "Set" or "Let"

Visual Basic 6.0 treats assigning an object type to a variable differently than assigning a value type; objects require the use of a special `Set` keyword, whereas value types can either use the `Let` keyword or just omit the keyword altogether. Listing 2.11 illustrates the different syntax required for value types and object types.

**LISTING 2.11**   In Visual Basic 6.0, You Had to Use the `Set` keyword to Assign an Object Reference to a Variable

```
Private Sub Command1_Click()
    Dim thisCurrentForm As Form
    Set thisCurrentForm = Me

    Dim myInteger As Integer
    myInteger = 3
    Let myInteger = 3 'same as previous line
End Sub
```

Visual Basic .NET makes no distinction between the two types of assignment (as shown in Listing 2.12); both are accomplished with the equals sign and no special keyword.

**LISTING 2.12**   No More Set or Let in Your Visual Basic .NET Code!

```
Private Sub Button1_Click( _
        ByVal sender As System.Object, _
        ByVal e As System.EventArgs) _
            Handles Button1.Click
    Dim thisCurrentForm As Form
    thisCurrentForm = Me

    Dim myInteger As Integer
    myInteger = 3
End Sub
```

# No More "As Any"

When creating declarations for external procedures (such as Win32 APIs) in Visual Basic 6.0, it was possible to declare a parameter As Any (see Listing 2.13). This indicates that multiple data type values were possible and you could pass in any one of them to the API call.

**LISTING 2.13**   In Visual Basic 6.0, As Any Allowed You to Declare an API Call Without Specifying a Specific Data Type

```
Public Declare Function SendMessage _
    Lib "user32" Alias "SendMessageA" _
    (ByVal hwnd As Long, ByVal wMsg As Long, _
    ByVal wParam As Long, lParam As Any) As Long
```

In Visual Basic .NET, you must be more specific; if a parameter of an API call can take more than one data type, you can declare more than one variation on the call and pick which one you want to use based on the data type. Declaring more than one version of a specific external procedure is possible due to the new OO features in Visual Basic .NET (specifically a concept called *overloading*), which is discussed in Chapter 7, "Object Oriented Programming in Visual Basic .NET."

**LISTING 2.14**   By Using Overloads in Visual Basic .NET, You Can Use Strongly Typed Values, While Still Supporting More than One Data Type

```
Public Overloads Declare Function SendMessage _
    Lib "user32" Alias "SendMessageA" _
    (ByVal hwnd As Long, ByVal wMsg As Long, _
    ByVal wParam As Long, ByVal lParam As Integer) As Long
```

**LISTING 2.14**   Continued

```
Public Overloads Declare Function SendMessage _
    Lib "user32" Alias "SendMessageA" _
    (ByVal hwnd As Long, ByVal wMsg As Long, _
     ByVal wParam As Long, ByVal lParam As String) As Long
```

# Miscellaneous Changes

For the most part, Visual Basic 6.0's operators and statements have made it into Visual Basic .NET without any changes, but a few have been altered or removed completely. A brief list of the removed language elements includes Imp, Eqv, GoSub, LSet, VarPtr, ObjPtr, StrPtr, AscB, ChrB, and MidB. If none of those elements sounds familiar, it is not surprising as they are all infrequently used. In addition to those elements that have been removed, several new language features have been added including new shortcut operators, new loop syntax, new bit shift operators and new short-circuiting versions of the standard And/Or Boolean operators.

A few other changes have occurred in the syntax for defining classes, calling procedures, specifying ByRef vs. ByVal parameters, and setting the return value of a function, all of which are covered in the "Class, Sub, and Function Changes" section later in the chapter.

## New Shortcut Operators

Visual Basic .NET introduces a new syntax for performing some simple mathematical operations, essentially shortcuts for the normal method of performing these operations. Each of the new operators is shown in the following table (the sample column assumes that X is equal to six and S is equal to "Hello World").

| += | Shorthand for adds a value and assigns the result | X += 2 (X holds 8) |
|---|---|---|
| [ms]= | Shorthand for subtracts a value and assigns the result | X [ms]= 3 (X holds 3) |
| *= | Shorthand for multiplies a value and assigns the result | X *= 6 (X holds 36) |
| /= | Shorthand for divides by a value and assigns the result | X /= 2 (X holds 3) |
| &= | Shorthand for combines with a string and assigns the result | S &= ", John" (S holds "Hello World, John") |

In each case, the result is the same as using the regular syntax (x += 2 is exactly the same as x = x + 2), but the shorter form appeals to many programmers, especially those who come from a C++ background. Although you might have also seen the ++ or − syntax (which increments or decrements a variable by one) in another language, that syntax has not been added to the Visual Basic .NET language.

## No More Default Properties

In Visual Basic 6.0 controls and classes could have default properties, which would be assumed if no property name was specified. These default properties allowed for quite a few code shortcuts, including omitting the Text property when working with a TextBox control, but they are no longer available in Visual Basic .NET.

*SHOP TALK*

### BEING EXPLICIT

As you read through the descriptions for each of the changes between Visual Basic 6.0 and Visual Basic .NET, you should start to notice a common theme. For many of these issues, what is changing is the *default* behavior, what happens when you haven't explicitly specified what you wanted. Consider the case of variables without a datatype, you are essentially stating that you don't know what you are going to use that variable for and leaving it up to the compiler to figure out what to do. There certainly are times when you need a variable that can hold anything (a Variant in Visual Basic 6.0 and an Object in Visual Basic .NET), but in most cases where I have seen undeclared variables or variables declared without datatypes, the use of the variable was very well known, but the programmer just didn't bother to specify a datatype. To save a bit of typing, the code of your project became a little harder to understand and now harder to upgrade.

The same goes for default properties, although you always knew you were interested in the .Text property of that TextBox, some programmers skipped it because they could and everything ended up working. Well, once again, a few characters of extra typing have been saved in return for more confusing source code. I have often been bugged by other programmers when they see me using .Text, ByRef/ByVal and other *unnecessary* bits of code in my Visual Basic 6.0 projects, but I have always tried to err on the side of being fully explicit. The less insider information a person needs about your code and the version of the compiler you were using when it was written the better.

Whenever possible, and you don't have a choice in most places in Visual Basic .NET, be explicit in your coding (and your documentation) and you will be thankful in the long run.

## New Loop Syntax

For and For Each loops each require special variables that represent the index of the loop in the case of the For loop or are populated with an element of an expression in the case of the For Each loop. In earlier versions of Visual Basic (and even in the original 2002 release of Visual Basic .NET), these control variables had to be declared before they could be used in the loop statement (assuming declaration of variable was required due to the Option Explicit statement). An example of declaring and then using a control variable in both the For and For Each loops is shown in Listing 2.15. Note that Debug.WriteLine (shown in the same listing) is the VB .NET equivalent of the Visual Basic 6 method Debug.Print (which has been removed from the language), and it will output values to the Output window of Visual Studio .NET.

LISTING 2.15    Declaring Control Variables Outside of the Loop

```
Dim idx As Integer
For idx = 0 To 10
    Debug.WriteLine(idx)
Next


Dim driveLetter As String
For Each driveLetter In Environment.GetLogicalDrives()
    Debug.WriteLine(driveLetter)
Next
```

Now, with the changes in the Visual Basic .NET 2003 release, you can declare your control variable as part of the loop statement. An example of the new syntax is shown in Listing 2.16 for a simple For loop with an integer control variable that is incremented from 0 to 10.

LISTING 2.16    Declaring the Control Variable as Part of the Loop Statement

```
For idx As Integer = 0 To 10
    Debug.WriteLine(idx)
Next
```

The syntax for the For Each statement is the same (and is shown in listing 2.17), although the type for a For loop must be a primitive numeric (Byte, Short, Integer, Long, Decimal, Single, or Double). In the case of For Each loop, the type is dependent on the particular expression being enumerated through.

LISTING 2.17    For Each Loops Benefit from the Same New Feature

```
For Each driveLetter As String _
        In Environment.GetLogicalDrives()
    Debug.WriteLine(driveLetter)
Next
```

This new loop variable, if defined within the For/For Each statement, is scoped to the loop block; meaning that it is unavailable outside of that section of code. The restricted scope of this new variable means that if you need access to the loop variable outside of the loop itself, you will need to use the pre-existing method; defining your variable prior to using it in the For or For Each statement. For example, Listing 2.18 compiles successfully and displays a value of 11.

**LISTING 2.18**   Control Variables Declared Outside of the Loop Are Available After the Loop has Completed

```
Dim idx As Integer
For idx = 0 To 10
    'do nothing
Next
MsgBox(idx)
```

If the variable had been defined as part of the For statement, it would be out of scope once the For loop ends. The code in Listing 2.19 will not even compile, as it results in a "Name 'idx' is not declared." error on the last line.

**LISTING 2.19**   Declaring Your Control Variable as Part of the Loop Means it Is Scoped to Just That Loop

```
For idx As Integer = 0 To 10
    'do nothing
Next
MsgBox(idx)
```

## New BitShift Operators

*BitShifting* is the modification of a number by moving all of its bits a specified number of positions to the left or right. Bits that fall outside of the size of the original value (on either the high or low sides of the binary value) are discarded. The code sample shown in Listing 2.20 illustrates shifting a binary value four positions to the left and then two to the right. Note the numberToBeShifted >>= 2 on line 10; this is a shortcut operator for numberToBeShifted = numberToBeShifted >> 2, and one exists for left shifting as well.

**LISTING 2.20**   BitShifting Manipulates Integers by Moving their Underlying Bits a Specified Number of Positions to the Left or Right

```
Private Sub btnBitShift_Click( _
    ByVal sender As System.Object, _
    ByVal e As System.EventArgs) _
        Handles btnBitShift.Click
    '&HFF = the hex value FF, which equals 255, and
    '1111 1111 in binary
```

**LISTING 2.20** Continued

```
    Dim numberToBeShifted As Integer = &HFF

    numberToBeShifted = numberToBeShifted << 4
    numberToBeShifted >>= 2
    MsgBox(numberToBeShifted)
End Sub
```

Although BitShifting has been a commonly used technique in computer mathematics for a very long time, Visual Basic has never had direct support for this operation before the release of Visual Basic .NET 2003. Before these two operators were available, you could achieve the same effect as a BitShift by multiplying or dividing your value by a power of 2 (the exponent represents the number of positions to shift), but an actual BitShift such as these new operators provide is faster.

## New Short-Circuiting Conditionals

Similar to an election outcome in the United States, the result of a Boolean expression is often known before the complete expression has been evaluated. Consider this Boolean expression: (X > 1) AND (X < 10). If X is one, as soon as you evaluate the left side of the expression (returning False), you know that the right side is irrelevant. Due to the nature of the AND operator, there is no need to evaluate the other side. The entire expression will be False, no matter what value is returned on the other side. This is something that a human would do without much thought when evaluating Boolean expressions, but it is not always so clear for the computer.

The behavior that we expect, not evaluating the unnecessary portion of an expression, is called *short-circuiting,* but neither Visual Basic 6.0 nor Visual Basic .NET work this way by default. To make Visual Basic .NET short-circuit a Boolean expression, you need to use alternative forms of the AND and OR operators, ANDALSO and ORELSE. You do not need to just trust that it behaves in this fashion though; some simple test code (see Listing 2.21) can be used to see exactly what happens.

**LISTING 2.21** Short-Circuiting Promotes the Most Efficient Processing of Boolean Expressions by Skipping Unnecessary Expression Evaluations

```
Private Sub Button1_Click( _
        ByVal sender As System.Object, _
        ByVal e As System.EventArgs) _
            Handles Button1.Click
    If Test("Left") AndAlso Test("Right") Then
        'do something
    End If
```

**LISTING 2.21**  Continued

```
End Sub

Function Test(ByVal sInput As String) As Boolean
    Debug.WriteLine(sInput)
    Test = False
End Function
```

If the Test() function returns False, as it does in Listing 2.21, you know what the overall expression will return simply by evaluating the left side. Running the code in Listing 2.21 will produce only one line of debug output, in this case, "Left". If Test() returns True, both sides need to be executed, and the program will output both "Left" and "Right". To test the behavior of Boolean operators, try both True and False for the return value of Test and switch between AndAlso/And/Or/OrElse in the If statement to see what results you get.

| VALUE RETURNED BY TEST() | OUTPUT WITH AND | OUTPUT WITH ANDALSO |
|---|---|---|
| False | Left<br>Right | Left |
| True | Left<br>Right | Left<br>Right |

| VALUE RETURNED BY TEST() | OUTPUT WITH OR | OUTPUT WITH ORELSE |
|---|---|---|
| False | Left<br>Right | Left<br>Right |
| True | Left<br>Right | Left |

In this sample code, it wouldn't be a terrible hit to the program's performance if both sides of the expression were evaluated every time the If statement was executed, but if the function(s) in question were more complicated and more time consuming, using a short-circuiting operator could really help performance. For maximum benefit, you should structure your expressions so that the most complicated portions appear to the right of the short-circuiting operator.

## Class, Sub, and Function Changes

There have been a few changes to how you create classes, define procedures, and set function return values in Visual Basic .NET, covered in the following sections.

### Files No Longer Define Classes, Forms, or Modules

Classes , modules, and forms are no longer file based; now they are based on statements in the code file that mark the beginning and end of the particular item in question. This means that a single code file can contain any number of classes, forms, or modules, as illustrated in Listing 2.22.

**LISTING 2.22**    A Single .VB File Can Contain Multiple Classes, Modules, and/or Forms by Using the `Class…End Class` and `Module…End Module` Keywords

```
Public Class Class1
    Public Sub DoSomething(ByVal howManyTimes As Integer)
    End Sub
End Class

Module Module1
    Sub Main()
        Dim x As New Class1
        x.DoSomething(5)
    End Sub
End Module
```

Although it is now possible to include more than one class in a single .vb file, it is generally considered best to stick with only one class per file.

### ByVal by Default

Parameters in procedure declarations default to `ByVal` (passed by value), whereas they defaulted to `ByRef` (pass by reference) in Visual Basic 6.0 and earlier. The best way to handle this change is to always explicitly state `ByRef` or `ByVal` for each of the parameters in your procedure. Listing 2.23 shows two pieces of code, one in Visual Basic 6.0 and one in Visual Basic .NET. They appear very similar but behave differently due to this change.

**LISTING 2.23**    The Same Code Can Produce Different Results Depending on the Version of Visual Basic Used

```
'VB6 Code
Private Sub Command1_Click()
    Dim myInteger As Integer
    myInteger = 5
    TestByVal myInteger
    MsgBox myInteger
End Sub

Private Sub TestByVal(inty As Integer)
```

**LISTING 2.23**   Continued

```
    inty = inty * 2
End Sub
'VB.NET Code
Private Sub Button1_Click( _
        ByVal sender As System.Object, _
        ByVal e As System.EventArgs) _
        Handles Button1.Click
    Dim myInteger As Integer = 5
    TestByVal(myInteger)
    MsgBox(myInteger)
End Sub

Private Sub TestByVal(int As Integer)
    int = int * 2
End Sub
```

The Visual Basic 6 code displays a result of 10, whereas the Visual Basic .NET code would display 5. Note that it would be difficult to even produce the Visual Basic .NET code from Listing 2.23 in Visual Studio .NET. Visual Studio .NET automatically adds the ByVal next to your variable name, when you write code like the procedure declaration shown on Line 11 of the VB .NET code.

**Parentheses Are Now Required**

When invoking a procedure in Visual Basic 6.0 and earlier, parentheses were required around the arguments when calling functions, but were not allowed when calling Sub procedures unless you used the Call statement in front of your call to the Sub procedure. In Visual Basic .NET, parentheses are required (and will be automatically added by Visual Studio .NET) around the arguments for both Sub and Function calls. Listing 2.24 demonstrates the difference, showing you a valid MsgBox call in both VB6 and VB.NET.

**LISTING 2.24**   Parameter Arguments

```
'VB6
MsgBox "MsgBoxPrompt", vbCritical, "MsgBoxTitle"

'VB.NET
MsgBox("MsgBoxPrompt", vbCritical, "MsgBoxTitle")
```

### Returning a Value from a Function

To return the result from a function in Visual Basic 6.0, you assigned the result to the function name, and that value would be returned to the calling program when the function exited. This syntax is still available in Visual Basic .NET, but now you can alternatively use a Return statement to send back the result of the function and exit the function all at the same time. Listing 2.25 provides an illustration of the Return statement in action.

**LISTING 2.25**  Visual Basic .NET Supports the Return Statement to End a Function and Specify a Return Value

```
Function ComputeSalesTax(ByVal amount As Double, _
    ByVal tax As Single) As Double
    'could use ComputeSalesTax = amount * tax
    Return amount * tax
End Function
```

# References, Namespaces, and Imports

As you move through the rest of this book, it is important that you understand this set of concepts—references, namespaces, and imports. These are relatively complex concepts, but they come up right from the beginning so they need to be covered now.

## References

If you have programmed in Visual Basic 6.0, the concept of references should not be new to you; you add a reference to an external library (usually a DLL or an OCX) so that your code can use the classes contained within that library. This concept still exists in Visual Basic .NET, and you even have an Add Reference dialog box, which allows you to add references to either .NET or COM libraries. We will get into the difference between adding a reference to a COM object and a .NET object in Chapter 9, "Integrating with COM," but for now the two can be treated as the same.

Visual Studio .NET adds a few references to your project(s) by default, but you can always see what references have been added by viewing a project's references folder in the Solution Explorer window.

**FIGURE 2.2**  The References folder lists all the library references that have been added to a specific project.

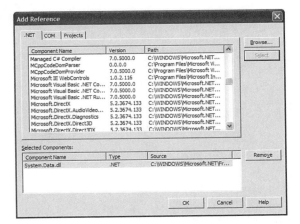

**FIGURE 2.3**  The References dialog box allows you to specify external libraries for use in your project.

To add a new reference, right-click the References folder (see Figure 2.2) and pick Add Reference from the menu that appears. This will bring up the Add Reference dialog box (see Figure 2.3) where you can select a .NET or COM reference from the list of available libraries, or browse the file system to find the appropriate file.

Adding a reference to a library is required if you are going to use any of its features, just like in Visual Basic 6.0. What can be confusing is how the classes contained within a library are named and structured, and that is all based around the concept of namespaces.

## Namespaces

A *namespace* is an abstract concept used to group a number of classes or modules, allowing you to logically categorize all these objects within a single higher-level object. So, by having a Namespace Chapter2 at the top of your classes and a corresponding End Namespace at the bottom, you effectively create a grouping called Chapter2 that contains all the classes within it. After this namespace exists, it is used by default for object references made in code within the same namespace, but can also be explicitly stated (Dim objMyClass as Chapter2.Class1).

There are many reasons why you might want to create and use namespaces, not the least of which is the basis for the moniker "namespace," as a way to create a private area to ensure that your class names are unique. By defining a namespace, the class Class1 becomes Chapter2.Class1, and therefore will not conflict with any other class created with the name Class1.

Another more subtle reason to use namespaces is because they produce easier code to maintain. The grouping of classes under higher-level namespaces leads to code that is clearly defined by some categorization scheme and is therefore more readable and easy to maintain. Note that the .NET Framework itself is defined as a deep hierarchy of namespaces. For example, System.Data.SqlClient.SqlConnection is a class within the Framework, it is really the class SqlConnection within the System.Data.SqlClient namespace.

This method of grouping classes is similar to the concept of variable scope; a class only has to be unique within its particular namespace. If you do happen to make a class that shares its name with a class that exists in another namespace, you will need to make sure that you are specifying the full name of the class whenever you reference it from outside its own namespace. So if you had a Class1 in the namespace NS1 and another Class1 in the namespace NS2, you would have to use the full name of the class (NS1.Class1) in any situation where there could be confusion.

Namespaces are hierarchical, which allows you to create a multiple level scheme for grouping your classes and objects, just like within the .NET Framework. There are two ways to create a lower-level namespace: Either define the namespace using the fully qualified name as in Listing 2.26, or nest namespace definitions (see Listing 2.27).

LISTING 2.26    Declaring a Multipart Namespace

```
Imports System
Namespace MyApp.Console
    Module Main
        Sub Main()
            Dim objHW As New MyApp.Console.Utilities()
            objHW.PrintOut()
        End Sub
    End Module

    Public Class Utilities
        'Run the application
        Public Sub PrintOut()
            Console.WriteLine(Environment.MachineName)
            Console.WriteLine(Environment.SystemDirectory)
            Console.WriteLine(Environment.GetLogicalDrives())
            Console.WriteLine(Environment.Version.ToString())
        End Sub
    End Class
End Namespace
```

LISTING 2.27    Using Nested Namespaces to Create Object Hierarchies

```
Imports System
Namespace MyApp
    Namespace Console
        Module Main
            Sub Main()
                Dim objHW As New MyApp.Console.Utilities()
```

**LISTING 2.27**   Continued

```
                objHW.PrintOut()
            End Sub
        End Module

        Public Class Utilities
            'Run the application
            Public Sub PrintOut()
                Console.WriteLine(Environment.MachineName)
                Console.WriteLine(Environment.SystemDirectory)
                Console.WriteLine(Environment.GetLogicalDrives())
                Console.WriteLine(Environment.Version.ToString())
            End Sub
        End Class
    End Namespace
End Namespace
```

Within your applications, you can use namespaces as a way to group conceptually related code together, but other than their effect on the scope of classes, namespaces are not required for building a system. You will usually end up using at least one namespace whether you want to or not, because your entire project is considered to be contained within a single namespace. That namespace is defined on the General tab of the Project properties dialog box; whatever value is in the Root Namespace field (see Figure 2.4) becomes the overall namespace for your entire project. It is possible to blank this field and therefore remove the concept of a root namespace completely for a given project.

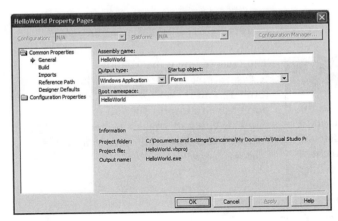

**FIGURE 2.4**   The Root Namespace contains all of your classes and other code contained within your project.

It can be either a single name (like HelloWorld) or you can use a multi-level namespace as the root for your project (SAMS.Samples.VB.HelloWorld would be fine). Any additional namespaces you create in your code are nested below that project-level namespace, as are your classes and other items. As long as you are working only in a single project, you likely won't notice or care about the root namespace. All of your project code is contained under the root and therefore it is not necessary to specify the root namespace when referring to code within the same project.

## Imports

The Imports statement is often confused with the concept of references, but they are not the same thing. As discussed in the section on namespaces, the full name of a class includes its namespace. The Form class, for example, is actually System.Windows.Forms.Form. We don't want to use the full name throughout our code though, and that is where the Imports statement comes in. An Imports statement specifies a namespace; by placing one or more Imports statements at the top of your code file, you can use classes from those namespaces without using the full path. So, if you want to refer to the System.Windows.Forms.Form class as just Form (as shown in Listing 2.28), you can add an Imports System.Windows.Forms statement to the top of the code file (.VB file).

**LISTING 2.28**    Using Imports Avoids the Need for Fully Specified Class Names

```
Imports System.Windows.Forms

Public Class ShowStuff
    Sub ShowAForm(ByVal myForm As Form)
        myForm.Show()
    End Sub
End Class
```

## DEFAULT IMPORTS CAN BE CONFUSING

Visual Studio .NET and Visual Basic can make the whole imports concept more confusing than it already is, because they include a set of "default" imports when you create a new project. If you check out the project properties window (select Properties from the Project menu on Visual Studio's main menu bar) and select the Imports option, you will see a list of default imports that are considered to be always on (see Figure 2.5).

The Imports line (Line 1) allows you to refer to System.Windows.Forms.Form as just Form (Line 4), and makes for cleaner code. You don't have to import the full namespace name, if you had Imports System at the top of the code file, you could refer to a form as Windows.Forms.Form.

61

Should You Use Existing Visual Basic Syntax or the New .NET Equivalents?

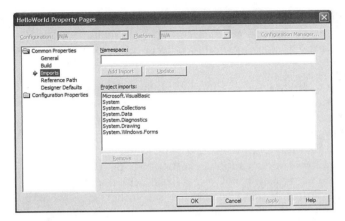

**FIGURE 2.5** Project can include a default list of imports that are considered to be always on.

I have seen quite a few posts on Internet forums and newsgroups that confuse the concept of imports and references. If you want to use a library (System.Xml for example), you need to have a reference to it, either by default due to the wonders of Visual Studio .NET, or because you explicitly added one. That is it; if you have the reference, you can use the classes contained within that library. No Imports statement is required; just use the fully qualified name of the class (System.Xml.XmlDocument) and everything should work fine. Now, once you have a reference, if you want to use the classes within a certain namespace without having to fully qualify them, you need to add an Imports statement.

Two general points about Imports:

- Add Imports statements to the individual code files, not to the project-level settings (as shown in Figure 2.4). That way if you pass a (.VB) code file around independently of the project, the imports won't be lost.

- The System.Xml namespace is contained within System.Xml.dll. That is just a happy alignment of namespace and filename due to a naming convention within Microsoft, it is not required to be this way and it often won't be; you will often find that the namespace and the library filename don't match.

# Should You Use Existing Visual Basic Syntax or the New .NET Equivalents?

Visual Basic .NET includes many language features of earlier versions for which corresponding functionality exists in the .NET Framework. This includes major areas such as file IO, for which there is a completely new model available in the Framework, and minor items such as the `MsgBox` statement, which has an almost exact counterpart in the Framework method `MessageBox.Show()`. For each of these cases, where the same functionality exists in both the "native" Visual Basic commands and in the Framework, you have to decide which one you are going to use.

As you read this book, we will attempt to guide your decision by showing you which of the options we use in each code sample. For most of the areas where there is a choice, it is essentially a personal preference, but in some cases one or the other is better and we will let you know why that is. You may hear the opinion expressed that you should not use any feature that is Visual Basic specific, but we feel that is a definite mistake. The language-specific features are what makes Visual Basic unique and you should use them whenever they work for you. It is also worth noting there are many features of Visual Basic .NET that are not included in the .NET Framework. For example, Visual Basic's conversion functions (`CInt`, `CStr`, `CDec`, and so on) do a lot more than the `Int32.Parse` routine supplied by the Framework, and `IsNumeric` is a powerful function that many C# programmers would love to use (and they can, if they reference the `Microsoft.VisualBasic.dll` from their projects).

Take advantage of all of the functionality your language of choice offers; if you are programming in Visual Basic, program the Visual Basic way.

# In Brief

This chapter has provided a whirlwind tour of the key language changes in Visual Basic .NET including:

- The new `Option` statements
- Changes in how variables and arrays are declared
- New operators, loops, and conditionals
- Changes to the basic data types between Visual Basic .NET and previous versions
- Changes in how procedures, parameters, and classes are declared and executed
- How imports, references, and namespaces work

# Building Windows Applications

## 3

## The Way Things Were

For most of Visual Basic's history, you did not need to specify you were building a rich-client application—all the applications you built were rich-client apps. Web development has never been the purpose of Visual Basic. This focus on developing stand-alone or client/server applications with a Windows user interface created a very tight bond between the VB language and the forms engine within it. There was no need to distinguish between the language and the tools for building an interface in VB6, but there certainly is in .NET.

In Visual Basic .NET, the technologies that enable you to create "standard" windows applications are part of the .NET Framework, available to any .NET language. This is a huge change from the way things were. In each of the following sections, before going into detail on how the new Forms technology works in Visual Basic .NET, I briefly describe some of the relevant details about Visual Basic 6.0 forms.

## The Windows Forms Model

Forms in Visual Basic 6.0 were distinct files from other types of code (such as modules and classes) stored in two parts—a .FRM file that contained the code and the layout of the form and a .FRX file, which was a special kind of resource file that held any embedded resources needed by the form. When you designed a form using the visual tools, controls were added to forms and properties were set (such as the size and position of various controls) without any visible effect on your code. Changing the position of a button would change some hidden (not shown in the IDE at least) text (shown below for a simple one button "Hello World" application) that you could access and change using a text editor, but all of these properties were not part of your code. Setting a property in code was therefore very different than setting it through the visual interface.

**LISTING 3.1**   The Code Behind a Visual Basic 6.0 Form

```
VERSION 5.00
Begin VB.Form Form1
   Caption         =   "Form1"
   ClientHeight    =   3090
   ClientLeft      =   60
   ClientTop       =   450
   ClientWidth     =   4680
   LinkTopic       =   "Form1"
   ScaleHeight     =   3090
   ScaleWidth      =   4680
   StartUpPosition =   3  'Windows Default
   Begin VB.CommandButton Command1
      Caption      =   "Hello World"
      Default      =   -1  'True
      Height       =   495
      Left         =   840
      TabIndex     =   0
      Top          =   480
      Width        =   1335
   End
End
Attribute VB_Name = "Form1"
Attribute VB_GlobalNameSpace = False
Attribute VB_Creatable = False
Attribute VB_PredeclaredId = True
Attribute VB_Exposed = False
```

This special area of the form would also contain object references (in the form of GUIDs) for any ActiveX controls you used. Although editing the .FRM file directly was not encouraged, that was exactly what you had to do to fix a corrupt form.

Forms in .NET change everything just described. Forms are no longer "special" files; they are just code (.VB files in .NET), although they certainly can have associated resource files with them. Editing the properties of the form or of the controls on the form does not add hidden text to the form file; it generates real VB .NET code that sets the properties in the same way that you would in your own code. If you follow along with me and create a sample VB .NET form, you can explore the new forms designer and browse the code generated by your visual editing.

## Building a Hello World Sample

First, go ahead and fire up Visual Studio .NET. Although it is possible to create Visual Basic .NET applications without using any IDE (another example of how VB has changed in its move to .NET), this book assumes that you have at least VB .NET Standard Edition and are therefore using the Visual Studio IDE.

Once it is loaded, you should see a start page. This start page has a few tabs and several different areas of information, but the main area (which is displayed by default) has all of the functionality you need at this point, including a list of recently opened projects and a New Project button. Click the New Project button, or select File, New, Project from the menu to bring up the New Project dialog box.

If you are new to Visual Studio .NET, this dialog box contains a lot more options than the equivalent from Visual Basic 6.0, including the capability to create Web Services, Windows Services, Console Applications, and more. For now though, pick the standard project for creating a new Windows Application: Windows Application. Selecting this project type (and picking a name and location, and then clicking OK) creates a new solution containing a single project that contains one blank Windows form and a code file called AssemblyInfo.vb. At this point, if you look around the Visual Studio .NET IDE, you will see an interface that is somewhat similar to Visual Basic 6.0, but many things have changed. In the first chapter of this book, I covered the IDE, detailing the key changes from Visual Basic 6.0 and many of the important features.

Moving along with this quick sample, you will build the application's user interface by placing a button onto the form. To work with the form, you need to use its design view, which is accessed through the same steps as in VB6. Double-click the form (in the Solution Explorer) to bring it up in the design view or right-click it and pick View Designer (this was View Object in VB6, but the meaning is the same) from the context menu.

Once you have the form's design view up, you can use the toolbox to select controls and place them onto your form. The toolbox looks a little different from the one in VB6. It has sliding groups to categorize all the different types of controls and lists the controls with an icon and text by default. It works a little differently as well. When you worked with the toolbox in Visual Basic 6.0, you had two choices of how to interact with it:

- You could double-click a control and a new instance of that type of control would be added to the form with a default size and location.

- You could also select a control and then click the form to set the top-left location and drag an outline out to represent the size of the control.

In the Windows forms designer, you have those two methods of placing a control and an additional option:

- You can drag a control from the toolbox onto the desired location on your form and it will be placed at that position with a default size.

Using any one of the three possible methods, place a single button from the toolbox onto the form. It is a minor change, but it is worth noting that the CommandButton control from Visual Basic 6.0 has changed to the Button control in VS .NET 2002 and 2003. Just like in Visual Basic 6.0, you can double-click this new button to start writing an event handler for its most common event (in this case Click). All you want to do is pop up a message box, which you can do with the exact same line of code that you would use in Visual Basic 6.0 (see Listing 3.2).

**LISTING 3.2**   Hello World Does Not Look Too Different in .NET

```
Private Sub Button1_Click( _
        ByVal sender As System.Object, _
        ByVal e As System.EventArgs) _
        Handles Button1.Click
    MsgBox("Hello World!")
End Sub
```

You can run the project at this point if you want; F5 works fine for that purpose or you can select Start from the Debug menu. The real reason for building this form was to look at the code generated by your actions in the designer.

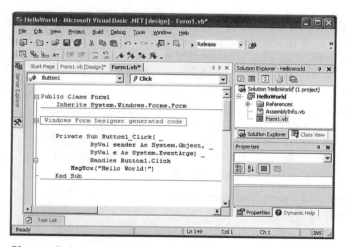

**Figure 3.1**   Regions allow you to hide blocks of code.

## Exploring the Designer Generated Code

Switch to the code for the form (right-click the form in the designer or the Solution Explorer and select View Code) and you will see your button's click procedure and an area called Windows Form Designer generated code, as shown in Figure 3.1.

That area is a *region*, a new feature of the code editor in Visual Studio .NET that allows you to collapse areas of code down to a single line to simplify the experience of browsing code. We discussed regions in Chapter 1, but all you have to know now is that the designer (the visual tool for creating forms) has used this feature to hide all of the code that it generated as you built the form. As a rule, you are not supposed to go into this area of code, which is why it is hidden by default, but you should at least understand the code in this area. In some cases, you might even need to change it. You can expand the designer code region by clicking the plus symbol next to the region name.

Inside the region, you will find a few key elements:

- A constructor for the form (a Sub New())

- A Dispose procedure

- Declarations of all of the controls on the form

- A sub called InitializeComponent

The Constructor and the Dispose routines are new to Visual Basic .NET, but they are relatively equivalent to the Class_Initialize and Class_Terminate events of Visual Basic 6.0 classes. The constructor is called when an instance of your form is created; the dispose is called before the form is destroyed. The real meat of the designer-generated code is the other two code elements—the list of declarations for all of the controls on the form and the InitializeComponent routine that sets up the properties of the controls on the form and of the Form itself. You did not set up many controls or even change many properties when creating this simple sample, but let's take a look at the generated code, shown in Listing 3.3.

**LISTING 3.3**   In VB .NET, You Can View and Even Edit All the Code that Builds Your Form's Interface

```
'NOTE: The following procedure is required by the Windows Form Designer
'It can be modified using the Windows Form Designer.
'Do not modify it using the code editor.
Friend WithEvents Button1 As System.Windows.Forms.Button
<System.Diagnostics.DebuggerStepThrough()> _
Private Sub InitializeComponent()
    Me.Button1 = New System.Windows.Forms.Button
    Me.SuspendLayout()
    '
    'Button1
    '
    Me.Button1.Location = New System.Drawing.Point(96, 88)
    Me.Button1.Name = "Button1"
    Me.Button1.TabIndex = 0
    Me.Button1.Text = "Button1"
    '
```

**LISTING 3.3**  Continued

```
    'Form1
    '
    Me.AutoScaleBaseSize = New System.Drawing.Size(5, 13)
    Me.ClientSize = New System.Drawing.Size(292, 273)
    Me.Controls.Add(Me.Button1)
    Me.Name = "Form1"
    Me.Text = "Form1"
    Me.ResumeLayout(False)
End Sub
```

The comment on the top of this routine lets you know that you can modify anything in here by using the visual designer, and that you should not change the code directly. This is pretty good advice, but let's ignore it for a moment and see what happens. If you look at lines 12-15 in Listing 3.3, you can see that they are setting the properties of the button, including the size. If you add some of your own code in there, even something as simple as outputting some text to the debug window, it could produce surprising results.

In this case, just adding a line (see Listing 3.4) causes the Windows Form Designer to fail when trying to parse the code, producing the helpful little error message shown in Figure 3.2.

**LISTING 3.4**  Editing the Windows Forms Designer Generated Code May Produce Unexpected Results

```
    '
    'Button1
    '
    Me.Button1.Location = New System.Drawing.Point(96, 88)
    Me.Button1.Name = "Button1"
    Debug.WriteLine("Testing!")
    Me.Button1.TabIndex = 0
    Me.Button1.Text = "Button1"
```

Other, less fatal, changes to the code are often undone the next time you change something in the designer (because the InitializeComponent procedure is regenerated), which can be quite frustrating. Code generators (such as the designers in Visual Studio .NET) work well in many situations, but when they have to support *round tripping* (where the code isn't just generated once; it is read back in and used by the designer whenever the form needs to be displayed), they tend to be very fragile. In this case, you cannot make code changes to most of the designer-generated area. The place where you can change code is in the constructor;

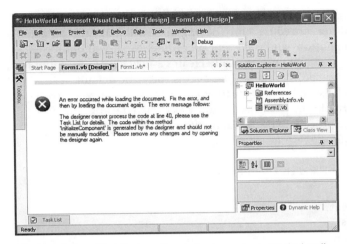

you can freely add code after the call to InitializeComponent as long as you do not remove that line! The best bet is to ignore all of the code inside this special region, other than the constructor, and make all of your property changes through the visual interface. Now let's go back to the button's click procedure and take a closer look at how .NET is handling events.

**Figure 3.2**   The Windows Forms Designer does not deal well with someone changing its code.

# Handling Events in .NET

Event handling has changed, for the better, in .NET. I never really thought anything of it, but event procedures in Visual Basic 6.0 were attached to the appropriate object and event based solely on the procedure's name. This reliance on names meant that if you had already created and written code for CommandButton1_Click and you renamed your button to the more meaningful saveFile, your event procedure would no longer be attached to this button.

If event handling is no longer based on procedure names, how do you connect a specific event handler with an object's event? There are two ways; one combines the familiar WithEvents keyword in your variable declarations with a new keyword Handles, and the other dynamically connects an object's event to an event handling procedure at runtime.

## Using WithEvents and the Handles Keyword

Although event handling in VB .NET has changed, as I described, using the Handles keyword is the closest model to pre-.NET Visual Basic and it is the model used by default by the Windows forms designer. Objects, such as controls, that expose events are declared using the WithEvents keyword, like they were in Visual Basic 6.0, and event procedures provide a Handles myObj.myEvent clause after the procedure declaration. Those two parts, the Handles and WithEvents, wire up a specific event handling procedure.

Returning to the first example, a simple button on a form, look at the code generated by the Windows forms designer to see how the designer wired the Button's Click event to a code procedure. The first line to look at is the declaration of the button itself:

```
Friend WithEvents Button1 As System.Windows.Forms.Button
```

The button is declared using the WithEvents keyword, which is required if you want to use the Handles keyword on the event handling procedure. Only having both will make the proper connection between this object (the button) and the event procedure. Next, you double-click the Button1 and the Windows forms designer automatically creates a new event procedure for the default event (Click). Controls can specify one of their events to be the default. If they do, the Windows forms designer will assume you want to work with that event when you double-click the control. The designer knows that the button was declared using the WithEvents keyword, so it creates the procedure declaration with Handles Button1.Click appended to the end (see Listing 3.5).

**LISTING 3.5**   Designer Generated Event Handlers Use the Handles Keyword

```
Private Sub Button1_Click( _
        ByVal sender As System.Object, _
        ByVal e As System.EventArgs) _
        Handles Button1.Click
    MsgBox("Hello World!")
End Sub
```

Up to this point, the syntax might be a little different, but the general idea is the same as in Visual Basic 6.0. The only change, the addition of the Handles keyword, is just a way to get around relying on the name of your event handling procedure. Even using WithEvents and Handles though, there is a new feature built into this method of handling events. It is possible to specify that a specific event procedure handle more than one event. If you were to add a second button to the form, (automatically named Button2) and to double-click it, the Windows forms designer would create a second event procedure (see Listing 3.6).

**LISTING 3.6**   The Windows Forms Designer Automatically Creates a Handler for the Default Event When You Double-Click a Control

```
Private Sub Button2_Click( _
        ByVal sender As System.Object, _
        ByVal e As System.EventArgs) _
        Handles Button2.Click
End Sub
```

This procedure declaration is followed by Handles Button2.Click, but you could instead modify the first Click procedure to handle both buttons' Click events, as shown in Listing 3.7.

**LISTING 3.7**  Listing More than One Object's Events After a Procedure Declaration Allows You to Consolidate Code

```
Private Sub Button1_Click( _
        ByVal sender As System.Object, _
        ByVal e As System.EventArgs) _
        Handles Button1.Click, Button2.Click
    MsgBox("Hello World!")

End Sub
```

Now, when either button is clicked, the same code will run. Any number of events can be handled by the same event procedure, assuming that all of the events have the same signature (the same set of arguments to their event procedures). It is also possible to have a single event handled by multiple procedures (see Listing 3.8) by having that event specified in multiple Handles clauses.

**LISTING 3.8**  One Event, Such as a Button's Click, Can be Handled by Multiple Routines

```
Private Sub ClickEvent1( _
        ByVal sender As System.Object, _
        ByVal e As System.EventArgs) _
        Handles Button2.Click
    MsgBox("ClickEvent1")
End Sub

Private Sub ClickEvent2( _
        ByVal sender As System.Object, _
        ByVal e As System.EventArgs) _
        Handles Button2.Click
    MsgBox("ClickEvent2")
End Sub
```

When Button2 is clicked, the code in both ClickEvent1 and ClickEvent2 is executed. You will use the first concept (multiple events being handled by a single event handler) more often than the second (multiple handlers for a single event), but it is good to know that the functionality exists if you need it. In the case of multiple events all being handled by a single event handler, you will likely need to know which specific control is raising (firing or causing) the event. For most events, the object that raises the event is passed in as the first parameter (usually named "sender") to the event procedure. The sender parameter is typed as an object, which means that you have to convert it into a more useful type (such as a Control or a Button) before you can work with it. Listing 3.9 shows a sample event procedure that is handling the Click event of 10 buttons; it *casts* (views an object as a different type) the sender parameter from Object to Button to determine the Button's text (caption).

**LISTING 3.9**   If You Handle the Events of Many Different Objects, the Sender Parameter Tells You which Object Caused the Current Event

```
Private Sub LotsOfButtons( _
        ByVal sender As System.Object, _
        ByVal e As System.EventArgs) _
        Handles Button1.Click, Button2.Click, _
                Button3.Click, Button4.Click, _
                Button5.Click, Button6.Click, _
                Button7.Click, Button8.Click, _
                Button9.Click, Button10.Click
    Dim clickedBtn As Button
    If TypeOf sender Is Button Then
        clickedBtn = DirectCast(sender, Button)
        MsgBox(clickedBtn.Text)
    End If
End Sub
```

It is worth noting, although perhaps a bit confusing, that you could have also written this routine using Control instead of Button, and this alternative is shown in Listing 3.10.

**LISTING 3.10**   All Windows Forms Controls Inherit from Control, so a Variable of that Type Can Be Used to Hold Any Control on Your Form

```
Private Sub LotsOfButtons( _
        ByVal sender As System.Object, _
        ByVal e As System.EventArgs) _
        Handles Button1.Click, Button2.Click, _
                Button3.Click, Button4.Click, _
                Button5.Click, Button6.Click, _
                Button7.Click, Button8.Click, _
                Button9.Click, Button10.Click
    Dim clickedCtrl As Control
    If TypeOf sender Is Control Then
        clickedCtrl = DirectCast(sender, Control)
        MsgBox(clickedCtrl.Text)
    End If
End Sub
```

The reason this works, and it does work, is due to the way in which Windows Forms controls have been written. All Windows Forms controls share the same base class, System.Windows.Forms.Control, and that class provides them with a set of common properties, events, and methods. Text is one of those common properties, so you can cast to Control instead of Button and everything will still work. What does that mean to you? It means you can write code to handle any control on a form and you never have to know what type of control it is. Without casting it to a specific type of control, you can work with any of the common properties available on the Control class including position and size properties, color properties, and many more. Combining the new flexibility in event handling with this common control class, there is a lot you can accomplish using WithEvents and handles. There are a few cases though, when even more flexibility is required, and that is where the other method of event handling comes in.

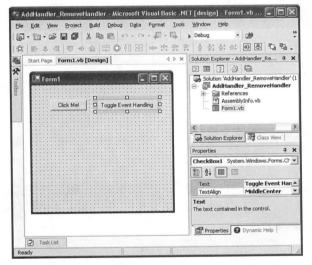

**Figure 3.3** The check box on this form, which is using the new toggle button appearance, turns event handling on and off for the button.

## Wiring Up Events Manually with AddHandler/ RemoveHandler

The WithEvents/Handles method of event handling is designed for when you know at design time which controls and which event handling procedures you are dealing with. If you are going to be working with objects and event procedures in a more dynamic fashion, you can use the AddHandler and RemoveHandler statements to connect an object's event to an event procedure at runtime. This is more of an advanced technique, and it will not likely be necessary in most applications, but here is a basic example to illustrate how these statements could be used. In this example, there is a Button and a CheckBox (set to look like a button) on an otherwise empty form (see Figure 3.3). When the CheckBox is pressed (see Listing 3.11), the button's Click event is attached using AddHandler to a simple event handler that displays a MsgBox. When the CheckBox is in its up position, the button is detached from its event handler using RemoveHandler.

**LISTING 3.11**   The CheckedChanged Event of the Check Box Is Used to Add and Remove an Event Handler for the Button's Click Event

```
Private Sub CheckBox1_CheckedChanged( _
        ByVal sender As System.Object, _
        ByVal e As System.EventArgs) _
        Handles CheckBox1.CheckedChanged
    If CheckBox1.Checked Then
        AddHandler Button1.Click, _
            AddressOf myClickHandler
    Else
        RemoveHandler Button1.Click, _
            AddressOf myClickHandler
    End If
End Sub

Private Sub myClickHandler( _
        ByVal sender As System.Object, _
        ByVal e As System.EventArgs)
    MsgBox("Event Handled!")
End Sub
```

Adding and removing an event handler is a more useful technique with non-form classes that raise events, but the procedure is the same.

## SHOP TALK

### DYNAMIC EVENT HANDLING

The AddHandler/RemoveHandler statements open up a completely new form of event handling, one that wasn't available in Visual Basic 6.0. There are many occasions where you will find yourself dynamically creating objects such as controls, but also including such things as forms, database objects, socket objects for TCP/IP communication, and more. By using AddHandler, you can still trap events from these objects even though you never declared them using WithEvents.

Behind the scenes, AddHandler and RemoveHandler are doing work with the delegate related Framework classes, wrapping the functionality of adding and removing additional methods (event handlers) to the same delegate (event). If you need to, you can still work natively with the System.Delegate class instead of, or in addition to, using AddHandler and RemoveHandler.

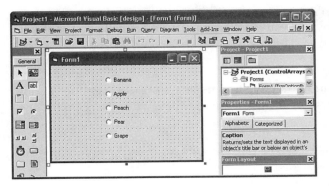

**Figure 3.4**  A group of options buttons on a VB6 form can all be part of a control array.

# Coding Without Control Arrays

One of the more noticeable changes for a Visual Basic 6.0 developer who is getting started in Windows forms is the lack of control arrays. This feature of pre-.NET VB allowed you to configure a set of controls with a single name by assigning index values to each control. Once a control array was created, a single event procedure could be used to handle the events of all the controls in the array and you could also loop through the controls in an array based on index. These features made control arrays useful for a great many projects, but I mostly remember using this feature to handle groups of option buttons (radio buttons in .NET). Consider this form in VB6 (see Figure 3.4), which displays a six-item option button (radio button) collection using a control array. A single event handler (see Listing 3.12) can be written for this array that will run whenever any of the options are selected, or the array can be looped through to find the one option button with a `Value = True`.

**LISTING 3.12**  VB6 Event Handler for an Option Button Control Array

```
Private Sub optFruit_Click(Index As Integer)
    MsgBox "Selected Item: " & optFruit(Index).Caption
End Sub
```

Due to the changes in event handling, allowing multiple objects' events to be mapped to the same event handler, achieving the same effect in Windows forms is not impossible, but it is not quite as simple as it was in VB6. Combining the event handling features of .NET with the use of a standard array, here is a walkthrough of handling some radio buttons on a .NET Windows form. This example creates an array to hold a set of radio buttons and shows you how you can use that array along with a shared event handler to determine which option button is currently selected. If you follow along with these steps, you can try out the code for yourself.

1. Create a new Visual Basic .NET Windows application.

2. A blank `Form1` will be created and opened in Design View. Select the form and then drag a new radio button onto it from the toolbox.

3. Copy and paste the radio button four times onto the form. This is likely the fastest way to end up with five radio buttons, but you can also drag four more radio buttons from the toolbox.

4. Add a label to your form.

5. Double-click one of the radio buttons to jump into its CheckedChanged event (see Listing 3.13) and modify the Handles clause to include all five of the radio buttons' events.

**LISTING 3.13**   Creating an Event Handler for All Five Radio Buttons

```
Private Sub RadioButton1_CheckedChanged( _
        ByVal sender As System.Object, _
        ByVal e As System.EventArgs) _
        Handles RadioButton1.CheckedChanged, _
                RadioButton2.CheckedChanged, _
                RadioButton3.CheckedChanged, _
                RadioButton4.CheckedChanged, _
                RadioButton5.CheckedChanged

End Sub
```

6. Declare an array of radio buttons as a private member variable in your form (put the declaration anywhere in your code outside of a procedure):

```
Dim radioButtons(4) As RadioButton
```

7. Declare an integer private member variable as well:

```
Dim selectedOption As Integer = 0
```

8. Add code into the constructor of the form (the sub New() procedure contained within the Windows Forms Designer generated area) to fill up the array with the radio buttons (see Listing 3.14).

**LISTING 3.14**   Filling Up Your Own Radio Button Array

```
Public Sub New()
    MyBase.New()

    'This call is required by the Windows Form Designer.
    InitializeComponent()
```

**LISTING 3.14** Continued

```
        'Add any initialization after the InitializeComponent() call
        radioButtons(0) = RadioButton1
        radioButtons(1) = RadioButton2
        radioButtons(2) = RadioButton3
        radioButtons(3) = RadioButton4
        radioButtons(4) = RadioButton5
End Sub
```

9. Finally, write code into the shared `CheckedChanged` event handler that will loop through the radio button array and determine the currently selected option (shown in Listing 3.15). Store the appropriate array index into `selectedOption` and change the `Text` property of the label control.

**LISTING 3.15** Loop Through the Radio Buttons and Determine which One Is Clicked

```
Private Sub RadioButton1_CheckedChanged( _
        ByVal sender As System.Object, _
        ByVal e As System.EventArgs) _
        Handles RadioButton1.CheckedChanged, _
                RadioButton2.CheckedChanged, _
                RadioButton3.CheckedChanged, _
                RadioButton4.CheckedChanged, _
                RadioButton5.CheckedChanged
    Dim i As Integer = 0
    Dim found As Boolean = False
    While i < radioButtons.GetLength(0) And Not found
        If radioButtons(i).Checked Then
            found = True
            selectedOption = i + 1
            Label1.Text = CStr(selectedOption)
        End If
        i += 1
    End While
End Sub
```

If you were to run this code, you would see the label changing every time a different option was selected. The flexibility of event handling in .NET allows you to work with a set of five radio buttons without having to have five different event handlers.

# Configuring Your Form for Resizing

Every time I built a resizable form in Visual Basic 6.0 (which includes every form I built except for the simplest of dialog boxes), I had to write code into the form's Resize event.

---

**USING THE LAYOUT EVENT IN WINDOWS FORMS**

This section is all about avoiding the code you used to have to write into your Resize event handler, but even if you did write code, it wouldn't be in the same event handler in .NET. A new event, Layout, is available in Windows forms, and if you need to write code that adjusts the form after a resize, the Layout event is the best place for it.

---

I had to decide how I wanted each control to adjust to the new size of the form, what size was too small for my interface to be usable, and I had to remember to check if the form had been minimized before trying to do any resizing. This code was not particularly hard to write, and after 50 or 60 forms I could do it without much thought, but it still took time and effort for every form I created. In Windows forms, a variety of features have come together to allow you to configure your controls for auto-resizing without having to write a single line of code. By combining the docking and anchoring features with the careful use of panels, you can set your form up to resize in almost any way you can imagine. If you add in the auto-scroll feature, you can even have parts of the form that do not resize at all, but instead extend right off the visible area of the form.

The following sections explain how each of these three features works and how the use of panels can increase your flexibility of control arrangement. Once you have learned about all the features, the chapter will detail a few of the more common form layout scenarios, showing you how to set them up for proper resizing.

## Using Docking to Handle Resizing

Docking windows and toolbars have been in use for quite some time, so the general concept is not new; a docked item is attached to one of the edges of its container (such as a form). Consider a form that contains only a single ListBox control. If you set the ListBox's Dock property to Left (see Figure 3.5), the height of the control will be fixed to the height of the form's client area (causing the list box to fill the form from top to bottom), while the position of the control will be locked to the left side of the form. The only thing you can change about the size of the list box at this point is its width, controlling how far out from the left side it extends. Docking to the right is essentially the same; the list box becomes attached to the right side of the form, but you can still change its width as desired. Docking to the top or bottom will cause the width to be fixed to fill the width of the form, but the height of the control can still be modified.

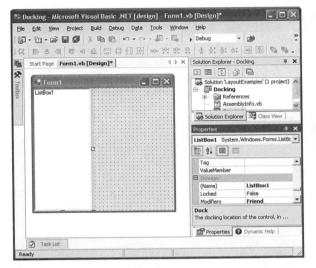

**Figure 3.5** Docking a control to the left makes it stick to the left side, while filling the vertical space of the container.

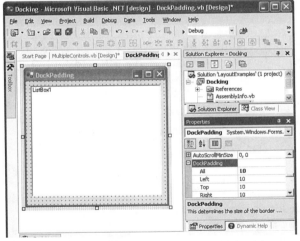

**Figure 3.6** DockPadding allows you to dock, without sacrificing a bit of white space around the edge of your controls.

In addition to docking to one of the four sides, controls also support a fifth (sixth if you count None for no docking) docking setting, Fill. If you set the Dock property to Fill, that control becomes attached to all four sides of the container, adjusting itself automatically as the form is resized. You cannot adjust any size or position settings for a control that has been docked to fill the container.

Remember that you are docking the control to its container, which in this example is the Form, but could be a container control such as a GroupBox or Panel. This flexibility leads to more layout options, as you will see later in the section on "Using Panels."

The container (form, panel, or other type of container control) has a DockPadding property, which allows it to specify a certain amount of padding between it and docked controls. The padding values can be specified individually for the four sides of the container, or an overall padding value that applies to all of the sides at once. If a container has specified a DockPadding value of 10, for example, a control docked to the left will be positioned 10 pixels away from the left edge. The DockPadding setting is great for creating a more visually pleasing user interface as it results in a border around the form while still enabling the automatic resizing of docked controls (see Figure 3.6).

Docking gets a little more complicated when multiple docked controls are involved. If you dock more than one control to the same edge, the second control will dock alongside the first instead of directly to the container. Going back to the example with the ListBox on a form, you can try multiple

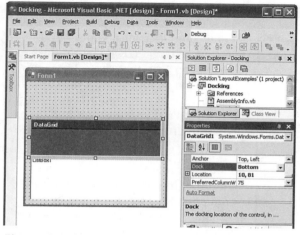

**Figure 3.7**    Multiple controls docked to the same side will stack instead of overlap.

docked controls to see what happens. If you docked the ListBox to the bottom and then added a new DataGrid to the form, setting its Dock property also to Bottom, you would have produced an interface similar to Figure 3.7, where the ListBox appears below the DataGrid.

Both of the controls are docked to the form and will resize as the form is resized. If you have controls docked to one or more sides of your container, and then you set another control's Dock property to Fill, the control set to Fill will be automatically sized to use all of the remaining area of the container. If you have multiple controls docked on a form, you might want to use the Splitter control. Splitter is a special Windows Forms control that, when docked between two other controls, allows you to resize the two controls at runtime. Using the Splitter control and a few other key controls, you can create a standard Explorer view form in a matter of minutes.

To add a splitter to your form, you need to be careful of the order in which you add your controls. Try adding a ListBox to an empty form, and docking it to the left. Then add a splitter control, and dock it to the left as well (it is by default). Finally, add a DataGrid control, dock it to the left as well, or set its dock property to Fill, and you will have a working example of using a splitter!

A little confusing? It can appear very complex, but the best bet is to try it out on your own, adding a variety of controls to a blank form and playing around with the various Dock/DockPadding settings.

## Anchoring as an Alternative Resizing Technique

After docking, this has to be the coolest layout feature. Anchoring is a little simpler than docking, but it can be a powerful tool. Using a graphical property editor (see Figure 3.8), you can set the Anchor property for a control to any combination of Top, Left, Bottom, and/or Right.

To anchor a control to a specific side means that the distance between the control and that side of its container becomes fixed. Therefore, if you anchor a control to a specific side and

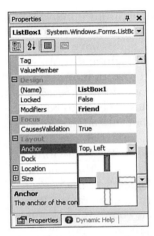

**Figure 3.8** The property editor for anchoring is a nice little graphical control.

then resize the form, the control's distance from the anchored side(s) will not change. To maintain a constant position relative to one or more sides of your container, the control might have to be resized when the form's size changes.

By default, controls are anchored to the top and left, which makes them behave exactly as controls did in previous versions of Visual Basic. When you resize the form, they do not move or resize. If you want to create a TextBox that grows as you make your form wider, you can anchor it to the top, left, and right sides. If you want the TextBox to grow in height as well as width, anchor it to the bottom as well. Figure 3.9 shows a form with some anchored controls, and Figure 3.10 shows what happens when that form is resized. You will see a few more examples of how anchoring can be used to lay out your form in the samples throughout the rest of this book.

**Figure 3.9** Anchored controls maintain a fixed distance between themselves and the container edge(s) they are anchored to.

**Figure 3.10** As the form changes size, the controls move and resize automatically.

## AutoScrolling Forms

Docking and anchoring are designed to resize your controls when the form is resized, but resizing the contents of your form is not always appropriate. In some cases there is a minimum size at which your form is usable, so resizing below that needs to be avoided. There are also situations when the content on your form is a fixed size, making resizing

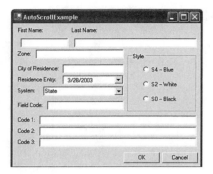

**Figure 3.11**    This form would be hard to resize, so the solution is to allow users to scroll.

**Figure 3.12**    AutoScroll automatically adds scroll bars when the form becomes small enough to hide any part of any of the controls on the form.

inappropriate. Windows forms provides a few additional features to allow you to deal with these situations. Forms have minimum/maximum height and width properties (allowing you to constrain resizing to a specific range of sizes) and the AutoScroll feature. AutoScroll allows a form to be resized by the users, but instead of shrinking the controls on the form, scroll bars appear to allow the users to view the entire form area even if they have resized the window. The form shown in Figure 3.11 is a perfect candidate for AutoScroll; it contains a large number of controls and buttons and cannot be resized using docking or anchoring.

If the user were to resize this form, making it smaller than the area required for all of its controls, the AutoScroll feature of Windows forms will save the day by adding horizontal and/or vertical scroll bars as required (see Figure 3.12).

In addition to the AutoScroll property, which you set to True to enable auto scrolling, there are two other properties, AutoScrollMargin and AutoScrollMinSize, that are used to configure exactly how scrolling occurs.

## Using Panels

Panels enhance all of the other layout features discussed so far because they can act as a container for other controls, much like a form does. Because they are containers, panels have their own DockPadding property and all of the auto-scroll features described for forms. A control can be placed into a panel and anchored to the bottom-right corner of that panel, while the panel itself was docked or anchored to a specific location on a form. By combining panels with forms, you can design more complicated layouts that still support resizing. Panels are used in several of the examples in the next section.

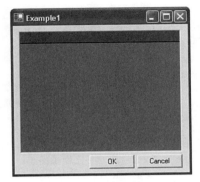

**Figure 3.13** Allowing the users to resize your form makes your application work better on a range of screen sizes.

# Some Common Resizing Scenarios

Now that you have been told what docking, anchoring, and auto-scrolling are, here are a few forms that demonstrate using the new layout features.

### A Standard One-Large-Control Dialog Box

A large control, such as TextBox, ListBox, or DataGrid, needs to resize properly on a Form with two buttons (OK and Cancel), as shown in Figure 3.13.

If it were not for those two buttons, docking would be a possible answer, but anchoring saves the day here. Assuming a desired border around the form's contents of 10 pixels:

- Position the large control with its top, left, and right edges 10 pixels in from the corresponding form edges. Note that you don't have to be exact about these positions, anchoring will lock the control in whatever place you put it. A precise border is just for aesthetics.

- Add your two buttons to the bottom of the form, placing their bottom edge 10 pixels up from the bottom of the form. The right edge of one button should be 10 pixels in from the right edge of the form. Place the other button so that its right edge is five pixels away from the left edge of the first button.

- Adjust the height of the large control so that its bottom edge is 10 pixels from the top of the two buttons.

- Now, set the large control's Anchor property to "Top, Bottom, Left, Right" and both buttons' Anchor property to "Bottom, Right".

### A Long List of Questions

You have a long list of questions that must be answered before a user can submit an order, and additional questions keep being added. There also needs to be an OK and Cancel button on the form; OK to move onto submitting the order, and Cancel to close the form and cancel the order.

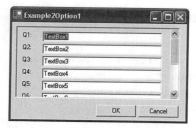

**Figure 3.14**   A panel allows you to restrict which parts of the form scroll and which parts are always visible.

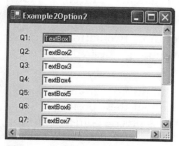

**Figure 3.15**   You can use the entire form surface for your scrolling area.

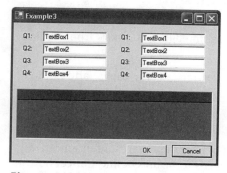

**Figure 3.16**   Multiple columns are trickier to resize.

AutoScroll is the key for this layout, either for the entire form or for a panel, depending on whether you want to keep the OK and Cancel buttons visible at all times or if you want the user to have to scroll down to find them.

- For the first option (Figure 3.14), where you want the buttons to be visible at all times, set up your form just like in Example 3.1, but use a Panel control as the large control.

- Set the panel's AutoScroll property to True and then place all of your individual questions into the panel.

- For the second option (Figure 3.15), set the Form's AutoScroll property to True and place all of your questions onto the form.

- Add your OK and Cancel buttons at the very bottom of your form below all of the questions.

**A Multi-Column Form**

You have a form with multiple columns of text boxes, each with associated labels, a single large text box, and the OK and Cancel buttons at the bottom (see Figure 3.16).

This gets a little trickier because of the two columns at the top of the form, but panels can make it all work out.

- Create a panel (mainPanel) that is tall enough to contain all of your controls for the top section of the form.

- Create two more panels (rightPanel and leftPanel) and place them in the first panel you created.

- Select one of new panels (rightPanel) and make its Dock property equal to Right; make the other panel's Dock property equal to Fill.

- Now, leftPanel will always fill the space not taken by rightPanel, but there is no way (in the designer) to force those two panels to equally share the available space. Instead you have to go to code.

- View the code for your form, and then select mainPanel from the object drop-down list (left side) and Layout from the event drop-down list (right side). Enter the code from Listing 3.16, assuming your panel names are mainPanel, rightPanel, and leftPanel, into the Layout event handler.

**LISTING 3.16**    Using Code to Make Two Panels Share the Available Space

```
Private Sub mainPanel_Layout( _
        ByVal sender As Object, _
        ByVal e As System.Windows.Forms.LayoutEventArgs) _
            Handles mainPanel.Layout
    rightPanel.Width = mainPanel.Width \ 2
End Sub
```

Note that I used the Layout event, which is a new event in Windows forms that was not available in Visual Basic 6.0. In Visual Basic 6.0, I would have used the Resize event, but Layout is actually more precise as it occurs when the position and size of controls within a container might need adjusting, as opposed to occurring upon every resize of the form. If a form were set to AutoScroll, for example, the Resize event would fire whenever the form was resized (as it should), but the controls inside the form would not need to be rearranged.

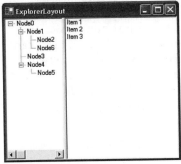

**Figure 3.17**    The standard Explorer style of form layout.

### An Explorer-Style Application

You are attempting to produce an interface in the format of the Windows Explorer, Outlook, and other applications. This interface will have a TreeView along one side of the form and a ListView on the other, and have the capability to move the dividing line between the two controls to resize them (see Figure 3.17).

This style of layout is easy to accomplish with the new features of Windows forms, but the specific order in which you add items to your form is important.

- Starting with a blank form, add a `TreeView` control and set its `Dock` property to `Left`.

- Add a `Splitter` control; it will automatically dock to the left and take its place along the right side of the `TreeView`.

- Add a `ListView` control and set its `Dock` property to `Fill`.

That's it. The `ListView` will fill whatever space isn't being used by the `TreeView` and the `Splitter` will allow you to adjust the relative size of the two areas.

That is all of the sample resizing scenarios covered in this chapter, but that certainly is not the extent of layouts that can be created.

# Programming Without Default Form Instances

Classes and objects existed in Visual Basic 6.0, but they were not as pervasive as they are in .NET. Objects are everywhere when you are developing in Visual Basic .NET, and that large change has lead to many small changes that can trip you up when you are coming from a VB6 background. One of the more commonly encountered problems for a VB6 developer is the lack of default form instances in .NET, but the term default form instance is confusing enough that I will need to go into more detail about the problem before we look at any solutions.

When you are dealing with classes and objects, it is helpful to think of a class as the blueprint of a house, whereas an object is an instance of a specific class and is more like an actual house that was built from the blueprint. In general, you don't work with classes, just like you don't live in blueprints. You create instances from your classes and it is those instances that get used throughout your applications. This is not a .NET issue; this is just how classes and objects work, even in VB6. Even in VB6, forms are considered classes, which is why you can create multiple copies (instances) of a single form in your VB6 code if you wish. The two snippets of code in Listings 3.17 and 3.18, assuming you have a `Form1` in your project, would produce the same result (11 open copies of `Form1`) in VB6 or VB .NET. The only differences between these two examples are syntax issues; they are otherwise identical.

**LISTING 3.17**   VB6 Code to Display 11 Copies of a Form

```
'VB 6 Code
Dim i As Integer
Dim myFrm As Form1

For i = 0 To 10
    Set myFrm = New Form1
    myFrm.Show
Next
```

**LISTING 3.18**    The Very Similar VB .NET Code for Displaying 11 Copies of a Form

```
'VB .NET Code
Dim i As Integer
Dim myFrm As Form1

For i = 0 To 10
    myFrm = New Form1()
    myFrm.Show()
Next
```

In each case, the code examples created 11 new instances of the class Form1 and then called a method (Show) on each of those new instances. Code you wrote in VB6 that worked with multiple instances of a single Form class will probably work in .NET without too many changes, but consider this VB6 code:

```
Form2.Show
Form2.TextBox1.Text = "dfsdf"
```

That code would not work in .NET, because it is treating the class Form2 as if it were an instance of Form2. In Visual Basic 6.0 and earlier versions, a special default instance of each form is automatically created, and allows you to use the form's name to access this instance. What this means is that the Visual Basic 6.0 code Form2.Show has the effect of showing the "default" instance of Form2, but it doesn't work in Visual Basic .NET. If you want to show a form in VB .NET, you need to create an instance, writing code like this to make Form2 visible:

```
Dim myFrm As New Form2()
myFrm.Show()
```

This is a major behavioral change from VB6, but the difference in code is not extreme. The removal of default instances changes more than just the code to show a form though. The second part of the problem is that these special default form instances were global to your entire project in Visual Basic 6.0. Taking the two facts together means that (in Visual Basic 6.0 or earlier) you can refer to any form in your project from anywhere in your code and you will always be referring to the same instance of that form.

In Visual Basic .NET, if you need to access an instance of Form2 from some other part of your application (such as another form or a module), you need to pass the reference to Form2 around your application. The next section explores some of the ways in which you can work with multiple forms.

# Working with Multiple Forms in VB .NET

The previous section described a major change in the forms model from VB6 to VB .NET—the removal of default form instances. This is not a major technical problem; programmers (including VB6 programmers) have been working without default instances of non-form classes for a very long time, but it is a big change if you are used to building Windows applications using VB6. The result of this change is that you need a reference to a particular instance of a form to be able to use it. I will start with a very simple example to illustrate the concept. I will create a new Windows application that contains two forms. Form1, which will be shown automatically when the project runs, will create and display an instance of Form2 when you click a button. To illustrate communication from one form to another, Form2 will also have a button, and it will change the caption of Form1 whenever it is clicked. To get things started, create the new project and add a new form.

Select File, New, Project from the main menu in Visual Studio .NET, and then pick a Visual Basic Windows Application to create. A form will be created with a default name of Form1. Add a second form by right-clicking the project and selecting Add, Add Windows Form from the menu that appears. Accept the default name of Form2 for the new form and click the Open button to finish the wizard.

## Creating and Displaying an Instance of a Form

The first step is to add code to Form1 to create and display an instance of Form2. Add a button to Form1, leaving it with a default name of Button1. Now, double-click the button to enter its event procedure for the Click event. If you used the code shown in Listing 3.19, a new form would open every time you click the button, which is likely not the desired result.

**LISTING 3.19**   Simple Code for Displaying a Form

```
Private Sub Button1_Click(ByVal sender As System.Object, _
    ByVal e As System.EventArgs) Handles Button1.Click
    Dim myForm As New Form2
    myForm.Show()
End Sub
```

Instead, you will move the Form variable to a module level value, and then determine if it already exists in the Click event (Listing 3.20). Then, you will create the form if it does not already exist and show it either way.

**LISTING 3.20** Code That Will Create and Display Only One Copy of a Form

```
Dim myForm As Form2


Private Sub Button1_Click( _
        ByVal sender As System.Object, _
        ByVal e As System.EventArgs) _
            Handles Button1.Click
    If myForm Is Nothing Then
        myForm = New Form2
    End If
    myForm.Show()
End Sub
```

Using the myForm variable allows you to hang on to a reference to your newly created form.
Hanging onto the reference returned from creating a new form is useful so that you can talk
to this second form if need be. The main reason for using this variable though, is so that you
can create and track a single instance of Form2, instead of creating a new one on every button
click. Now, let's make Form2 talk back to Form1.

## Communicating Between Two Forms

If you want Form2 to be able to communicate with Form1, you need to supply a reference to
Form1. Once you do this, you will be set up for two-way communication, as both forms will
be holding a reference to the other. The simplest way to accomplish this is to add a public
variable (of type Form1) to Form2, like this:

```
Public Class Form2
    Inherits System.Windows.Forms.Form

    Public myCaller As Form1
```

Then, right after you create an instance of Form2 in the button click event (see Listing 3.21),
you can set this property.

**LISTING 3.21** You Can Pass a Form Reference with a Property

```
Dim myForm As Form2


Private Sub Button1_Click( _
        ByVal sender As System.Object, _
        ByVal e As System.EventArgs) _
        Handles Button1.Click
```

**LISTING 3.21** Continued

```
    If myForm Is Nothing Then
        myForm = New Form2
        myForm.myCaller = Me
    End If
    myForm.Show()
End Sub
```

If code in Form2 needs to access Form1, it can now do so through the myCaller variable. Add a button to Form2 and put this code into it, as shown in Listing 3.22.

**LISTING 3.22** Now that Form2 Has a Reference to Form1, it Can Access Form1's Properties

```
Private Sub Button1_Click( _
        ByVal sender As System.Object, _
        ByVal e As System.EventArgs) _
        Handles Button1.Click
    If Not myCaller Is Nothing Then
        myCaller.Text = Now.ToLongTimeString
    End If
End Sub
```

Clicking the button on Form1 will create an instance of Form2 and populate Form2's myCaller variable with a reference to Form1. Clicking the button on Form2 will access Form1 through the myCaller variable (if it was set) and change its window title. This was a very simple example of communicating between multiple forms, but there will be additional examples as part of the sample applications in Chapters 4 and 5. The next section covers creating and using a form as a dialog box.

## Creating and Using a Form as a Dialog Box

Technically speaking, every window/form in an application could be called a dialog box. When I use the term, however, I am referring specifically to a window that is displayed to request some information from the users and return that information back to the application that displayed the dialog box. For the most part, the calling application does not care what happens between displaying the form and the user clicking OK or Cancel to close it; all it is concerned with is the information gathered by the dialog box. To illustrate how you can create a standard dialog box using Visual Basic .NET, this section walks you through the creation of a dialog box that is designed to allow the users to enter in an address (see Figure 3.18).

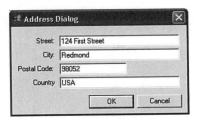

**Figure 3.18**    An Address entry dialog box.

### Setting Up Your Form

First, you create the sample application and form. Open a new project, a Visual Basic Windows Application, and add a new form named `GetAddress`. There should now be two forms in your project, which is exactly what you want because we will launch the `GetAddress` dialog box from `Form1`. Now, you need to set up the look of `GetAddress` to match the expected appearance of a dialog box. Set up four text boxes named `txtStreet`, `txtCity`, `txtPostalCode`, and `txtCountry` on your form and arrange them somewhat like the form shown in Figure 3.18. Now, add two buttons to your form, `saveAddress` and `cancelAddress`, with captions of OK and Cancel, respectively. The two buttons should be positioned in the lower-right corner. If you are planning to make your dialog box resizable, you will want to anchor the two buttons to bottom and right. Select the form itself (click any empty area of the design surface) and set its `AcceptButton` and `CancelButton` properties to the `saveAddress` and `cancelAddress` buttons. Setting these properties allows the users to use the Enter and Escape keys as the equivalent of OK and Cancel. The `AcceptButton` property also makes the `saveAddress` button into the default for the form, which causes it to be highlighted. So that you can tell what button was pressed to exit the form, you should also set the `DialogResult` property of both buttons. Set the `DialogResult` property for `saveAddress` to `OK`, and set it to `Cancel` for `cancelAddress`.

If you want your dialog box to be resizable, select the `Sizable` option for the `FormBorderStyle` property. For a fixed sized dialog box, you select `FixedDialog` for `FormBorderStyle` and set `MinimizeBox` and `MaximizeBox` both to `False`.

Once you have created your dialog box, the key to using it is to determine a method for putting starting data into the dialog box and for pulling out the information the user entered. You could access the various controls (the text boxes) directly, but I strongly advise against it. If you work directly with the controls, you will have to change that code if you ever modify the dialog box. Instead, I suggest one of two approaches. Either create a property procedure for each of the values you are exchanging (street, city, postal code, and country in this example) or create a new class that holds all of these values and then create a single property for that object.

This section shows you both methods; you can use whichever one you prefer. For the first case, using multiple properties, create a property for each of the four values you are dealing with, as shown in Listing 3.23.

**LISTING 3.23**    You Can Insert and Remove Values from Your Dialog Box Using Properties

```
Public Property Street() As String
    Get
        Return Me.txtStreet.Text
```

**LISTING 3.23** Continued

```
        End Get
        Set(ByVal Value As String)
            Me.txtStreet.Text = Value
        End Set
    End Property

    Public Property City() As String
        Get
            Return Me.txtCity.Text
        End Get
        Set(ByVal Value As String)
            Me.txtCity.Text = Value
        End Set
    End Property

    Public Property PostalCode() As String
        Get
            Return Me.txtPostalCode.Text
        End Get
        Set(ByVal Value As String)
            Me.txtPostalCode.Text = Value
        End Set
    End Property

    Public Property Country() As String
        Get
            Return Me.txtCountry.Text
        End Get
        Set(ByVal Value As String)
            Me.txtCountry.Text = Value
        End Set
    End Property
```

For now, these property procedures are just working with the text boxes directly. The value in using property procedures instead of direct control access is that you can change these procedures later, without affecting the code that calls this dialog box. The properties are all set up now, but to make the dialog box work correctly, you also need some code (shown in Listing 3.24) in the OK and Cancel buttons.

**LISTING 3.24**   Don't Forget to Provide a Way to Close Your Forms

```
Private Sub saveAddress_Click( _
        ByVal sender As System.Object, _
        ByVal e As System.EventArgs) _
        Handles saveAddress.Click
    Me.Close()
End Sub

Private Sub cancelAddress_Click( _
        ByVal sender As System.Object, _
        ByVal e As System.EventArgs) _
        Handles cancelAddress.Click
    Me.Close()
End Sub
```

Although both button click events do the same thing, close the dialog box, the DialogResult property of each button is set appropriately so it will result in the correct result value being returned to the calling code. In the calling procedure, a button click event on the first form, you populate the dialog box using the property procedures, display it using ShowDialog(), and then retrieve the property settings back into the local variables. ShowDialog is the equivalent of showing a form in VB6 passing in vbModal for the modal parameter, but with the added benefit of a return value. ShowDialog returns a DialogResult value to indicate how the user exited the dialog box. The example in Listing 3.25 checks for the OK result code before retrieving the properties from the dialog box.

**LISTING 3.25**   If Users Click OK, You Must Copy the Values Back, Otherwise You Don't Want to Change Anything Because They Must Have Clicked Cancel

```
Private Sub Button1_Click( _
        ByVal sender As System.Object, _
        ByVal e As System.EventArgs) _
        Handles Button1.Click

    Dim address As New addressDialog

    Dim Street As String = "124 First Street"
    Dim City As String = "Redmond"
    Dim Country As String = "USA"
    Dim PostalCode As String = "98052"

    address.Street = Street
    address.City = City
```

**LISTING 3.25**    Continued

```
        address.Country = Country
        address.PostalCode = PostalCode

    If address.ShowDialog = DialogResult.OK Then
        Street = address.Street
        City = address.City
        Country = address.Country
        PostalCode = address.PostalCode
    End If
End Sub
```

The other method I mentioned, using a class to hold a set of values instead of passing each value individually, requires just a few modifications to the code. First, you need to create the class. Add a new class to your project, named Address, and enter the class definition shown in Listing 3.26.

**LISTING 3.26**    With a Class being Used to Hold Multiple Values, You Can Add New Properties to it without Having to Change the Code to Pass it Around

```
Public Class address
    Dim m_Street As String
    Dim m_City As String
    Dim m_PostalCode As String
    Dim m_Country As String

    Public Property Street() As String
        Get
            Return m_Street
        End Get
        Set(ByVal Value As String)
            m_Street = Value
        End Set
    End Property

    Public Property City() As String
        Get
            Return m_City
        End Get
        Set(ByVal Value As String)
            m_City = Value
        End Set
    End Property
```

**LISTING 3.26**   Continued

```
    Public Property PostalCode() As String
        Get
            Return m_PostalCode
        End Get
        Set(ByVal Value As String)
            m_PostalCode = Value
        End Set
    End Property

    Public Property Country() As String
        Get
            Return m_Country
        End Get
        Set(ByVal Value As String)
            m_Country = Value
        End Set
    End Property
End Class
```

This class is nothing more than a convenient way to package data into a single object, but it allows you to have only a single property procedure (Listing 3.27) in the dialog box and to simplify the calling code in Form1 (see Listing 3.28).

**LISTING 3.27**   The Number of Properties Is Reduced to One if You Switch to Using a Class Versus Individual Properties on Your Form

```
Public Property Address() As address
    Get
        Dim newAddress As New address
        newAddress.City = txtCity.Text
        newAddress.Country = txtCountry.Text
        newAddress.PostalCode = txtPostalCode.Text
        newAddress.Street = txtStreet.Text
        Return newAddress
    End Get
    Set(ByVal Value As address)
        txtCity.Text = Value.City
        txtCountry.Text = Value.Country
        txtPostalCode.Text = Value.PostalCode
        txtStreet.Text = Value.Street
    End Set
End Property
```

**LISTING 3.28**   A Single Property to Exchange Data Simplifies the Calling Code as well as the Form

```
Private Sub Button1_Click( _
        ByVal sender As System.Object, _
        ByVal e As System.EventArgs) _
        Handles Button1.Click

    Dim addr As New address
    Dim address As New addressDialog

    Dim Street As String = "124 First Street"
    Dim City As String = "Redmond"
    Dim Country As String = "USA"
    Dim PostalCode As String = "98052"

    addr.Street = Street
    addr.City = City
    addr.Country = Country
    addr.PostalCode = PostalCode

    address.Address = addr
    If address.ShowDialog = DialogResult.OK Then
        addr = address.Address
    End If
End Sub
```

The simple addition of a return code when displaying a modal form makes it easier to implement dialog boxes within Visual Basic .NET, but the lack of default form instances can make all multiple form applications difficult.

# In Brief

This chapter presented a detailed overview of the new Windows client development model in Visual Basic .NET. Here are the important points of this chapter:

- Windows forms is the new forms model for Visual Basic. Although it is similar to the forms model for Visual Basic 6.0, it supports many new features.

- In .NET, you can see and sometimes edit all of the code that creates and configures your user interface.

- Event handling in .NET is no longer based on the name of the event-handler procedure, instead a new `Handles` keyword has been added.

- Form layout is more powerful in .NET than in VB6 due to the addition of new features for docking and anchoring.

- There are no default instances of forms in VB .NET, which means you cannot work with the form's name as if it were always available.

# Working with Files

# 4

## The Way Things Were

File handling before Visual Basic 6 had not changed significantly since Visual Basic 1 came onto the stage. In fact, it had not changed significantly since Kemeny and Kurtz first defined BASIC back at Dartmouth College in 1964. You used the Open statement to open or create a file, the Print and Put statements to write to the file, and the Read and Get statements to retrieve information. It all worked (most of the time), but it was somewhat clunky. You had to associate a file with a handle (a number from 1-16), and then use that handle to print #1 to the file. There was no easy way to get directory information, or even file information (beyond size).

In Visual Basic 6.0, a library called the File System Object greatly simplified file manipulation and access. With Visual Basic .NET, most of the features of the File System Object are included but through an entirely new set of classes built into the .NET Framework.

## Using Streams

As you read the documentation on Visual Basic .NET, you will continually read about things called streams. A stream is simply a series of bytes to be read or written, just as a water stream is a series of water droplets (if you look very closely). There are several types of streams, some read-only, others read-write. The one benefit of them is that they all act more or less the same. For example, a file can be thought of as a stream. In this case, it's a stream of bytes written to disk. There are other streams that represent in-memory collections of bytes, network traffic, encrypted information, and many others. The benefit of learning the Stream object is that you learn it once, and then can apply that knowledge to many places throughout Visual Basic .NET. Some of the more common types of streams are listed in Table 4.1.

**TABLE 4.1**

**Types of Streams**

| STREAM | DESCRIPTION |
|---|---|
| Stream | This is the basic Stream object. It contains all the common methods and properties of all streams. You cannot explicitly create one of these stream types. |
| FileStream | Represents a stream stored in a physical file on a disk. This can be a simple text file, or an executable program; either way, FileStream allows you to read from and write to the file. |
| MemoryStream | Represents a stream that's stored in memory. This is a handy object to use when you want to hold a large amount of data in memory, but don't want to incur the slowdown caused by dealing with writing the information to a disk. One thing to keep in mind, however, is that if the program shuts down, or the computer is turned off, the data is lost. |
| NetworkStream | Represents a stream of data across the wire. This is often used when communicating at a low level between computers. |
| CryptoStream | Used when encrypting information. Writing to a CryptoStream encrypts the information; reading from it decrypts. |
| BufferedStream | When you write to any of the other streams, the information is passed immediately to the stream. BufferedStream is intended to be added around the other stream, to reduce the actual number of reads and writes. For example, if you are using a FileStream, and are writing a single byte at a time to the file, the operating system will write each byte as requested. This means that there will be a disk write (remember that disks are relatively slow to work with) for each byte. Applying a BufferedStream around the FileStream would mean that the BufferedStream would send information on to the FileStream in chunks, reducing the number of disk reads and writes, and thus improving performance. |

Some Streams differ in their capabilities. For example, a MemoryStream is simply a block of memory. If you think about a block of memory, moving randomly around that block should make sense. Technically, this means the Stream is seekable (or rather, the CanSeek property is true). However, think about a NetworkStream—a flow of information through a network cable. It doesn't make sense that you can jump forward, skipping a set of bytes at will, or move back to re-read bytes you missed the first time. A NetworkStream is not seekable (CanSeek is false). You can discover which features each type of stream supports through its properties. The most important properties for each stream type are outlined in Table 4.2.

**TABLE 4.2**

**Common Stream Properties**

| PROPERTY | STREAM | VALUE |
|----------|--------|-------|
| CanSeek | FileStream | Generally `true`. If the underlying file supports seeking (any file on a disk), it is `true`. If it's on something (like a tape drive) that is not random access, it is `false`. |
| | MemoryStream | True |
| | NetworkStream | False |
| CanRead | Any | Generally depends on the stream. For example, if the underlying file does not permit reading, it is `false`. |
| CanWrite | Any | Generally depends on the stream. For example, if the underlying file does not permit writing, it is `false`. |

# Reading and Writing to Streams

Streams are lovely things, and I admire the person who came up with such a generic, but poetic, idea. However, being so generic, they are a pain to work with. You can only read and write to them one byte (or an array of bytes) at a time. There is no easy way to say, "Give me everything you've got as a string." What you need is an easier way to do the basic tasks of reading from and writing to the stream. Enter TextReader and TextWriter, and other related classes for reading and writing. Whereas you can think of a stream as a low-level series of bytes, readers and writers provide an easier way of getting to them. If you have worked with Active Server Pages, think of the Request and Response objects as being similar to readers and writers. If you haven't used ASP, just follow along and I'll explain the concept of readers and writers in more detail.

There are actually a number of different readers and writers (classes designed to simplify reading and writing with streams), but the ones I tend to use most often are the StreamReader and StreamWriter, so I will stick with them here. The StreamReader is designed to make reading from a stream easier (guessing what the StreamWriter is for is left up to you). You create a StreamReader object from any stream type, and then use its methods to retrieve data. This is where I feel the idea of streams becomes most powerful. The generic nature of streams means that you can now take a StreamReader and work with memory, files, networks, and other streams of information in exactly the same way.

As described previously, you create a StreamReader from a Stream. This is accomplished using a constructor, which is covered in more detail in Chapter 7, "Object Orientated Programming in Visual Basic .NET." A constructor allows you to supply one or more arguments when you are creating a new instance of an object, setting that object up right at the time it is created. The following code creates a StreamReader given an existing Stream (which is based on a file and opened using the Open method of the System.IO.File class) that you want to read from:

```
Dim str As Stream = File.Open(path, FileMode.Open, FileAccess.Read)
Dim sr As StreamReader
sr = New StreamReader(str)
```

Once you have a StreamReader, you obviously want to read something from it. Fortunately, the designers of the class named these methods appropriately—they all begin with the word Read:

- Read—Reads one or more characters from the underlying stream.

- ReadBlock—Reads a number of characters from the underlying stream. The difference from Read is that ReadBlock waits until the requested characters are available. Read returns the number available, up to the requested amount.

- ReadLine—Reads a line from the underlying stream. Of course, this makes sense only with streams that organize information by lines (such as with a text file).

- ReadToEnd—Reads all remaining information from the underlying stream.

Similarly, the StreamWriter supports writing to a Stream:

- Write—Writes one or more characters to the underlying stream.

- WriteLine—Writes one or more characters to the underlying stream, and ends that line with a carriage return-line feed (CRLF) combination.

This probably all seems quite abstract right now, so it's time to write some code. In this case, you'll learn how to create the code needed to read and write simple text files.

# Reading and Writing to a Text File

To illustrate the use of streams, I will walk you through creating a simple Windows Forms application that reads in and writes out text files. Of course, text files (and even files in general) are just one example of streams. The code to work with streams is generic enough that the same techniques demonstrated in this sample to read and write files would work against something more interesting such as a MemoryStream.

## Configuring a New Windows Application

For the first step, create a new Windows Forms project. Call it ReadWriteFile. Add one each of the MainMenu, OpenFileDialog, SaveFileDialog, and TextBox controls to the form. Set the properties as in Table 4.3, by selecting each control and then changing the values displayed in the Properties dialog box (press F4 to make the Properties dialog box visible if it's hidden).

**TABLE 4.3**

**Property Settings**

| CONTROL | PROPERTY | VALUE |
|---------|----------|-------|
| TextBox | Multiline | True |
| | Scrollbars | Vertical |
| | Dock | Fill |
| OpenFileDialog | Filter | Text files¦*.txt¦All files¦*.* |
| | DefaultExt | txt |
| SaveFileDialog | Filter | Text files¦*.txt¦All files¦*.* |
| | DefaultExt | txt |

In addition to the properties listed in Table 4.3, change the names of the controls from the defaults (TextBox1) to fileContents for the TextBox, topMenu for the MainMenu, openDialog for the OpenFileDialog, and saveDialog for the SaveFileDialog.

Next, create the menu structure for the form as in Table 4.4. To work with menus, simply click the Menu design view at the top of the form (first selecting the MainMenu control, named topMenu, in the component design area below the Form), type the menu names into the "Type Here" area of the menu, and continue until you have created a top-level File menu and all four of the options (items to be placed onto the FileMenu) shown in Table 4.4. As you work on the menu, you should change the names of each menu item to something more descriptive than the default names (MenuItem1). Suggested names are provided in the second column of Table 4.4, and those same names are used in the sample code that follows.

**TABLE 4.4**

**Main Menu for the Sample Application**

| MENU CAPTION | MENU NAME |
|--------------|-----------|
| &FILE | FILEMENU |
| &Open... | openFile |
| &Save | saveFile |
| Save &As... | saveFileAs |
| E&xit | exitApp |

**VISUAL STUDIO .NET PROVIDES SEVERAL METHODS TO ACCOMPLISH ALMOST ANY TASK**

Never content with a single method for accomplishing a task, Visual Studio .NET enables you to get into the code editor also by right-clicking the form in the Solution Explorer and choosing View Code, by selecting Code from the View menu, or by pressing the F7 key. This same phenomenon, an abundance of UI paths to a single feature, exists in many areas of Visual Studio, but you will tend to find the one method that most suits you and then stick with it. For example, I always run my applications by pressing F5; if the corresponding menu item was to disappear I would probably never notice.

Once the form is set up, it is time to move onto writing code. Right-click the form and select View Code to switch to the code editor.

Now that the form is set up and the controls are in place, it is time to start writing code.

## Opening the Text File

The first coding task is to add a private `FileName` variable to the form. Later, in the rest of the code, this variable will be used to store the filename of the currently opened file. Anywhere in the form code, outside of any existing procedures, create a private variable to store the `fileName` value.

```
Dim fileName As String
```

Next, you add code to the Open File menu item's `Click` event to load the contents of a text file using a `Stream` and `StreamReader`. Before writing that code though, you need to add a reference to the `System.IO` namespace to the project and an `Imports` of `System.IO` to the form. Open the `References` folder in the Solution Explorer. You should see a `System` namespace included in the listing, but not `System.IO`, which is fine. The items in the References dialog box represent the actual libraries (DLLs) that are used to locate code when you are compiling your application. Each of these DLLs might actually contain multiple namespaces. This is one of those cases. The `System` library, or assembly, contains many namespaces. One of them is `System.IO`, and it is already added to the reference To make life easier when coding, however, you can also import the namespaces you will be using. This allows you to use shortcuts when referring to classes. For more details on `Import` and `References`, see the following sidebar. Import the `System.IO` namespace to save some typing. Add the line `Imports System.IO` to the top line, before the `Public Class frmMain` line.

Now, with the new `Imports` statement added, it is time to move onto writing the `openFile` menu's `Click` event procedure. To get to the right procedure in the code editor, select the name of the menu (`openFile`) from the left drop-down list at the top of the code editor window and then select the desired event (`Click`) from the right drop-down list. Alternatively, you can get to this event from the visual form designer by double-clicking the appropriate menu item. Whichever method you use to get to it, add the code shown in Listing 4.1 to the event procedure.

Now that all of the text is loaded, you add code to the `saveFile` menu item's `Click` event to save it back out to the original file.

## Saving Out to a Text File

Using a `StreamWriter`, writing out to a file requires only a few lines of code. This will alter the original file, so be careful not to test with an important file. The code in Listing 4.2 uses the `fileName` variable to find out where the current text was loaded from, and then saves the text back out to that same file. If the `fileName` variable is not set, the `Click` event for the Save As menu item is called instead.

### IMPORTS VERSUS REFERENCES

The difference between references and the `Imports` statement can be confusing when you start working with Visual Basic .NET. You add references using the Solution Explorer (by right-clicking the Reference folder and picking Add Reference), or from the Project menu. They represent components that your application will use. If you are going to use code that exists in another DLL—either one of the namespaces that come with the .NET Framework that isn't automatically added, or code that was written by another developer or company—you must add it to the references for your project. The `Imports` statement can be thought of as a tool for shortening your code. By using the `Imports` statement, you can avoid having to write long class names. For example, when you add a `TextBox` to a form, Visual Basic .NET writes:

```
Private WithEvents txtText As
System.Windows.Forms.TextBox
```

Thus, the full class name of a text box is `System.Windows.Forms.TextBox`. However, if you add `Imports System.Windows.Forms` to the top of the file, you could shorten this to:

```
Private WithEvents txtText As TextBox
```

When Visual Basic .NET sees the `TextBox`, it uses the namespaces added with the `Imports` statement to search for the `TextBox` class.

If you use a namespace, it must be included in the References section. If you want to shorten your code, use the `Imports` statement.

**LISTING 4.1**    Use OpenFileDialog and a Stream to Open a Text File

```
Private Sub openFile_Click(ByVal sender As Object, _
    ByVal e As System.EventArgs) Handles openFile.Click
    Dim str As FileStream
    Dim sr As StreamReader

    If Me.openDialog.ShowDialog = DialogResult.OK Then
        Me.fileName = Me.openDialog.FileName
        str = New FileStream(Me.openDialog.FileName, FileMode.Open)
        sr = New StreamReader(str)
        Me.fileContents.Text = sr.ReadToEnd
        sr.Close()
        str.Close()
    End If
End Sub
```

**LISTING 4.2**    A StreamWriter Allows You to Write to a FileStream and Save the Contents of the TextBox

```
Private Sub saveFile_Click(ByVal sender As System.Object, _
    ByVal e As System.EventArgs) Handles saveFile.Click
    Dim str As FileStream
    Dim sw As StreamWriter

    If Filename.Length >= 0 Then
        str = New FileStream(Filename, FileMode.Create)
        sw = New StreamWriter(str)
        sw.Write(Me.fileContents.Text)
        sw.Close()
        str.Close()
    Else
        saveFileAs_Click(Nothing, Nothing)
    End If
End Sub
```

What if you don't want to save over the file you loaded the text from? Or what if you never loaded a file at all (you've just typed text)? The Save As menu item handles that possibility by allowing the users to enter or select a filename before saving. Add the code in Listing 4.3 to use the saveDialog to obtain a filename. Once the user has entered a filename (which has been stored into the private form variable fileName), the Click event for the Save menu item (see Listing 4.2) is called, and it handles the actual save back to a file.

**LISTING 4.3**   The SaveFileDialog Control Allows You to Provide a Professional Appearance

```
Private Sub saveFileAs_Click(ByVal sender As Object, _
    ByVal e As System.EventArgs) Handles saveFileAs.Click
    With Me.saveDialog
        .FileName = Me.fileName
        If .ShowDialog = DialogResult.OK Then
            Me.fileName = .FileName
            'let the other procedure save the file
            saveFile_Click(sender, e)
        End If
    End With
End Sub
```

That is all the code you need; run the application by selecting Start from the Debug menu or by pressing F5. You should be able to load text files and then save them (changed or not).

## Basic Concepts for Opening/Closing Files

Although there are quite a few lines of code in that sample application, the basic code to open a text file and read its contents into a textbox is as shown.

```
tr = New FileStream(Me.OpenDialog.FileName, FileMode.Open)
sr = New StreamReader(str)
Me.TextField.Text = sr.ReadToEnd
```

This is the most common scenario when working with streams. You create the stream, attach a StreamReader to it, and then read from the StreamReader. Similarly, writing is almost the exact same three lines, replacing a StreamWriter for the StreamReader, and the Write command for the ReadToEnd. To be safe, the code should have checked the stream to ensure it was readable or writable before performing any actions. Note that you can shorten your code by a few lines by eliminating some extra steps; you can pass a file path in when you create a new instance of StreamReader or StreamWriter, eliminating the need for a separate FileStream object for most purposes.

The downloadable version of this application provides you with a few more bits of useful code, including a fully functional edit menu (Cut, Copy, Paste, and Select All) and even a working Exit option.

# Working with the File System

You have now seen reading and writing with files, but Visual Basic .NET (through the .NET Framework classes) provides a large set of useful file operations outside of the stream classes. This section looks at how to find, create, and delete directories and files.

As I briefly discussed in Chapter 2, "Visual Basic .NET Language Changes," the .NET Framework is divided into a series of namespaces and each of the namespaces contains a number of related classes. The file and directory (and stream) classes are bundled into the System.IO namespace. The System.IO namespace is, as you might gather from the name, all about input and output. The System.IO namespace is one of the most heavily used namespaces in the .NET Framework for this reason. Anytime you want to open, read from, write to, or otherwise deal with a file or stream, you need this namespace. Fortunately, the System.IO namespace is included inside System.DLL and Visual Basic .NET includes a reference to System.DLL by default in any new project, so you should always have the IO classes available.

## Manipulating Files and Directories

If you look in the online help at the System.IO namespace, you will see two classes named File and Directory. These two classes map to files and directories, as you probably gathered from the name, and using their methods, you can work with the file system. For example, the Directory class has methods for retrieving subdirectories, getting the list of files in the directory, and so on, whereas the File class has methods for copying a file, deleting a file, and for retrieving file information. Table 4.5 lists the important methods of the Directory object and Table 4.6 shows the important methods of the File class.

**TABLE 4.5**

**Methods of the Directory Class**

| METHOD | DESCRIPTION |
|---|---|
| CreateDirectory | Creates one or more directories. One of the more powerful uses for this class is to create an entire tree of directories. |
| Delete | Removes a directory. |
| Exists | Returns True if the directory exists. |
| GetCurrentDirectory | Returns the full path to the current directory. |
| GetDirectories | Returns a String array containing the names of the child directories under a specified path. |
| GetFiles | Returns a String array containing the names of the files in the specified path. |

## TABLE 4.6

**Methods of the File Class**

| METHOD | DESCRIPTION |
|---|---|
| Copy | Copies a file. |
| Create | Creates a new file. |
| CreateText | A special version of Create that creates a text file. |
| Delete | Deletes a file. |
| Exists | Returns True if the file exists. |
| Open | Opens a file for reading, writing, or both. |
| OpenRead | Specialized version of Open that always opens the file for reading. |
| OpenText | Specialized version of Open that opens text files only for reading. This would be a handy shortcut if you were writing an application that needed to read configuration information, or a log file. |
| OpenWrite | Specialized version of Open that always opens the file for writing. |

The methods of the File and Directory classes are Shared, which means that you don't have to create an object to use them. To work with a Shared class member, you simply use the class name to access them. For example, because the Exists method of the File class is Shared, you do not need to declare an instance of the File class to access it; you just use the File class itself. So, rather than writing this:

```
Dim isMyFileThere As Boolean
Dim oFile As New File()
isMyFileThere = oFile.Exists("somefile.txt")
```

You determine whether a file exists with the following code:

```
Dim isMyFileThere As Boolean
isMyFileThere = File.Exists("somefile.txt")
```

## The Path Class

Another key class used for working with the file system is also located in the System.IO namespace, Path. As the name implies, Path provides a set of useful functions (all shared like the File and Directory classes) used for working with file paths. Table 4.7 lists the various methods of the Path class, along with brief explanations.

**TABLE 4.7**

**Methods of the** `Path` **Class**

| METHOD | DESCRIPTION |
|---|---|
| `ChangeExtension` | Given a path that includes a filename, changes the filename's extension (.TXT, .JPG, and so on). |
| `Combine` | This often-used function merges two paths, such as `C:\Docs` and `myfilename.txt` (which would produce `C:\Docs\myfilename.txt`), correctly adding or removing path separators (\). |
| `GetDirectoryName` | Returns the directory (folder) information out of a path, essentially stripping off any filename if one is included. |
| `GetExtension` | If a filename is included in the supplied path, this method returns the file's extension. |
| `GetFileName` | Returns the filename if one is included in the path. |
| `GetFileNameWithoutExtension` | Returns the filename, minus its extension. |
| `GetFullPath` | Returns the absolute path equivalent of the path supplied, which is useful for converting a relative path such as `..\bin\myapp.exe`. |
| `GetPathRoot` | Returns the root directory information for the supplied path. |
| `GetTempFileName` | Determines a unique temporary filename and creates an empty file in your temp directory with that name. |
| `GetTempPath` | Returns the path of the current system's Temp folder. |
| `HasExtension` | Returns `True` if the `fileName` portion of a path includes a file extension (.TXT, for example). |
| `IsPathRooted` | Returns `True` if the supplied path is an absolute path, `False` if it is a relative path. |

I will not go into any more detail on the `File`, `Directory`, or `Path` classes, but a demo application that shows some of the functionality of these classes is included on this book's Web site.

# Using Structured Exception Handling Instead of On Error

Older versions of Visual Basic support trapping and raising errors using the `On Error` statement. Starting with Visual Basic .NET 2002, it also supports a better concept in programming languages—structured exception handling. It is worth noting that the `On Error` statement still works in Visual Basic .NET, and you can use it if you want, but it is not the recommended way to deal with errors.

# Digging Into Structured Exception Handling

Before you can understand what structured exception handling (SEH) is, you should understand just what a *structured exception*—or even *a non-structured exception*—is. Otherwise, you won't know what you're handling. An *exception* is something that happens out of the ordinary (and usually unexpectedly) in your applications. Exceptions can occur in many circumstances: a file wasn't found, an invalid parameter was passed into a function, and so on. In each of these cases, the running code detects that something unexpected has occurred and it raises an exception.

*Structured exception handling* is a strategy for handling these unexpected events. You perform structured exception handling by "protecting" sections of code that are likely to experience exceptions. For example, when you are about to make a division, you could protect the code that does the division. If the program attempts to divide by zero—either because of an error you've made in the program, or a value the user has entered—the protected code could deal with the resulting exception. Other times when you should use exception handling include when reading from databases; when opening, reading from, or writing to files; or at any other time you think that an error could occur.

## SHOP TALK

### GUIDELINES FOR USING EXCEPTION HANDLING

I am of the belief that it is difficult to overuse exception handling. The benefits you get by protecting yourself, your programs, and your users from errors far outweigh the minimal slowdown that results from using exception handling. On the other hand, be reasonable. If there really is not any possibility for an error to occur, do not bother with the extra typing. You also shouldn't use exception handling in situations where it isn't really an exception. For example, if you want to know if a string contains a number, don't try to convert it to an integer and use the exception as your indicator; use IsNumeric instead to check if the string contains a numeric value.

A bigger question is, "what should you do when you catch an error?" I like to handle exceptions differently during the initial development, early (preview/beta) releases, and final production releases. During development I display as much information as I can, and I try to catch errors as close to the source as possible. During early releases, I generally display the raw error message but I log the detailed information available from the Exception object (such as the stack trace). Finally, in a production release, I try to classify exceptions in terms of their effect—should the application exit, should the current action be aborted, or is it purely informational. In each case, I throw my own error using some friendly text to describe what has occurred and what is going to happen next; I don't want users to have to interpret the raw error messages. Depending on the complexity of the application, some form of selectively activated error logging can be very useful. It is not complicated to add your own error logging, just use the file-writing code from earlier in this chapter to write all of the desired information from the Exception object out to a text file.

## Errors and Exceptions

So, how is an exception different from an error? If you are familiar with other versions of Visual Basic, or indeed most other programming languages, you have likely come across the idea of an error, but not an exception. What is the difference? Why do you need a new word, and something as fancy sounding as structured exception handling?

First, an exception really is an error. Part of the problem, though, is that an error is so much more. An error can be when the function returned a result that you were not expecting, or when the programmer used the wrong algorithm. An exception is more formal. An exception, to repeat the previous definition, is when something happens in your code outside the normal flow of control. Structured exception handling defines a particular way of dealing with exceptions, ensuring that everything is cleaned up after the fact. Another benefit of moving Visual Basic .NET to this new style of handling errors is for consistency across other .NET programming languages. All languages on the .NET platform (including VB .NET, C#, J#, and others) use the same model for raising and handling exceptions. This means that an exception could occur in a piece of code written in one language, and that exception could be raised and dealt with in a different language.

Most errors in Visual Basic have traditionally been dealt with using the On Error statement. On Error is *unstructured* and can lead to confusing code that jumps around in a procedure. As the name implies, structured exception handling uses a more organized approach.

## The Try Block

You protect a section of code to trap whenever an exception occurs with the Try…End Try block. Begin the code you want to protect with Try, and end the section with End Try.

### The Syntax for Try…End Try

The following code block, which you can create in VS.NET 2003 just by typing **Try** and pressing Enter, shows the syntax for the Try…End Try block:

```
Try
.
Catch ex As Exception
.
End Try
```

Try is the beginning of the section of code to protect, and End Try ends the block of code. The Catch line marks the section of the block that actually deals with any exceptions that might occur.

## The Catch Section

Simply marking a section of code with Try…End Try does not actually do anything. If an exception occurs in the protected code, it must be "caught" and dealt with. You catch the exception with the Catch keyword.

Each Try…End Try block can have one or more Catch sections. Each Catch section targets a specific type of exception, as indicated by the type of variable declared in the Catch line. If you decide to have multiple Catch sections in your Try blocks, each Catch section should catch different types of exceptions. Having multiple Catch sections allows you to have different code for handling different types of exceptions. After all your specific Catch sections, you should also have one generic Catch section that will catch any exception that does not fit into any earlier section. This form of the Try…End Try block would look similar to that shown in Listing 4.4.

**LISTING 4.4**   Exceptions Are Caught by the First Catch Block that Matches the Type of Exception that has Occurred

```
Try

Catch ex As IO.FileNotFoundException

Catch ex As IO.IOException

Catch ex As Exception

End Try
```

The Try…Catch Block shown in Listing 4.4 is designed to trap errors for a file-processing procedure. There are separate sections for handling FileNotFound exceptions, IO exceptions, and then a final "catch all" block for all other exceptions. With this type of error handling, it is more obvious which code targets each type of exception. This example also shows another important concept, you need to provide your Catch blocks in the correct order; put them from most specific to the most generic. When an exception occurs within a Try block, it is caught by the *first* compatible Catch, so if you put the most generic block first, every exception would be caught by that block and the code in the other blocks would never run.

To illustrate error handling in action, you can create a program that can produce a variety of errors all through the act of opening a file. First, you will start without any error handling, and then wrap the code in a Try…Catch block, as follows:

1. Create a new Windows application. Call it StructuredExceptionHandling.

2. Add a text box named fileName, a text box named fileContents, and a button called loadFile.

Put code into the Click event for the loadFile button that grabs the filename (including path) from the fileName text box and loads the file's contents into the fileContents text box. Many exceptions can occur when you try to open a file, so this is a good place to add exception handling. For the first version of the code, do not add any error handling; you can add that later. Look at the finished code (with exception handling) in Listing 4.5 if you need some help writing the first version.

Once you have written the code, try the following scenarios: type a filename that doesn't exist, a directory that doesn't exist, and (if possible) try one that you don't have rights to (just specifying C:\ should produce an access exception, if you don't have any secured files). In each case, you will have seen a standard error dialog box and, regardless of whether you chose Break or Continue, these simple errors will have forced you to abort the entire program. Now, add structured exception handling to the code and see how it can allow you to catch these exceptions intelligently. Listing 4.5 shows the lines used to open the file and read its contents wrapped in a Try...Catch block with three Catch clauses. The Catch clauses, which are in order from the most specific to the least, are set up to handle the very specific FileNotFound exception, any IO exception (IO.IOException), and finally to handle anything else that might occur (Exception).

**LISTING 4.5**   Handling Exceptions When Opening a File

```
Private Sub loadFile_Click( _
    ByVal sender As System.Object, _
    ByVal e As System.EventArgs) _
    Handles loadFile.Click

    Try
        Dim sr As New IO.StreamReader(fileName.Text)
        fileContents.Text = sr.ReadToEnd()
    Catch ex As IO.FileNotFoundException
        Dim errorMessage As String
        errorMessage = _
            "Whoops, that file wasn't found"
        MsgBox(errorMessage, MsgBoxStyle.Information, _
            "Error Loading File")
    Catch ex As IO.IOException
        Dim errorMessage As String
        errorMessage = _
            "Whoops, I had a little trouble loading that file." _
            & vbCrLf & ex.Message
        MsgBox(errorMessage, MsgBoxStyle.Information, _
            "Error Loading File")
    Catch ex As Exception
```

LISTING 4.5   Continued

```
        Dim errorMessage As String
        errorMessage = _
            "Whoops, something bad happened: " & ex.Message
        MsgBox(errorMessage, MsgBoxStyle.Information, _
            "Error Loading File")
    End Try
End Sub
```

In keeping with the concept of exceptions representing unexpected events, IO.FileNotFound is a good example of an exception that should never occur in your code. Whenever you open a file there is a chance it will not be where you expect. This is not an exception; it is just a fact when dealing with files. By adding a check with the File.Exists(filePath) function, you can catch a non-existent path before you even try to open it.

Table 4.8 lists some other common exceptions.

**WHAT ELSE CAN GO WRONG?**

Table 4.8 is not a complete list of all the possible exceptions. There are many others; please look in the Visual Basic .NET help for more details. In addition, you can create your own exceptions to add to this list if you need to, by creating a class that inherits from System.Exception.

**TABLE 4.8**

**Common Exceptions**

| EXCEPTION TYPE | WHEN IT OCCURS |
| --- | --- |
| ArgumentException | General category for errors that occur when the wrong type (or value) is passed to a method. Includes ArgumentNullException and ArgumentOutOfRangeException. Can occur because of programmer error or user data entry. |
| ArgumentNullException | Occurs when you pass a null to a method when it will not accept it. |
| ArgumentOutOfRangeException | Occurs when you pass a variable that is either too large or too small for the method; for example, if you pass the number −1 to a method that is designed to expect a month number (that is, between 1 and 12). |
| DivideByZeroException | Occurs when attempting to divide by an uninitialized variable, or a variable holding zero. Usually occurs because of programmer error. |
| IndexOutOfRangeException | Occurs when attempting to access the member of an array that does not exist. Usually occurs because of programmer error, but can also be caused by invalid user entry. |

**TABLE 4.8**
Continued

| EXCEPTION TYPE | WHEN IT OCCURS |
|---|---|
| NotImplementedException | Normally used as a placeholder when a developer is first working on a program. You can create the shell for your application, and then throw this exception from all methods. As you continue on the application, you replace the exception with the actual code. This ensures that you complete each of your procedures. |
| OutOfMemoryException | Occurs when your program runs out of memory. This can happen when you are filling large arrays, or when performing a loop. |
| OverflowException | A common exception that occurs when you try to put a value that is too large into a variable, for example, if you attempt the following assignment:<br><br>`Dim iSmallishNumber As Short = 50000` |
| FileNotFoundException | An example of an error that is not defined in the System namespace. In this case, the exception is defined in the System.IO namespace. This exception occurs when you attempt to access a file that does not exist. It could be because it has not been created, or because the path is incorrect. |

## Using the Finally Section to Clean Up

As you write Try blocks, you sometimes come across situations when, even if an exception occurs, you *must* do something. For example, if you are writing code that writes information to a file, you should close the file, whether or not an error occurs during the write. You add this functionality with the Finally section. This is a good place to close files, dispose of memory intensive objects (like database connections), and otherwise clean up after yourself. Listing 4.6 shows the addition of a Finally section to the code in Listing 4.5.

**LISTING 4.6**   Using the Finally Section

```
Private Sub loadFile_Click( _
    ByVal sender As System.Object, _
    ByVal e As System.EventArgs) _
    Handles loadFile.Click

    Dim sr As IO.StreamReader
    Try
        sr = New IO.StreamReader(fileName.Text)
        fileContents.Text = sr.ReadToEnd()
```

**LISTING 4.6**   Continued

```
     Catch ex As IO.FileNotFoundException
         Dim errorMessage As String
         errorMessage = _
             "Whoops, that file wasn't found"
         MsgBox(errorMessage, MsgBoxStyle.Information, _
             "Error Loading File")
     Catch ex As IO.IOException
         Dim errorMessage As String
         errorMessage = _
             "Whoops, I had a little trouble loading that file." _
             & vbCrLf & ex.Message
         MsgBox(errorMessage, MsgBoxStyle.Information, _
             "Error Loading File")
     Catch ex As Exception
         Dim errorMessage As String
         errorMessage = _
             "Whoops, something bad happened: " & ex.Message
         MsgBox(errorMessage, MsgBoxStyle.Information, _
             "Error Loading File")
     Finally
         sr.Close()
     End Try
End Sub
```

The `Finally` block closes the `StreamReader` even if errors occur. Although not required, it's good practice to clean up after you're done with a variable by closing it or calling `Dispose()` if the object has such a method. Scope can be a bit of a confusing issue with error handling blocks in general, including both `Catch` and `Finally` blocks. Keep in mind that you can't access variables that are declared within the `Try` portion of code, because variables are scoped to be visible only within the block where they are created. To account for the scoping issue while still allowing the `Finally` block to close the `StreamReader`, notice that Listing 4.6 has the `StreamReader` variable (sr) declared before the start of the `Try` block, making it available in the `Finally` section.

## Raising Exceptions

Occasionally, you might want to notify a user that something drastic has gone wrong. This might be something related specifically to your application, or it might be a "normal" exception. In Visual Basic 6.0, this was accomplished by raising an error using the `Err.Raise` method, but in .NET you don't raise an error, you *throw* it. To throw a new error, you call `Throw` with an `Exception` object (as shown in Listing 4.7).

**LISTING 4.7**   Throwing an Exception up the Calling Chain

```
Public Sub DoSomething( _
        ByVal ID As Integer)
    If ID < 0 Then
        Throw New ArgumentException( _
            "ID must be a positive Integer", "ID")
    End If
End Sub
```

If you are throwing your own exception because of another lower level exception, you can (and often should) include that original exception object by passing it in when you create the new exception. Listing 4.8 shows an example of wrapping an existing exception object when you are throwing a new one.

**LISTING 4.8**   Wrapping an Existing Exception

```
Public Sub DoSomething( _
        ByVal ID As Integer)
    Try
        ID = 365 / ID
    Catch ex As DivideByZeroException
        Throw New ArgumentException( _
            "ID must not be zero!", "ID", ex)
    End Try
End Sub
```

One general rule for exception handling is to catch errors only if you are planning to do something with them; do not catch an error and then just throw it again (as in Listing 4.9). Just catching and throwing does not add any value, and you can achieve the same result by removing error handling completely. If you want to throw it again, it would be best to make a new exception with your application's friendly error message and then stick the old error in as an InnerException (as in Listing 4.8).

**LISTING 4.9**   Just Catching and Throwing Is not Very Useful in the .NET Development World

```
Public Sub DoSomething( _
        ByVal ID As Integer)
    Try
        ID = 365 / ID
```

**LISTING 4.9**   Continued

```
    Catch ex As DivideByZeroException
        Throw ex
    End Try
End Sub
```

Note that your errors might contain sensitive information, such as database server or table names, file paths, and so on, which makes it a good idea to provide your own Exception object, complete with friendly error message, whenever you want to throw an exception to your user interface.

## Making Use of "On Error" in Visual Basic .NET

If you are moving from Visual Basic 6.0 to Visual Basic .NET, structured exception handling is a big change. The previous method of handling errors, using On Error Goto [section] or On Error Resume Next, is still supported in Visual Basic .NET, but it is not recommended. In general, you should be able to replace On Error code with structure exception handling without too much difficulty (keep in mind that you might need multiple Try blocks within a single procedure), but On Error Resume Next is harder to duplicate. Essentially, On Error Resume Next is the equivalent of wrapping a Try…Catch block around each line of code in a procedure, which you're not likely to need. Instead, only a smaller set of the procedure's code needs the Resume Next functionality. In many cases, you can rewrite the code to remove the need for resuming without acting on the error.

# In Brief

This chapter provided an in-depth discussion of working with files. Here are the primary things that were discussed:

- Streams are a key concept in .NET programming. Streams are used for read and write access to files, network streams, memory buffers, and more.

- The classes in the System.IO namespace, including File, Path, and Directory, contain shared methods that allow you to access and manipulate the file system.

- Structured exception handling replaces the On Error model for catching errors at runtime. Used correctly, it can be much more powerful than Visual Basic 6.0's On Error.

- Multiple Catch blocks in a Try…Catch allow for granular handling of exceptions. The first matching Catch block handles the exception and the rest are skipped. It is critical that you arrange your Catch blocks in order from the most specific to the most generic.

# Data Binding

**5**

## Working with Data

Being able to create data-management applications quickly and effectively using Visual Basic has always been at the heart of Visual Basic development. At some point all Visual Basic developers will work with data in some form. Visual Basic 6 had some good ways to work with data, as well as all the features available in ADO. Visual Basic .NET is no exception. In fact, there are many great improvements in the way you can work with data in the .NET Framework, in addition to great improvements in the area of DataBinding. However, the concepts used in ADO have somewhat changed in ADO.NET and is often viewed as one of the larger sections of .NET to learn while moving from VB 6.

This chapter introduces the new object model in ADO.NET and how it relates to ADO, while pointing out why these changes were made and how you can take advantage of them. It also explains how to take advantage of data binding in a Windows Forms application and how powerful and flexible it is. Visual Studio .NET has a lot of tools built-in to help you when working with data in your VB.NET projects; this chapter goes through these features and discusses how to use them as well.

## What's New in ADO.NET?

There's a whole lot to cover, but before getting into the obvious object model changes from ADO to ADO.NET, it would be good to talk about the general changes from the Visual Basic developer's standpoint.

Don't you hate it when you create a new project in VB6 and have to add a project reference to the Microsoft ActiveX Data Objects DLL? Luckily, this is no longer an issue when creating a new project (with the exception of the "Empty Project" and "Empty Web Project"). The classes in ADO.NET that are located in the System.Data.DLL Assembly, which is already included in every project type that you create in Visual Studio .NET. The namespace that you'll be getting familiar with throughout this chapter, as you might have guessed, is System.Data. This namespace contains everything in ADO.NET that you need for your data access applications. Another item that must be understood before jumping in the deep end is the new layout of providers—how they work and how they are built-in on top of the same interfaces for consistency.

## Understanding the Concept of Providers

Oneof the new concepts in ADO.NET is that there are separated providers now built specifically for certain data sources. In ADO, this wasn't really the case. You could connect directly to any OLE DB or ODBC provider through the Connection Object. Now that ADO.NET has evolved into provider specific implementations, you will need to pick the best provider for the job. Table 5.1 shows a list of the available providers (each of which is implemented as classes within the System.Data namespace), with separate entries for each key use of that provider.

**TABLE 5.1**
**Available Providers and their Key uses**

| NAMESPACE | USES |
| --- | --- |
| OleDb | Working with data against an OLE DB data sources. A couple good examples of this is an Access file using the Jet 4.0 OLE DB or pulling information from an Excel file. |
| Odbc | Working with data against an ODBC data source, such as an ODBC connection to DB2 or MySQL, using a Data Source Name (DSN) or fully-specified ODBC connection string. In general you will use ODBC when an OLEDB (or Native) driver is not available for your database, as ODBC should be available for almost every type of database system. |
| SqlClient | Working specifically with data from SQL Server. Built to work fast, efficiently and natively with SQL Server, avoiding the extra OLE DB or ODBC interfaces. |
| OracleClient | Working specifically with data from an Oracle database. |

You can still use the OleDb provider in ADO.NET to connect to a SQL Server database using the SQLOLEDB provider, but this is not recommended because the SqlClient provider classes are built specifically for SQL Server and work much better and faster.

What it comes down to for you and your understanding of this new structure is that all classes that are related to the provider, such as the Connection class and others, will be inside the provider's namespace. One thought about this approach though is that there will now be so many different classes that might all work differently. Jumping from one provider to another is not going to be easy. This actually isn't true. Each provider must implement the same interfaces and follow a typical naming convention. This is typically the namespace (or a shortened version of it) as a prefix to the actual object. Examples of this are the `SqlConnection` and `OleDbConnection` classes, both of which represent the connections for their specific provider. To help these classes all follow the same patterns, so it is easier for you to work with them, the classes in each provider implement the interfaces that are located in the `System.Data.Common` namespace.

For questions about what an interface is, refer to Chapter 7. By implementing these common interfaces, you ensure that opening a connection will work in the same way in each provider.

## Where's My Recordset?

One of the biggest questions that comes up with Visual Basic 6.0 (or earlier) users is the fact that ADO.NET does not have a Recordset object. ADO.NET has been rebuilt from the ground up to allow you to do all the things you used to and much more, but in the process some of the things you are used to working with have been taken away or moved.

Previously, in ADO, the recordset was aimed at being able to work directly with connected data; typically a single result set either using a client cursor or a server cursor. It had the ability to work in a disconnected environment, but disconnected support was limited and sometimes would not work very well. There was also the ability to export XML from a record-set, but you were not given much control over how this XML was created, as it was limited to a single proprietary format. The lack or limitations of built-in support for these two features alone could be major hurdles for accomplishing some of the advanced functionality that many projects required.

## Why so Many Changes?

You're probably wondering why Microsoft changed everything you had grown so accustomed to. This is a valid question. Although sometimes change is a good thing, it can also be frustrating because of the time necessary to learn the new object model and new methods of data access in .NET, not to mention just wrapping your head around some of the new concepts.

ADO.NET has many changes, which can be disturbing to experienced ADO developers looking to learn the next big thing. I'm here to tell you that these changes are worth learning—they'll help you get your job done faster and in a more organized fashion. Let's dive right into some of the new concepts and objects.

## Connected and Disconnected Data Models

As mentioned earlier, ADO was focused on connected data, meaning your connection to the database needed to be open while reading the result set you were working with. Even though it could work in a disconnected environment, such scenarios were difficult to accurately define and develop. In ADO.NET, connected and disconnected data have actually been split out into new objects that are more focused on the task at hand. This chapter mainly focuses on working with disconnected data, but first talks briefly about the new object used with connected data.

## Using DataReaders to Pull Back Read-Only Data

There are often times when you want to retrieve data extremely quickly and don't have the need to send updated data back to your database. When using ADO, this type of situation called for the use of a "firehose" Recordset, one that was opened as forward-only and read-only. The DataReader classes (SqlClient.SqlDataReader and OleDB.OleDbDataReader) are the ADO.NET equivalent to the "firehose" Recordset, but defined as classes on their own, instead of just a particular combination of options used to open a Recordset.

As described above, DataReaders are connected-only, forward-only, and read-only views of your data. While this is an equivalent to the ADO "firehose" concept, it is important to note that this is the only really connected option in the ADO.NET set of functions.

The DataReader easily supports multiple result sets  (from batched SQL commands) along with much better support for retrieving specific types of data out of it. The most important of these differences is that it is much faster when accessing data than the Recordset.

DataReaders are often used when developing ASP.NET applications, because a forward-only, read-only connection to the database is perfect when you are retrieving data for display on a web page. However, they are best for fast access to data and can be used in your Windows Forms applications as well. For a more in-depth look at the DataReader and how to use it, refer to Chapter 6.

Now let's talk about the new objects that you will use more often in Visual Basic .NET Windows Forms application development. The following items are part of the disconnected model of working with data. Because all providers can work with these items, they are "out in the open" and located in the System.Data namespace and again are not provider specific.

## DataTable

The first class to describe in ADO.NET's disconnected data model is DataTable. Like DataReaders, DataTables also resemble Recordsets, but in this case DataTables are more like a disconnected Recordset than one set up for quick use. Unlike a recordset, however, the DataTable does not rely on a connection to your database to be worked with. You can think of a DataTable as an in-memory representation of a result set or table in your database. This set of data has no understanding of where it received the data from, nor of the original table's structure. What it does understand is what is already in it and how to work with it. There are many properties and methods to this class, but this chapter only covers some of the basic and most important ones.

The DataTable contains two collections which contain both the data itself (Rows) and the details about the data structure of the table (Columns). The Columns property is a DataColumnCollection that holds an instance of the DataColumn Class for each column (or field) of data in your DataTable. Each DataColumn object exposes all the properties of a field that you would normally see in a table designer, such as the one in Access or in SQL Server Enterprise Manager. These properties describe each field in your DataTable, including specifying details such as ColumnName, DataType, AllowDBNull and others. Not all DataColumn objects will include all of the details I described above. In fact, a single DataColumn can have only ColumnName and DataType set and be perfectly valid. ADO also provides you with the data type of each column, but ADO.NET's DataType property has an important difference from what was provided by ADO. ADO.NET providers return back native .NET Framework types, converted for you from whatever native format was being used by the data source. Having data conversions handled by the data provider means less work for you and also quicker, more efficient data access, because the Framework does the conversion for you as it's coming out of the database.

## PROPER NAMING CONVENTIONS

You've got to love the naming conventions that Microsoft has used in ADO.NET, as well as the entire Framework. One of the naming conventions you might have just noticed is that most collections in the Framework have the word Collection at the end of their name. Another important aspect to take into consideration when naming properties and methods is that you'll notice names of classes in the .NET Framework are typically quite a bit longer than in previous Microsoft development platforms. This is because using more descriptive names helps the consumer (you) better understand what a class is to be used for, without ever having to read through any documentation. You might hear someone say that this isn't a good idea, because it means more typing. There are a couple things you can say to that. If typing is an issue, you're probably in the wrong field, but also and more importantly, Enterprise developers are using Visual Studio .NET. Intellisense can auto-complete words for you, so the length of words isn't really an issue, except that the more descriptive, the better.

The Columns collection provides the list of columns in the DataTable, and the Rows collection provides the actual data. The Rows property returns a DataRowCollection object, which is a collection of individual rows from your data source, each of which is represented as an instance of the DataRow class.

Once you catch on to some of the patterns used throughout the Framework, it becomes pretty easy to guess what a class does without ever having to look at the documentation.

The DataRow class provides an Item property, which allows you to retrieve the contents of an individual field (column) using the integer ordinal or the field's name.

```
Dim Customers As DataTable
For Each customer As DataRow In Customers.Rows
    MsgBox(CStr(customer.Item("Full Name")))
```

```
    'CSTR(customer.Item(3)) would also work,
    'assuming Full Name was the 4th column
Next
```

The DataRow class also exposes another interesting property, RowState, which you can use to determine if the row has been modified, added, or deleted since it was retrieved from the data source.

```
Dim Customers As DataTable
Dim message As String
message = "{0} has been modified!"
For Each customer As DataRow In Customers.Rows
    If customer.RowState = DataRowState.Modified Then
        MsgBox(String.Format(message, CInt(customer("ID"))))
    End If
Next
```

With its collection of Columns and Rows, a DataTable could be considered an in-memory representation of a table from your data source. If you wish to represent multiple tables and the relationships between them, then you will want to look at the DataSet class.

## DataSet

The next item on the list is the DataSet. The DataSet is a collection of DataTable objects and the relationships between them. This is basically what a typical database does also, in that a database stores multiple tables of data. Again, just like the DataTable, the DataSet only holds the data, it is not connected back to the original data source in any way. The relationships between tables in a DataSet are exposed through the Relations property. This property allows you to add new DataRelation instances used for setting up relationships between different DataTables in your DataSet. A quick example of this is to have a Customer table and an Order table, which are related (in the data model) by a CustomerID column on the Order table. This column is a Foreign Key and relates the two tables by means of the CustomerID value. In the DataSet, you could set up a new relationship linking the two by the CustomerID column in the Order table to the ID column in the Customers table. Once you have established a relationship between two tables, you can use methods such as GetChildRows that will return the related rows to a specific parent row.

The DataSet also adds some extra functions to help you manage the state of your data. AcceptChanges, RejectChanges, GetChanges, and several others that deal with updating data back to the database. For more information on the update side of this disconnected data model, refer to Chapter 6.

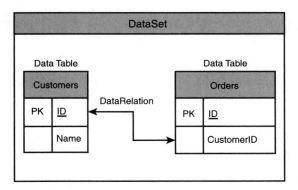

**FIGURE 5.1** Here you can see a representation of a DataSet that contains two DataTables with a DataRelation to associate them.

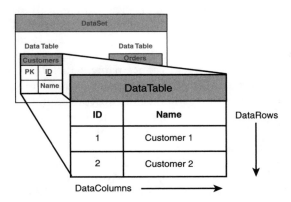

**Figure 5.2** Shows the details of a DataTable, pointing out the DataColumns and DataRows.

## Object Model Hierarchy

It's one thing to read about this new object model, but it's a whole other thing to see how it looks brought together. Here's an example for you. Imagine you have a Customers table and an Orders table. Now let's say you already went out to your database and retrieved the data and put it into a DataSet, which would have two DataTables in it. What would it look like? Take a look at Figures 5.1 and 5.2.

This is an extremely scaled down view of DataSets, but the general layout is easier to grasp in this visual approach. With this key understanding, you're ready to learn some of the details of the DataSet and learn how to take advantage of its power so you can write less code.

The next section explains how it all comes together and how to use the tools in Visual Studio .NET to build data management applications.

## Retrieving Data

With a good idea of the new object model, you're ready to take a look at the tools that Visual Studio .NET provides and learn how to use them. First stop, the Server Explorer. If you haven't seen it yet, it has a lot of functionality and use in Visual Studio. This chapter focuses on using it to get some data. Figure 5.3 shows you what the Server Explorer looks like.

The two sections you'll see are Data Connections and Servers. The Servers section allows you to connect to one or more Windows machines. Typically you will use it to connect to a server and get easy access to its services, SQL Server instances or maybe its event logs, but it is

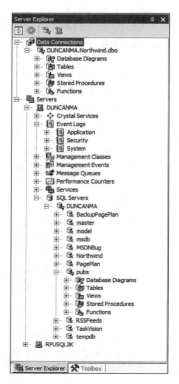

**FIGURE 5.3** This is the Server Explorer. If you don't see it anywhere you can click the View menu and choose Server Explorer.

not limited to servers. With a default installation of Visual Studio, your local machine will show up in the list of servers to play with. This section focuses on the Data Connections section. It helps you more with the task at hand of building data applications.

## Data Connections

First things first, before you can access any of your data, you need to create a connection to your database. To create a data connection in Visual Studio .NET, simply right-click the Data Connections node in the Server Explorer window and click Add Connection or click the Connect to Database button in the toolbar across the top. This will bring up the Data Link Properties dialog box, which will more than likely be pretty familiar because it has existed in most of Microsoft applications that work with data. You can add any type of connection you'd like to any data source, but for these examples, you're going to add a connection to the Northwind SQL Server database. To do so, enter the name of a SQL Server instance name, which by default is the name of the server. Then set up the appropriate authentication to connect to it. The type of authentication to use depends on how your SQL Server is configured, so check with your SQL administrator if you are unsure of what type of authentication to use. Finally, enter in the name of the database to connect to, in this case, "Northwind," or select it from the drop-down list and click the OK button. Assuming everything was set up properly, you will now see a new item under Data Connections in Server Explorer. By default, the name is in the form <SQLInstanceName>.<DatabaseName>.<DatabaseOwner>. You can easily change this to anything you'd like.

If you expand this new connection, you'll see most of the things you'd expect to see in SQL Server Enterprise Manager, including tables, views, and stored procedures. You can also edit all these items and perform queries, which can come in handy at times.

Now that you have a connection, let's get started. Create a new Windows Forms project. For this example, expand the Tables node in the Data Connection and select the Customers table. Make sure that the default Form1 is open and in design view. Now click and drag the table from the Server Explorer to the design surface of your form. You'll notice two new objects are created: a SqlConnection and a SqlDataAdapter.

## Establishing a Database Connection

The `Connection` (SqlConnection for SQL Server, or OleDBConnection for OLE DB data sources) class isn't very far off from the `ADODB.Connection`. It has a `ConnectionString` property and Open and Close methods that should be pretty familiar. It also has built-in support for dealing with transactions. When you create a Transaction through your Connection object, it creates a real database transaction, but it exists across more than a single database call, as opposed to handling transactions within your SQL calls and Stored Procedures. Having a transaction that you can control outside of your SQL statements allows you to commit or roll it back based on the results of non-database activities.

If you wanted to add a record to your table and at the same time add a file to the file system that was somehow related, you could wrap this pair of actions in a transaction. By placing a `Try Catch` statement around both statements, you can rollback the database action if the other activity fails. It is worth noting though, that in the reverse situation (if database action fails, but the non-database action succeeds) you will have to handle "rolling back" the non-database change in your own code. (There are exceptions to this rule though, check out the System.EnterpriseServices namespace for more information on COM+ and the concept of "distributed transactions".)

When wrapping both database and non-database actions together into a single transaction it is often easier to place the database work first, because it can be easily rolled back. If the database activity is first and either it or the non-database activity fails, then you only have to concern yourself with rolling back the database action. For more information on transactions, refer to Chapter 6.

## DataAdapter

You can think of the DataAdapter (SqlDataAdapter against SQL Server or OleDBDataAdapter against OLE DB data sources) as an excellent helper class for pulling data from a database to a DataSet or DataTable, but especially for updating data back to the database. The DataAdapter has two main methods: Fill and Update. It has a `SelectCommand` property that is of type `SqlCommand` (or `OleDBCommand` against an `OleDB` data source. The `Command` object (SqlCommand for SQL Server, OleDBCommand for OLE DB data sources) is another object that existed in ADO, but has been improved upon. In the `SqlDataAdapter`, the `SelectCommand` lets the Fill Method know how and what data it should be pulling from the database to put into the supplied DataSet. For now, focus on using the SqlDataAdapter for "filling" a DataSet, but first you need to understand the `SqlCommand` object. For a more in depth look at the SqlDataAdapter, refer to Chapter 6.

## STRONGLY TYPED DATASETS

While checking out the properties of the DataAdapter, you might notice a few hyperlinks at the bottom of the Property window. These are called DesignerVerbs and are special tasks to help you at design time when working with the currently selected component. There are a few handy items, including "Configure Data Adapter" to help you make common changes to your data adapter or "Preview Data," which will let you see the real data that your data adapter is going to retrieve. Then there's the Generate DataSet item, which will actually create a DataSet for you, but more importantly create a schema (or XSD file) to define all the fields and columns in the table of your dataset at design time. In the background, it is calling XSD.EXE to create a strongly typed collection, which is basically a code file that will give you an easier way to work with your data, because you can access your data and get design-time warnings if you're trying to cast a field to an invalid type. With a regular DataSet, you would not get the error until runtime and the offending line was actually executed, because all fields return an object, instead of say a string, integer, or GUID. If you were to create a strongly typed DataSet from the Customers table in the Northwind database, you would actually be able to access a field in your table with something more intuitive and strongly typed, such as Northwind.Customers(0).ContactName. This can be advantageous for certain projects. One thing to keep in mind is that if you're working with many databases and tables in a project, this probably won't be a good idea, because any time you change your data structure, you will have to remember to update all of your strongly typed DataSets.

## Using the Command Class

The Command (SqlCommand or OleDBCommand) class is at the core of working with data. It can be used to pull data as well as send data back to the database.

The key properties on the SqlCommand object are CommandType, CommandText, and Connection. The CommandType is an Enum that you can set to Text, StoredProcedure, or TableDirect. Setting the CommandType will tell the SqlCommand object how it should interpret the CommandText property, which is a string that either represents the SQL statement to execute, the stored procedure name to execute, or the name of the table to retrieve the result set from. In ADO, the precursor to ADO.NET (used in many Visual Basic 6.0 applications), if you didn't set the CommandType property correctly, then it would be determined for you, but in ADO.NET not setting the CommandType will result in an error.

One great advantage that you'll start to notice about ADO.NET over ADO is that the object model is much cleaner and objects better relate to each other and work together to get the job done.

The Parameter property is another important one with the Command object as it can hold parameters to be used with your queries that can be programmatically set. The power of this is that you won't have to build the queries as a string anymore to supply the values for the SQL where statement. Building the query as a string in the past has also had some security implications, such as SQL injection by hackers. The Parameters collection obviates this issue. For more information on using the Parameters collection, refer to Chapter 6.

# Filling a DataSet

Now that you have a good idea how all these objects work with the existing data model, let's continue with this example and query the Northwind database for some information about a customer.

Earlier, you used some of the cool RAD (Rapid Application Development) features of Visual Studio .NET to help set up the objects you need to retrieve some data from the Customers table. At this point, you should see in the component tray of Form1 two objects— SqlConnection1 and SqlDataAdapter1. You can use the Property window to browse around and check out some of the things that VS .NET sets up for you. The connection has its ConnectionString property already set to the proper string. You can also dig around in the DataAdapter to see what it has already set up. In the Property window, you can expand the SelectCommand property to see that it was nice enough to set up a SQL Select statement that selects all the fields from the Customers table. It also sets a reference to SqlConnection1, so when it executes, it will know what source to execute it on.

With that, you can now go get some data from the Customers table. Listing 5.1 demonstrates how to do this in the load event of the form.

**LISTING 5.1**    Retrieving data using the Fill method of the DataAdapter.

```
Private Sub Form1_Load( _
        ByVal sender As Object, _
        ByVal e As System.EventArgs) _
        Handles MyBase.Load
    Dim Customers As New DataTable
    SqlDataAdapter1.Fill(Customers)
End Sub
```

In the load event, you're declaring a new DataTable, which is appropriate because you're really only dealing with one table. If you were dealing with more than one table, using a DataSet would be appropriate. Because DataAdapter already knows what SQL statement to execute when you want to pull data out, because of the SelectCommand property of SqlDataAdapter1, all you have to do is call the Fill method and supply the DataTable as the parameter. The DataAdapter will then take care of everything. It will open the connection, execute the SQL statement on the connection, and place the results in the DataTable. Just to prove that it's really working, let's display a message that tells you the "CustomerName" value of the first record in our Customer table.

```
MessageBox.Show(Customers.Rows(0)("CustomerName").ToString)
```

Again, as discussed before, you're going to use the Rows collection to retrieve the row you're after, and then use the default indexer of the DataRow, supplying the name of the field to return the value. The returned value can be any object, so you'll need to make sure it's a string, because that's what you would like to display. If you run your Windows Forms application, you'll see that the name of the first customer is displayed.

Now that you've got a good handle on how to pull data from a table in a database and how simple it is, let's see how you can take advantage of data binding in the Windows Forms application.

## SHOP TALK

### FIGHTING THE FEAR OF DATA BINDING

If you have spent a great deal of time programming in pre-.NET versions of Visual Basic, then you might have a pretty poor opinion of Data Binding. Most experts you asked would say that it was a bad idea to use Data Binding in your Visual Basic 6.0 application, and many of the available articles and books reflected this same opinion. The key issues that surrounded Visual Basic 6.0 Data Binding were decreased performance and problems with connecting your user interface directly to the database, and these two issues no longer exist when you are working with ADO.NET. Performance is no longer an issue due to a completely new binding architecture, and also because you are working against a local set of data not directly against your database server. This disconnected data-model addresses the second issue as well, since you are not binding your UI directly to the database, preventing any issues with database connections being held open too long or other such issues. In addition to the two issues I just mentioned, I always had an additional issue with Data Binding in Visual Basic 6.0, which was that it was designed to work with ADO Recordsets, and couldn't work with collections of my own custom object classes. This limitation prevented systems from abstracting the database into their own system-specific classes and then still benefiting from data binding in the user interface. I won't be going into this topic in this chapter, but in .NET the binding model handles your own objects and custom collections of object in the exact same manner as it handles the results of a database query. Overall, despite its issues in earlier versions of Visual Basic, Data Binding is the way to go.

## Data Binding in Windows Forms

In the last section you learned how to retrieve data from the Customers table in the Northwind database, with barely any code. This is a good thing. Visual Studio .NET helps you do a lot of the repetitive work that you don't really want to, so you have more time to focus on more important aspects of your applications. Data Binding won't be an exception to that statement. Let's take the previous example and learn how to bind it to the UI. Because you now have a table of data to work with, you can display it in the control that is appropriate for that job—the DataGrid.

To shorten the code even further, you can move the DataSet that you declared in the load event earlier, to the Forms Designer. To create a new DataSet at design time, locate the

ToolBox window and click on the Data tab. You will then see the DataSet class and can drag a new one onto your form. A wizard will pop up asking if you'd like to create a typed dataset or an untyped dataset. Select untyped dataset and click the OK button. A new DataSet will now show up in the component tray. Change the Name property of this new DataSet to dsNorthwind and change the DataSetName property to Northwind. Now click the ellipsis at the right side of the Tables property and you will see the Table collection Designer. Click the Add button to add a new DataTable and change Name property to dtCustomers and the TableName property to Customers. You can now change the form's loading code to one simple line, as shown in Listing 5.2.

**LISTING 5.2**  Filling a DataSet

```
Private Sub Form1_Load( _
        ByVal sender As Object, _
        ByVal e As System.EventArgs) _
        Handles MyBase.Load
    SqlDataAdapter1.Fill(dsNorthwind)
End Sub
```

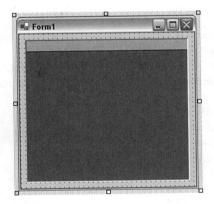

**FIGURE 5.4**  A DataGrid docked to fill in a form.

When you call the Fill method now, you will instead pass in the DataSet this time. The DataAdapter will notice that you're pulling from the Customers table to get the data and dsNorthwind has a Customers table in it, so it will fill in the columns and rows in that DataTable in the DataSet. What's great about this is that you can now access the DataTable by its name instead of by Index, which makes for more readable and dynamic code.

```
MsgBox(CStr(dsNorthwind.Tables
("Customers").Rows(0)("ContactName")))
```

With this aside, you are now ready to data bind. Add a DataGrid control to the form. Set its Dock property to Fill and change the DockPadding.All property of the form to 10. The end result should look like Figure 5.4. For more information on docking, refer to Chapter 3.

Select the DataGrid in the forms designer and check out the Property window. The properties of interest to you right now are in the Data section. If you click and select the DataSource property, you'll notice a little down arrow. Click that arrow and you will see the DataSet and DataTable you have created there. Select dsNorthwind from the drop-down list because you want to have the grid display data from it. Now click the DataMember property and click the down arrow. You should see a list of all the DataTables contained inside the DataSet selected

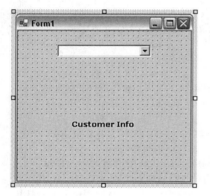

**FIGURE 5.5**    A form that displays all the customers.

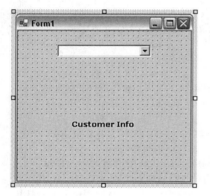

**FIGURE 5.6**    A form to display customers and information about them one at a time.

in the DataSource property. In this case, you will see Customers; select it. Now run this application and you will see that lo and behold, without writing but a single line of code, you now have a form that will show you all the customers as shown in Figure 5.5. How cool is that?

There are quite a few other ways you can use Data Binding for different types of data layouts and situations. The next section illustrates simple binding.

## Simple Binding

Simple binding refers to binding a set of data to a control that is capable of displaying only one piece of data at a time, such as the TextBox or ComboBox. To keep things simple, this example uses the same data structure as the last example. Create a new Windows Forms project on the default form, and place a ComboBox and a Label. Name them cmbCustomers and lblCustomerInfo, respectively. Your form should look like Figure 5.6.

After setting up the UI, you will need to set up the connection, DataAdapter, and DataSet again like you did for the first example. Once you have all of that set up, you're ready to write some code. This time around, you're going to do all the Data Binding in code instead of at design time so you can see that it works exactly the same. Like last time, you'll need to fill the DataSet when the form loads, but this time, you'll also write a bit of code to bind the Customers table to cmbCustomers. Listing 5.3 shows this process.

**LISTING 5.3**    Binding the ComboBox to the Customers Table

```
Private Sub Form1_Load( _
        ByVal sender As Object, _
        ByVal e As System.EventArgs) _
        Handles MyBase.Load
    SqlDataAdapter1.Fill(dsNorthwind)
    With cmbCustomers
        .DisplayMember = "ContactName"
        .ValueMember = "CustomerID"
        .DataSource = dsNorthwind.Tables("Customers")
    End With
End Sub
```

This code introduces a couple new properties—DisplayMember and ValueMember. These properties exist on several controls in Windows Forms that support Data Binding to a list of data, including the ListBox, CheckedListBox and the ComboBox. Both properties are strings and in the case of binding to a DataTable, represent the field names. The DisplayMember is the field that you would like to be shown in the control per row in the DataTable. ValueMember is the field you would like to use to identify the currently selected item. This is usually the identification field. As before, the DataSource property is set to the Customers table, because that's what you want to bind to.

That little bit of code is enough to properly bind to the ComboBox. If you run the application, you will see that cmbCustomers now has all the customers bound to it and because you set the DisplayMember property to ContactName, that field is displayed for you to visually recognize each row. Now let's see what the ValueMember field is going to do for you.

## SHOP TALK

### CREATING YOUR DISPLAYMEMBER

Quite often the requirements of a system I am building specify combo boxes that show a combination of database fields (first and last name, for example) instead of just one. In cases like these, having only a single field to use for DisplayMember doesn't show all the information you need. DisplayMember doesn't allow you to set any combination of two field names, so how can you display the person's full name? The quick and dirty solution is to use the AS keyword in the SQL Select statement to create a new field. In addition to selecting all the other fields in your table, you would then also have a field select that resembles this "FirstName + ' ' + LastName AS Name". Then, you simply set DisplayMember to Name and you'll get the desired results. If your data source is coming from a View or a Stored Procedure, so you can't modify it to include a new column definition, then you can also do it at the ADO.NET level. Once you've pulled back a table full of data, you can add a new column on the client side using the DataTable's Columns collection.

```
Private Sub Form1_Load( _
        ByVal sender As Object, _
        ByVal e As System.EventArgs) _
        Handles MyBase.Load
    SqlDataAdapter1.Fill(dsNorthwind)
    Dim allColumns As DataColumnCollection
    Dim displayCol As DataColumn
    allColumns = dsNorthwind.Tables("Customers").Columns
    displayCol = allColumns.Add( _
        "DisplayMember", _
        System.Type.GetType("System.String"), _
        "ContactName + ' (' + ContactTitle + ')'")
End Sub
```

Either way, either at the database server or on the client, adding a special column to give you your display member is a good technique when you are data binding.

In the SelectedIndexChanged event of cmbCustomers, you can add in the code listed in Listing 5.4 to set a value into the label on the form.

**LISTING 5.4**   Show the SelectedValue

```
Private Sub cmbCustomers_SelectedIndexChanged( _
    ByVal sender As Object, _
    ByVal e As System.EventArgs) _
    Handles cmbCustomers.SelectedIndexChanged
    lblCustomerInfo.Text = _
    cmbCustomers.SelectedValue.ToString
End Sub
```

**FIGURE 5.7**   The ComboBox is now bound to the Customers table and the SelectedValue returns the CustomerID.

Again, you're introduced to a new property called SelectedValue. This property returns the value of "ValueMember" field for the currently selected row, which in this case was CustomerID. The code snippet in Listing 5.4 takes the value of that field and displays it in the label. If you run the application, the result should look like Figure 5.7.

This is all really great, but there's a lot more power built into Data Binding than just getting the selected value from the ComboBox.

When you set the DataSource property, each DataRow in the Customers DataTable is actually getting bound to the Items collection of the ComboBox, so if you were to try to retrieve the first item in the Items collection of the ComboBox, it would actually return a reference to the first row. Using the SelectedItem property of the ComboBox you can obtain the currently selected row of the data source. So let's say you wanted to show the address instead of the CustomerID in the label; you could easily change the line from Listing 5.4 to this:

```
lblCustomerInfo.Text = _
    DirectCast( _
    cmbCustomers.SelectedItem, _
    DataRowView)("Address").ToString
```

SelectedItem returns an object so you must properly cast it to another type so that you can deal with it. In this case, it's actually an instance of the DataRowView class. This mirrors what is in the underlying DataRow and in fact has access to the actual DataRow through the Row property. The reason you're seeing a DataRowView instead of a DataRow is that when you bind to a DataTable in Windows Forms, you are actually binding to the default DataView, and a DataView's rows are exposed as DataRowView objects. This will become important and I will talk about it shortly. Now with the DataRowView of the currently selected DataRow, you can access whatever field you'd like in that row. In this case, you'll grab the value of the Address field; make sure it's a string and display it. The big picture here is that Data Binding in Windows Forms actually binds to the objects themselves, so you can easily access them and do whatever you want with it. This is extremely powerful.

This takes you to the final subject of this chapter. You can combine what you've learned so far to create an even more powerful DataBinding solution.

# Using the CurrencyManager to Manage your Data Binding

Now that you've learned how to bind an entire table to a DataGrid and bind a table to a ComboBox for viewing one row at a time, the next step is to learn how to use the CurrencyManager. No, this has nothing to do with money. Currency refers to the current state, including the currently active row and mode (editing, adding, etc.) for a specific data source. Windows Forms has built-in support for keeping track of the current state of bound data on your form, and the CurrencyManager object exposes that state information to you. Using the methods and properties of the CurrencyManager object, you can add navigation support to your form.

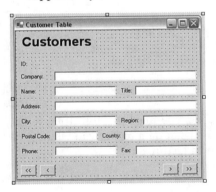

For this demo, you are again going to use the Customers table in the Northwind database, so create a new Windows Forms application and set up the data objects as you did before. First things first, you need to lay out the controls the way you want to display the details of a single customer. Also, if you're still a little bit confused by what I mean by adding navigation, Figure 5.8 shows controls that will be used to move forward and backward through the data source.

**FIGURE 5.8**  The Access-like interface for navigating through the data in the Customers table.

In this example I have used a standard naming convention for all the controls. All controls that you are going to bind to are the same name as the field you are going to bind to it, but with a control prefix in front of it. The prefixes I used are lbl for Labels and txt for TextBoxes. The buttons and label across the bottom are named btnFirst, btnPrevious, lblPosition, btnNext and btnLast, respectively.

Currency Management in Windows Forms is on a per-form basis, so you can get a reference to the currency manager object from the form itself through the BindingContext property.

```
MyBindingManager = _
    Me.BindingContext(dsNorthwind, "Customers")
```

The first parameter is the DataSource you want to get the binding manager for. The second and optional parameter is used if you need to specify a specific DataMember. In this case, you're only going to be dealing with the Customers table inside the dsNorthwind DataSet. This will return the instance of the BindingManagerBase class that you will need to keep track of the currency of the data. The BindingContext property represents the collection of all the BindingManager instances for the current Windows Form, one for each datasource that is data bound on that Form. This collection returns a BindingManagerBase type, but you can cast it into a CurrencyManager object as that is its true underlying type. You will be accessing the CurrencyManager object quite a lot in your code, so it is best to store it as a private form level variable so that you can use it as needed. Listing 5.5 demonstrates obtaining the CurrencyManager object and storing it as a form level variable.

**LISTING 5.5**  Saving an Instance of the CurrencyManager Class for our Customers Data Source

```
Dim cmCustomers as CurrencyManager
Private Sub Form1_Load(ByVal sender As Object, _
        ByVal e As System.EventArgs) _
        Handles MyBase.Load
    SqlDataAdapter1.Fill(dsNorthwind)
    cmCustomers = DirectCast( _
        Me.BindingContext( _
            dsNorthwind, "Customers"), _
        CurrencyManager)
End Sub
```

Now that you have cmCustomers to use throughout your code, you need to "link" the controls on the form to the binding manager, so it will know what data to show in what control. For this, you will create a new procedure, as shown in Listing 5.6.

**LISTING 5.6**  Set up the bindings on all controls.

```
Private Sub SetupControlBindings()
    lblID.DataBindings.Add("Text", _
        dsNorthwind, "Customers.CustomerID")
    txtCompanyName.DataBindings.Add("Text", _
        dsNorthwind, "Customers.CompanyName")
    txtContactName.DataBindings.Add("Text", _
```

**LISTING 5.6**   Continued

```
            dsNorthwind, "Customers.ContactName")
        txtContactTitle.DataBindings.Add("Text", _
            dsNorthwind, "Customers.ContactTitle")
        txtAddress.DataBindings.Add("Text", _
            dsNorthwind, "Customers.Address")
        txtCity.DataBindings.Add("Text", _
            dsNorthwind, "Customers.City")
        txtRegion.DataBindings.Add("Text", _
            dsNorthwind, "Customers.Region")
        txtPostalCode.DataBindings.Add("Text", _
            dsNorthwind, "Customers.PostalCode")
        txtCountry.DataBindings.Add("Text", _
            dsNorthwind, "Customers.Country")
        txtPhone.DataBindings.Add("Text", _
            dsNorthwind, "Customers.Phone")
        txtFax.DataBindings.Add("Text", _
            dsNorthwind, "Customers.Fax")
End Sub
```

Each control has a DataBindings property, which is a collection of bindings. Each binding is basically a map that links a property of the control to a specific property/field of the data source. So each line in the new SetupControlBindings procedure is setting up a mapping, in this case from the Text property, to whatever field in the table you want. Let's set up the load event for the form to load up the data and set up all of the bindings for the controls. See Listing 5.7.

**LISTING 5.7**   Load the DataSet and set up the Bindings

```
Dim cmCustomers as CurrencyManager
Private Sub Form1_Load(ByVal sender As Object, _
        ByVal e As System.EventArgs) _
        Handles MyBase.Load
    SqlDataAdapter1.Fill(dsNorthwind)
    cmCustomers = DirectCast( _
        Me.BindingContext( _
            dsNorthwind, "Customers"), _
        CurrencyManager)
    SetupControlBindings()
End Sub
```

Now that you have the data and all of the bindings, you need to give the user interface some control over the data. You need to link the buttons to some sort of action to the binding manager, to navigate through the data. The Position property is an integer and can be set to any number from zero to the number of records minus one. Like all arrays and collections in .NET, the Rows collection in the DataTable is zero-based, meaning that the first position is zero, instead of one. The basic idea of using the buttons to navigate is simple. If you want to go to the first record, set the position to zero. If you want to go to the next record, you'll just set the position to one number higher than it is already at and so on. Listing 5.8 shows how to use the cmCustomers variable you set up earlier to change the current position that you will be viewing in the data.

**LISTING 5.8** Change the Position Based on Which Navigation Button was Clicked.

```
Private Sub btnFirst_Click( _
    ByVal sender As System.Object, _
    ByVal e As System.EventArgs) _
    Handles btnFirst.Click
      cmCustomers.Position = 0
End Sub

Private Sub btnPrevious_Click( _
    ByVal sender As System.Object, _
    ByVal e As System.EventArgs) _
    Handles btnPrevious.Click
      cmCustomers.Position -= 1
End Sub

Private Sub btnNext_Click( _
    ByVal sender As System.Object, _
    ByVal e As System.EventArgs) _
    Handles btnNext.Click
      cmCustomers.Position += 1
End Sub

Private Sub btnLast_Click( _
    ByVal sender As System.Object, _
    ByVal e As System.EventArgs) _
    Handles btnLast.Click
      cmCustomers.Position = cmCustomers.Count - 1
End Sub
```

Now that you have the code to navigate through the data source using the currency manager, you need some visual cues to let the user know where they currently are and also make sure the buttons don't allow them to go past the end or beginning of the data source. Again, you'll use the currency manager, as shown in Listing 5.9, to come up with the text for the label as well as to determine whether each button should be enabled or disabled.

**LISTING 5.9**   Changing the State of the Navigation, so the User Knows Where They Are

```
Private Sub cmCustomers_PositionChanged( _
    ByVal sender As Object, _
    ByVal e As EventArgs)
    Dim CurrentPosition As Integer = cmCustomers.Position
    Dim CurrentCount As Integer = cmCustomers.Count

    lblPosition.Text = String.Format( _
        "Record {0} of {1}", _
        CurrentPosition + 1, CurrentCount)

    btnFirst.Enabled = CurrentPosition > 0
    btnPrevious.Enabled = CurrentPosition > 0
    btnNext.Enabled = CurrentPosition < CurrentCount - 1
    btnLast.Enabled = CurrentPosition < CurrentCount - 1
End Sub
```

You'll notice that the code retrieves the Position and Count properties from the binding manager and stores them in variables. This process saves a bit of typing and it's best to store the properties' values and reuse the values instead of accessing them over and over again. It's quite possible that they might have a bit of logic in them to determine their current state, so you're saving a little processing power, which can't hurt.

The code then sets the lblPosition.Text using String.Format, to more easily concatenate what would be four different pieces. Instead of combining the items using the & operator, you provide a format string using placeholders, and then provide the items to be inserted into those positions. The last four lines simply return a Boolean from an evaluation to make sure that the buttons aren't enabled when they shouldn't be; preventing the position to be changed when it would produce an invalid result.

The procedure looks like an event handler (with sender and EventArgs parameters) because it is going to be hooked up to handle an event raised by the CurrencyManager instance.

You will want this code to execute every time you change position in the data source, because you will need to update the label and button states. Luckily for you, there is an event of the CurrencyManager class called PositionChanged. Visual Basic .NET allows you to easily attach to events at runtime, so you can modify the load event (like in Listing 5.10) so the method will be attached to the PositionChanged event of cmCustomers.

**LISTING 5.10** Adding an Event Handler to the PositionChanged Event of the BindingManagerBase Class

```
Private Sub Form1_Load(ByVal sender As Object, _
                        ByVal e As System.EventArgs) _
            Handles MyBase.Load
    SqlDataAdapter1.Fill(dsNorthwind)
    cmCustomers = DirectCast( _
        Me.BindingContext( _
            dsNorthwind, "Customers"), _
        CurrencyManager)

    SetupControlBindings()

    AddHandler cmCustomers.PositionChanged, _
        AddressOf cmCustomers_PositionChanged
End Sub
```

The AddHandler clause will set it up so whenever the PositionChanged event of cmCustomers occurs, the method that you wrote to check button states and show what record you're on will also be called. For more information about dynamic event handlers, take a look at Chapter 3. Alternatively, you could declare the cmCustomers variable with the WithEvents keyword and then add an event handler using the left and right hand side combo boxes in the Visual Studio code editor. This would produce slightly different code, as shown in Listing 5.11.

**LISTING 5.11** Using WithEvents Removes the Need for Dynamic Event Handling in Some Situations

```
Dim WithEvents cmCustomers As CurrencyManager

Private Sub Form1_Load( _
    ByVal sender As System.Object, _
    ByVal e As System.EventArgs) Handles MyBase.Load
    SqlDataAdapter1.Fill(dsNorthwind)
    cmCustomers = DirectCast( _
            Me.BindingContext( _
            dsNorthwind, "Customers"), _
        CurrencyManager)
    SetupControlBindings()
End Sub

Private Sub cmCustomers_PositionChanged( _
```

**LISTING 5.11**  Continued

```
    ByVal sender As Object, _
    ByVal e As System.EventArgs) _
    Handles cmCustomers.PositionChanged
    Dim CurrentPosition As Integer = cmCustomers.Position
    Dim CurrentCount As Integer = cmCustomers.Count

    lblPosition.Text = String.Format( _
        "Record {0} of {1}", _
        CurrentPosition + 1, CurrentCount)

    btnFirst.Enabled = CurrentPosition > 0
    btnPrevious.Enabled = CurrentPosition > 0
    btnNext.Enabled = CurrentPosition < CurrentCount - 1
    btnLast.Enabled = CurrentPosition < CurrentCount - 1
End Sub
```

With all of this code in place, you can now run the application. You'll notice that immediately, there is data populated in the different controls of the form. You can click any of the buttons also and notice that the appropriate record is shown, along with the button's enabled states. The position label is updated accordingly. All of that code you would have needed to write to keep your UI in sync with your data source isn't necessary. You get that all for free, because it's built right into Windows Forms and ready for you to use. You might also notice that the binding manager even takes care of pushing any changed data from the UI back into the data source for you. There are additional methods on CurrencyManager that you might also want to take a look at. The AddNew method adds a new Row to your data source, as well as moves the position to that row. The RemoveAt method is used to remove a row at a specific position.

# Formatting Bound Data

There is one more topic I thought I'd cover, because it's a really cool feature, but also because it comes in quite handy when dealing with some types of data. If you remember back in the code where you set up the DataBindings for each control (Listing 5.6), the Add method returns the Binding class instance that it just created in the DataBindings collection. Normally, you can ignore this as shown in Listing 5.6 and move on; however, it's sometimes useful to hold onto that return value and add event handlers to a pair of useful events. the Format and Parse events of the Binding class work together to transform a value in the database to and from a different display format. The Format event is fired when the state of the binding changes and the binding manager is copying the current data out of the data source and into the UI, and then the Parse event fires when the binding manager is trying to take data from the UI and slam it back into the data source. One common use for the Format and Parse events is to transform a date time value stored in the database into the desired format and then to parse whatever information the user enters back into a datetime value before storing it into the data source. Listing 5.12 shows how you could use these two events to handle parsing a date.

**LISTING 5.12**  Attaching to the Format Event

```
Private Sub Form1_Load( _
    ByVal sender As System.Object, _
    ByVal e As System.EventArgs) Handles MyBase.Load
    Dim conn As New SqlClient.SqlConnection( _
        "Integrated Security=SSPI;" & _
        "Initial Catalog=Northwind;Data Source=(local)")

    Dim cmdOrders As New SqlClient.SqlCommand( _
        "Select OrderID, OrderDate, RequiredDate" & _
        " From Orders", conn)
    Dim daOrders As New SqlClient.SqlDataAdapter(cmdOrders)
    daOrders.Fill(Me.dsNorthwind, "Orders")
    cmOrders = DirectCast( _
            Me.BindingContext( _
            dsNorthwind, "Orders"), _
        CurrencyManager)
    SetupControlBindings()
End Sub

Public Sub SetupControlBindings()
    Dim myBinding As Binding
    myBinding = Me.orderDate.DataBindings.Add( _
        "Text", dsNorthwind, "Orders.OrderDate")
    AddHandler myBinding.Format, AddressOf Binding_Format
    AddHandler myBinding.Parse, AddressOf Binding_Parse
End Sub.
```

As you can see, the new code takes the return value from the Add method and places it in a temporary variable to facilitate . Then it adds an event handler so when its Format Event is fired, the Binding_Format method will be called. Go ahead and write out that method using the code in Listing 5.13.

**LISTING 5.12**  The Format and Parse Event Handlers

```
Private Sub Binding_Format(ByVal sender As Object, _
    ByVal e As System.Windows.Forms.ConvertEventArgs)
    Dim baseDate As DateTime
    baseDate = CDate(e.Value)
    e.Value = CStr(baseDate.ToShortDateString)

End Sub

Private Sub Binding_Parse(ByVal sender As Object, _
    ByVal e As System.Windows.Forms.ConvertEventArgs)
    Dim dateToSave As DateTime
    dateToSave = DateTime.Parse(e.Value)
    e.Value = dateToSave
End Sub
```

The "e" parameter has a DesiredType property so you can know what type the incoming binding wants the value to be, because it's defined in the data source of the binding manager. It also has a Value property, which is what the current value is at right now. The beauty of the Format Event is that you can set e.Value to whatever you want and that's what will be returned to the user interface to be displayed.

# In Brief

This chapter provided a detailed discussion of Data Binding. The important points include the following:

- ADO.NET has many structural changes from ADO, introducing some new concepts.

- Loading data from a database is easy using the built-in tools in Visual Studio .NET and the DataAdapter.

- DataBinding in Windows Forms binds to the actual objects themselves for ultimate flexibility.

- Using the Currency Manager, you can easily create data-management applications that support navigation through the available records.

# Data Without the Binding

**6**

## Data: What's Next?

The previous chapter discussed how to take advantage of some of the built-in features of Visual Studio .NET to help you get your job done. These features are great and should be taken advantage of whenever possible. However, to make the best use of these features and additional features of ADO.NET, you really need to know how it works underneath the covers and specifically how you can accomplish the same things (and more) on your own.

## Learning the Inner Workings of ADO.NET

Visual Studio .NET truly gives you a rapid-application-development (RAD) experience, with great design-time support for many of the features in ADO.NET and data binding in Windows Forms, but there are a lot of times where using these features just aren't going to cut it. You need to learn the underlying details of ADO.NET to harness its power. This chapter jumps right into some of these items, starting off with more details on some features of the two Connection classes: (SqlClient.SqlConnection and OleDB.OleDBConnection).

# More on Connections

Chapter 5, "Data Binding," explained that the connection specifies how to open a link to a database and also is how the SqlCommand object knows what data source to work with. The SqlConnection object contains a ConnectionString property that can be set in Visual Studio either manually using the Property window or it can be automatically set up when dragging objects such as a table from a database out of the Server Explorer. Often times, however, this doesn't provide enough flexibility. For example, consider what will happen when you need to deploy this system out to the users. Let's say that you have created a database management system that works well with the development SQL Server. The ConnectionString property would probably look something like this.

```
Data Source=DevServer;Initial Catalog=ProductDB;Integrated Security=True
```

Now, you'd like to sell this product to a customer. When they try to use the product, they will receive an error when the application tries to open a connection to the database, because the server and security information is hard-coded. This is, of course, no good. You need a way for them to be able to easily change the ConnectionString value. You could store it in the Registry and create an Admin interface for the customers to edit the value with, although that would take a lot of extra coding. If users wanted to manually change the value, they would have to work hard to determine where you stowed the value. The best way to accomplish the task at hand is to use an application configuration file. These are usually referred to as App.Config files and are used for storing various forms of application settings for your .NET application, but this chapter focuses only on using it to store a connection string. Therefore, anyone who installs this application can easily change the connection string to whatever works for their setup.

The config file sits in the same directory as the executable, in the case of Windows Forms applications, and follows the naming pattern of *MyExecutable.exe.config*. When working in Visual Studio .NET, projects do not usually include the bin directory in them, which is where the executable for an application is typically created. Because the config file must be in that folder, Visual Studio allows you to create a file named "App.config" that sits in the main project folder. You can make any changes to this file and when that project is built, VS .NET automatically copies the App.config file into the bin directory and renames it *MyExecutable.exe.config*. This idea can be a bit confusing, because the config file in the bin directory is overwritten every time the project is built.

The config file has a specific schema (format) that must be followed for it to work correctly. In the case of storing application settings, the format in Listing 6.1 demonstrates how to enter a ConnectionString variable.

LISTING 6.1    Sample App.config File with ConnectionString

```
<?xml version="1.0" encoding="utf-8"?>
<configuration>
    <appSettings>
        <add key="ConnectionString"
          value="Data Source=DevServer;
          Initial Catalog=ProductDB;Integrated Security=True" />
    </appSettings>
</configuration>
```

All settings for the config file are located inside the configuration node. The `appSettings` node is used to store a collection of settings that can be used throughout your application. You can have as many nodes as you want in the appSettings node, as long as each key is unique. By moving certain settings out of the application and into the config file, each instance of the application can be configured differently. In this case, it can be configured to work with a different SQL Server. Now you need to know how to retrieve this value from inside your application. Take a look at Listing 6.2 to see how you can access the `ConnectionString` stored in the previously mentioned config file.

LISTING 6.2    Accessing the ConnectionString Value from the config File

```
Dim cfg As Configuration.ConfigurationSettings
Dim connString As String
connString = cfg.AppSettings("Northwind.ConnectionString")
Dim NorthwindConnection As _
    New SqlClient.SqlConnection( _
    connString)
MessageBox.Show(connString)
```

`System.Configuration.ConfigurationSettings.AppSettings` is a `System.Collections.Specialized.NameValueCollection` that will easily allow you access the value of any of the "add" nodes in the appSettings section of the config file by the key attribute. Listing 6.2 also introduces a new idea of using the constructor of the `SqlConnection` class. This allows you to pass in the initial value for the `ConnectionString` property, thus saving a bit of code. All the classes in ADO.NET have overloaded constructors to help you initialize them with very few lines of code. After you've retrieved the value and created a new connection, you can use a message box to show the new connection's `ConnectionString` property value. Just for kicks, you can go into the App.config file, change the value of `ConnectionString`, and re-run the application. It will pick up the changes. With this, you can now copy the executable and the *MyExecutable.exe.config* file to any location and make changes to the config file for an easily configurable application.

If you want, you can take advantage of Visual Studio .NET's capability to work with the config file as well. Simply add a connection to a form, go to the Property window and expand the `DynamicProperties` item under the Configurations category. Change the `ConnectionString` property under `DynamicProperties` to the key you want to link it to in your config file, in this case, `ConnectionString`. This will accomplish the same sort of link between your config file and your `ConnectionString`. For more information on XML, refer to Chapter 10.

## SHOP TALK

### CONNECTION POOLING

In ADO.NET, connections to SQL Server are automatically pooled for you. You must use the same connection string for all of your database work to enable automatic connection pooling. When first working with ADO.NET, many people find that connection pooling works in an odd way. Most people expect that when they call the Open method of the `Connection` class, a new connection would be opened on the server and that when calling the Close method, the connection would be terminated and destroyed at the server. This isn't necessarily the case. Connection pooling follows some of the same patterns that the garbage collector does with memory consumption. When you call the Open method on your connection, it will check the connection pool for any connections it can use. The connection pool will then return either a new connection or one that already exists in the pool. This is also related to how connections are closed. When you call the Close method, the connection is marked as being available and returned back to the connection pool. This doesn't mean that the connection at the server is actually closed and destroyed. Because the pool manager is taking care of all of it for you, it will decide whether the connection should actually be destroyed. This greatly helps with efficiency, again, just as the garbage collector makes memory management more efficient. So if you sit down at your SQL Server and are watching connections, don't expect them to act as you'd expect, but know that it is working by design.

A common mistake when programming with .NET is to assume that all of these new features (such as garbage collection) will handle everything, but the key difference between a program that performs well and one that performs horribly is still the skill of the programmer building it. Do not assume that just because .NET does automatic garbage collection and connection pooling that you do not have to worry about managing your database connections. A connection is released back to the pool only when it is closed, which means that you still need to ensure that you call the `Close` method on your `SqlConnection` or `OleDBConnection` object immediately after you finish using it. The goal should be to have the shortest possible code path between the `Open` and `Close` of the connection. Don't include code in that path that might require a user interface prompt and block the `Close` indefinitely.

The `Connection` classes are very much related to the `Transaction` classes, as well as the `Command` classes. You'll read about `SqlTransaction` and `OleDBTransaction` later in this chapter, but for now, turn your attention to the `Command` classes (`SqlCommand` and `OleDBCommand`).

## More on Command

Chapter 5 discussed the `Command` object's purpose in the grand scheme of ADO.NET fairly in-depth. You saw how the `Command` object was used in the DataAdapter and a little bit about how it worked with the `Connection` class. In this chapter, you will learn more about how the `Command` classes can be used with parameters and to call stored procedures.

Like the `SqlConnection` example earlier in this chapter, the `Command` class also has a few over-loaded constructors that make creating instances of it a bit easier. Because all commands need to know what database they are going to be executing on, the `Connection` property must always be set. You can set it a few ways. The first of which is to directly set the `Connection` property to the reference of your connection.

```
Dim NorthwindCommand As New SqlCommand
NorthwindCommand.Connection = NorthwindConnection
```

The same thing applies for setting the CommandText, which again, is the SQL statement to execute on the database.

```
Dim NorthwindCommand As New SqlCommand
NorthwindCommand.Connection = NorthwindConnection
NorthwindCommand.CommandText = "SELECT * FROM Customers ORDER BY ContactName"
```

A better route is to take advantage of one of the overloaded constructors of the `Command` object.

```
Dim NorthwindCommand As New _
SqlCommand("SELECT * FROM Customers ORDER BY ContactName", NorthwindConnection)
```

You can see here that instead of having to write a separate line of code for setting each property, you can use the constructor to initialize the `Command` object with those properties so that it is ready to be used on the next line.

With the understanding of how to create a command, as well as create connections, it's time to dig a little deeper and see how you can actually get results from the `Command` object.

### Command Execute Methods

The `IDBCommand` interface, which is the interface implemented by all provider-specific `Command` objects, provides three common methods for executing the `CommandText` property against the command's connection.

The first is the ExecuteNonQuery method. Calling this method executes the specified CommandText and returns the number of rows that were affected by the SQL statement as an integer. This is used when executing a SQL statement that does not return any rows. Most SQL statements that do not return rows are designed to change a table in some way, be it inserting, updating, or deleting. You'll learn about updating data later in this chapter.

The second method is ExecuteReader. This will execute your SQL on the database, typically a query for data, and return an instance of a DataReader. The DataReader is provider-specific, so if you were using SQL Server you would get back a SqlDataReader. The ExecuteReader function has an optional parameter of type CommandBehavior. CommandBehavior is an Enum that can affect how the returned DataReader works. The most used item is CommandBehavior.CloseConnection. When this item is passed as a parameter of the ExecuteReader method, when you later call the DataReader's Close method, it will also close the connection that was attached to it. Let's quickly compare the two.

```
Dim MyReader As SqlDataReader

With NorthwindCommand
    .Connection.Open()
    MyReader = .ExecuteReader()
    'Use DataReader
    MyReader.Close()
    .Connection.Close()
End With
```

The previous example firsts open a connection, and then calls ExecuteReader to get a reference to the result set in a DataReader. Then, you write any code to actually use that data. This will be explained more in depth later in this chapter. Finally, call the Close method on the DataReader and the connection. Technically, you don't need to call the DataReader.Close because once you close the connection, the DataReader loses its connection to the database and would then be out of scope when the code was all done. Again, the DataReader is connected-only data. Alternatively, you can close the connection automatically using the CommandBehavior Enum.

```
Dim MyReader As SqlDataReader

With NorthwindCommand
    .Connection.Open()
    MyReader = .ExecuteReader(CommandBehavior.CloseConnection)
    'Use DataReader
End With

MyReader.Close()
```

Again, in this case, because of the extra parameter passed into the ExecuteReader method of the NorthwindCommand object, when you close MyReader, it will then close the connection. In that particular code example, it wasn't really that necessary, but there are often times when you don't have access to the original connection and being able to inherently close it is absolutely necessary.

The third method to retrieve data with the Command object is ExecuteScalar. This method is optimized for retrieving the first column of the first row in the result set, meaning a single value. Even if multiple rows and/or multiple columns are returned from the query, only the first column of the first row is returned from calling the ExecuteScalar method. The following is an example of calling ExecuteScalar and retrieving the result.

```
Dim ContactName As String

With NorthwindCommand
    .CommandText = _
        "SELECT ContactName FROM Customers " & _
        "WHERE CustomerID = 'ALFKI'"
    .Connection.Open()
    ContactName = DirectCast(.ExecuteScalar(), String)
    .Connection.Close()
End With

'ContactName contains "Maria Anders"
```

The SQL statement retrieves a specific customer by the CustomerID field and selects only that row's ContactName. When ExecuteScalar is called, that field is returned as a string. ExecuteScalar returns an object, however, so you must cast it to a string. In the case of this sample code, you know what the result is going to be. In the real world, however, you might not always know that a string will be returned. If the field in a table you are trying to access allows NULLs, you must first check to see if DBNull was returned or if an actual string was returned. According to the definition of the Northwind.Customers table, ContactName does allow NULL, so it is possible that you'll get DBNull back, so you need to check for it. Let's create a quick Windows Forms application to demonstrate this. First, you'll create a quick function that takes a parameter of the CustomerID and returns its name, as shown in Listing 6.3, and then displays it when you click a button.

**LISTING 6.3**   Calling ExecuteScalar and Checking for DBNull

```
Private Function GetCustomerContactName( _
    ByVal CustomerID As String) As String
    Dim NorthwindCommand As New _
        SqlCommand("SELECT ContactName FROM Customers " & _
        "WHERE CustomerID = '" & CustomerID & "'", _
```

## LISTING 6.3    Continued

```
            New SqlConnection( _
                ConfigurationSettings.AppSettings( _
                "Northwind.ConnectionString")))

        Dim ContactName As Object

        With NorthwindCommand
            .Connection.Open()
            ContactName = .ExecuteScalar()
            .Connection.Close()
        End With

        If IsDBNull(ContactName) Then
            Return String.Empty
        Else
            Return DirectCast(ContactName, String)
        End If

    End Function

    Private Sub btnFind_Click(ByVal sender As System.Object, _
                            ByVal e As System.EventArgs) _
                            Handles btnFind.Click
        MessageBox.Show(txtCustomerID.Text & " = " & _
            GetCustomerContactName(txtCustomerID.Text))
    End Sub
```

This code does what you need it to. It sets up a command with a connection, calls ExecuteScalar, which goes out to the Northwind.Customers table. If no records meet the WHERE criteria or if the field contains it already, DBNull is returned. This is why the ContactName variable is declared as an object. DBNull and String are not at all related, so you must declare a holder variable that is the lowest common denominator. In this case, it is Object. Then the code checks to see if ContactName is DBNull.Value. If it is, it's replaced with an empty set (String.Empty). ContactName is still declared as an object, even though you now know it has some string in it, so it must be cast to a string to be returned.

You might remember that Chapter 5 mentioned building query strings dynamically was a bad idea for a few reasons. This last example just went against this advice, because you have not yet read about how to use parameters. The time is now. Let's get started.

## Command Parameters

Each `Command` object has a `Parameters` collection, which is a collection of provider specific parameters. The main motivation for using parameters with your commands is organization. It is an easy way to parameterize your queries without having to build a string. It also automatically escapes characters for you. Doing this provides you an extra level of security in case you forget to escape them.

*SQL Injection* is a method of hacking where if your characters, such as the single quote, aren't escaped and you are dynamically building your query as a string, someone would be able to put in another single quote at the beginning of the value they enter, therefore ending the first single quote in your query. After that, they can do all sorts of evil things, like grab records with sensitive data in them or even dropping entire tables. Those two big reasons alone are enough to want to use parameters, so let's find out how.

Consider the previous example of looking up a Customer's contact name by the `CustomerID`. The next example demonstrates how to set up parameters for the `SqlCommand` object, but again, they are not provider specific and work with all providers. First, you need to have a placeholder in the query, so when you set up a parameter, it will know where it's supposed to be in the query.

```
SELECT ContactName FROM Customers
WHERE CustomerID = @CustomerID
```

In SQL Server, all parameters must start with the @ symbol. You now have a variable in the query, so you can set up a parameter to match that variable.

```
NorthwindCommand.Parameters.Add("@CustomerID", SqlDbType.NVarChar)
```

Because `Parameters` is a collection, it has an `Add` method, as all collections in .NET do. One of the overloads for it takes a string for the parameter name and the SQL data type that the field uses. That's all there is to it. Now you need to set its value, so the query returns the desired results:

```
NorthwindCommand.Parameters("@CustomerID").Value = CustomerID
```

The line simply calls the default indexer of the `Parameters` collections and requests the parameter named `@CustomerID`. It then returns the correct `SqlParameter`; you set its value to what you want to look for. Listing 6.4 brings it all together inside a form with a `TextBox` named `txtCustomerID` and a button named `btnFind`.

---

**LISTING 6.4**   Using a Parameter to Call a Query and Return a Value

```
Private NorthwindCommand As SqlCommand

Private Sub Form1_Load( _
        ByVal sender As Object, _
```

**LISTING 6.4**   Continued

```vb
            ByVal e As System.EventArgs) _
            Handles MyBase.Load
        SetupDataObjects()
    End Sub

    Private Sub btnFind_Click( _
            ByVal sender As System.Object, _
            ByVal e As System.EventArgs) _
            Handles btnFind.Click
        MessageBox.Show(txtCustomerID.Text & " = " & _
            GetCustomerContactName(txtCustomerID.Text))
    End Sub

    Private Sub SetupDataObjects()
        NorthwindCommand = New SqlCommand( _
            "SELECT ContactName FROM Customers " & _
            "WHERE CustomerID = @CustomerID", _
            New SqlConnection( _
                ConfigurationSettings.AppSettings( _
                "Northwind.ConnectionString")))

        NorthwindCommand.Parameters.Add( _
            "@CustomerID", SqlDbType.NVarChar)
    End Sub

    Private Function GetCustomerContactName( _
            ByVal CustomerID As String) As String
        Dim ContactName As Object

        With NorthwindCommand
            .Parameters("@CustomerID").Value = CustomerID
            .Connection.Open()
            ContactName = .ExecuteScalar()
            .Connection.Close()
        End With

        If IsDBNull(ContactName) Then
            Return String.Empty
        Else
            Return DirectCast(ContactName, String)
        End If

    End Function
```

For this time around, the code declares the NorthwindCommand in a different scope (global to the current form) so that you can have a method to easily set up the object. Therefore, the method will be ready to go for the function every time it's called. This makes it so it's easy to reuse also. In the method called SetupDataObjects, the code instantiates the command, and adds a parameter to its Parameters collection. Then, when it actually calls the GetCustomerContactName method when btnFind is clicked, the @CustomerID parameter's value is set. When ExecuteScalar is called, the appropriate query is called.

Parameters have a lot more properties that can be adjusted to better match them up with the actual fields in the table, but the name, type, and value properties are enough to get them working. You'll read later about a few other properties of the Parameter class, when discussing sending data back to the database.

The next section discusses another way to execute queries: using stored procedures.

## Executing Stored Procedures

If you are unfamiliar with stored procedures, now is a great time to learn. Although basically all SQL work can be done by calling SQL statements directly, using stored procedures can have some key advantages. First and foremost, there are some major performance boosts you can get just from simply moving all your SQL statements into stored procedures and calling them instead. Stored procedures are compiled and run from memory within SQL Server. They are also compiled with different parameter sets and placed into a priority queue, so the stored procedures that are called the most in your database and the ones called with the same parameters will get priority and execute faster than others. Overall though, all stored procedures just being compiled ahead of time will run faster than a plain SQL statement.

Secondly, they provide much great organization by separating all your data into the same layer of your application. This has a few good side-effects. One of which is that stored procedures can be stored in a source control database and versioned. Another big reason to use them is that they make complex combinations of SQL much easier to maintain. You can have a few different items that make changes to your database all within a transaction inside of SQL server.

**LET VS .NET DO THE WORK**

If you drag out Command and Connections from the Toolbox, use the Property window to set up the Connection, and then set up the Command, Visual Studio will actually do a lot of the work for you. Make sure you have a valid Connection set up. Then, set up the Connection property in the command. Next, select the CommandText property and click the ellipses button to the right. Voila, the Query Designer! Also, if you specified Parameters in your query, when you're done, Visual Studio .NET will ask you if you want it to set up the parameters for you. If you choose yes, it will go through and map all the parameters and set them up. In your code, you will only have to write the necessary lines to set their values.

The other big reason to have the SQL statements separated out into stored procedures instead of calling them directly is maintainability. When you initially create all of your SQL statements to work with your data, you may be okay, but what if tomorrow you decide you'd like to do some logging on each query. It would be hard to do for one thing, searching through all your code, for all the places you'd need to put some additional SQL to add a new record to a log table, not to mention having to re-create your executable. If all of it is already in stored procedures, you can easily go into each one in SQL Server and add the SQL statements and you will be done. None of your code will have to change.

If you ever called stored procedures in VB 6, you probably noticed that a lot of the properties of the Command object are the same. The big difference now and is that it's much more organized. Calling a stored procedure through the Command object is extremely straight-forward and nearly identical to calling a regular old SQL statement, except that the CommandType is set to StoredProcedure instead of Text and the CommandText contains the name of the stored procedure.

```
NorthwindCommand.CommandType = CommandType.StoredProcedure
NorthwindCommand.CommandText = "MyStoredProcedure"
```

By setting those two properties, everything that you learned earlier about ExecuteNonQuery, ExecuteReader, and ExecuteScalar works exactly the same. Now, you get all the advantages mentioned earlier. To see this in action, start a new Windows Forms project and add a ListView control to the main form. Change the name of the ListView to lvMain, set its View Property to Details and set the Dock Property to Fill. Add two columns with text of Product and Price and align the second column to the right, in lvMain. Change the Name Property of the form to ExpensiveProducts. Now add the code from Listing 6.5 to the form.

**LISTING 6.5**   Calling a Stored Procedure to Fill a ListView Control

```
Private Sub ExpensiveProducts_Load( _
        ByVal sender As Object, _
        ByVal e As System.EventArgs) _
        Handles MyBase.Load
    Dim NorthwindCommand As New SqlCommand("[Ten Most Expensive Products]", _
        New SqlConnection( _
        ConfigurationSettings.AppSettings( _
        "Northwind.ConnectionString")))
    Dim ProductList As SqlDataReader
    Dim TempLVItem As ListViewItem
    Dim ProductIndex, PriceIndex As Integer

    With NorthwindCommand
        .CommandType = CommandType.StoredProcedure
        .Connection.Open()
```

**LISTING 6.5** Continued

```
        ProductList = .ExecuteReader
    With ProductList
        ProductIndex = .GetOrdinal("TenMostExpensiveProducts")
        PriceIndex = .GetOrdinal("UnitPrice")
        While .Read
            TempLVItem = lvMain.Items.Add(.GetString(ProductIndex))
            TempLVItem.SubItems.Add( _
                .GetDecimal(PriceIndex).ToString("c"))
        End While
    End With
    .Connection.Close()
    End With
End Sub
```

**FIGURE 6.1** Ten most expensive products displayed in ListView from the Northwind database.

When you run the application, you should see something along the lines of Figure 6.1.

Looking back at Listing 6.5, you will see a few new items that you haven't seen yet. The first section of code, however, is just about the same as you've been working with. It sets up a command, passing in the name of the stored procedure you're going to call and a new connection. The other declarations will be used a bit later. The section of code is within a With block to make it a little easier, with less typing, because you'll be dealing with the Command object a lot.

First things first. The code sets the Command's CommandType property to StoredProcedure, that way it knows how to execute the CommandText against the database. Next, the code opens the connection and returns a DataReader into a variable called ProductList.

The next part is new. You'll notice another With block. You can embed as many With blocks as you want. They can be quite advantageous at times and can easily access items from the parent With block; however, blocks are used here to help separate out the code and make for a bit less typing. First, let's look at the While loop. The condition for it is a new method of the DataReader called Read. At first, the Read method can be a bit confusing to work with. In the recordset world of ADO, you can think of the Read method as MoveNext combined with Not EOF. When called, the Read method advances the DataReader to the next record. It also returns True if there are more records or False if there are no more records. The power of this, as you can see in Listing 6.5, is that looping through data in a DataReader is really easy and requires very little code.

Now inside of the loop, you add two lines of code to create a new `ListViewItem` and add it to the `ListView`, as well as add a `SubItem` to it, to show another column. The methods being called here (such as `GetDecimal`) are a bit different than calling the default indexer and simply passing in the name of the field.

Using the default indexer to access the value of the field you want for the current row returns an object. Because of this, it's possible that while coding, you'll accidentally make a mistake and cast the results to the wrong type, which would throw an exception. To avoid this problem, the `DataReader` provides methods that start with `Get` and end with the CLR type name that it will return. This allows Visual Studio .NET to know the type that will be returned, hence avoiding any possible problems with casting at design time instead of runtime. The problem with these methods is that they only take a parameter of an integer, which is the index of the field.

```
ProductList.GetDecimal(1)
```

What's really great about this is that in this case the `GetDecimal` method actually returns a decimal, so there is no need to convert the return value before using it. There is a method to make the code a bit more readable though, called `GetOrdinal`. This method returns the index of a field by the field's name. As demonstrated earlier, it is best to store this value to use it later.

```
Dim PriceIndex As Integer = ProducstList.GetOrdinal("UnitPrice")
ProductList.GetDecimal(PriceIndex)
```

One important thing to take note of: When you use the default indexer to access a field by its name, under the covers it is actually calling this same `GetOrdinal` method to make it a bit easier for you. However, because of this, if you access a field using the indexer in a loop, it is actually performing a field look up to get the index for every iteration of your loop, which can slow it down. This is why in Listing 6.5, `GetOrdinal` is called and its values are stored before entering the loop. This way, the code is always accessing the fields by their index, while still being able to access the fields by name.

The last new thing in Listing 6.5 is calling an overloaded `ToString` method on the returned `UnitPrice` decimal. By passing in "c", you're requesting the string version of this decimal, but formatted as currency. You can also use this instead.

```
FormatCurrency(.GetDecimal(PriceIndex), 2)
```

`FormatCurrency` and `ToString("c")` are similar and both take into account the current culture.

# Updating Data

You've pretty much mastered pulling data out of a database, you've used it for data binding and even worked with the data to get the desired result. The next big task is to send data back to the database. There are a few methods of doing this, either issuing your own individual SQL statements to update the database, or by setting up the DataAdapter and letting it handle all of the updates for you. When you use the DataAdapter's Update method, it handles executing the required SQL statements for each insert, delete, or modification in your DataTable(s). The DataAdapter method is usually what you will use with Windows Forms development, but executing SQL statements one at a time can also be useful, and is often used in Web applications. Let's check out the process for executing a single SQL statement first, before moving onto the DataAdapter process.

## Single-Execution Update

Using a command to execute an update on your database is really easy. As you can probably guess, as before, it simply involves changing the CommandText and setting a few parameters. Here you can see a new command being instantiated and initialized with a connection and an Insert statement.

```
Dim AddCustomer As New SqlCommand( _
    "INSERT INTO Customers " & _
    "(CustomerID, CompanyName, ContactName) VALUES " & _
    "(@CustomerID, @CompanyName, @ContactName)", _
    NorthwindConnection)
```

All that's left is to add the parameters and set their values.

```
AddCustomer.Parameters.Add( _
    "@CustomerID", SqlDbType.NChar _
    ).Value = "ERIKP"
AddCustomer.Parameters.Add( _
    "@CompanyName", SqlDbType.NVarChar _
    ).Value = "ErikPorter.com"
AddCustomer.Parameters.Add( _
    "@ContactName", SqlDbType.NVarChar _
    ).Value = "Erik Porter"
```

With all the parameters set up and their values set, simply call ExecuteNonQuery and the statement will be executed against the database.

```
AddCustomer.Connection.Open()
AddCustomer.ExecuteNonQuery()
AddCustomer.Connection.Close()
```

In this case, a new record is inserted with a `CustomerID` of `ERIKP` and the `ContactName` set to `Erik Porter`, whereas all other fields are `NULL`. If you want to insert another record, you simply change the values, because everything else is already set up and you're ready to go.

```
With AddCustomer
    .Parameters("@CustomerID").Value = _
        "STACD"
    .Parameters("@CompanyName").Value = _
        "Professional Voice Instruction, Inc."
    .Parameters("@ContactName").Value = _
        "Stacey Dyer"
    .Connection.Open()
    .ExecuteNonQuery()
    .Connection.Close()
End With
```

Because you already set up the parameters, all you needed to do was change their values and execute it again and it will work exactly the same. The concept is no different if you're calling an `UPDATE` or `DELETE` statement, except that the `CommandText` would be a different SQL statement. Now that you understand the concept of single execution on a database, you can take these concepts to the next level and perform multiple executions at once, while taking advantage of the tools in ADO.NET.

## Multi-Execution Update

Take the following scenario: You would like to create an editor for the `Customers` table in the Northwind database, much like some of the examples from Chapter 5. However, this time, you must be able to edit data, delete records, add new ones as much as you want and then have a save button to send it all back at once. The `DataAdapter` is perfect for this scenario. There are better UI designs out there than using a `DataGrid` for this scenario, but because these examples focus on ADO.NET and not Windows Forms, the `DataGrid` will make it much easier to code against.

Start a new Windows Forms application and add a `DataGrid` to `Form1`. Name it `dgCustomers`. Place two buttons on `Form1` and name them `btnSave` and `btnCancel`. Make sure they both default to Enabled properties set to `False`. At this point, you can use Visual Studio .NET to automatically set up the connection and use a `Data Adapter` to work with the `Customers` table. However, it's important to learn how to do it yourself, so that when a more complex scenario arises, you'll know how to handle it. This example uses a `DataTable` to store the data, because you will only be working with one table. If you happened to be working with more than one `DataTable`, the `DataSet` would definitely be the way to go. Listing 6.6 is all the code you will need to accomplish this.

**LISTING 6.6**    Setting up a Form to Edit Customer Data

```
Private NorthwindCustomers As DataTable
Private NorthwindCustomersAdapter As SqlDataAdapter

Private Sub ProductEditor_Load( _
        ByVal sender As Object, _
        ByVal e As System.EventArgs) Handles MyBase.Load
    SetupDataObjects()
    LoadData()

    dgCustomers.DataSource = NorthwindCustomers

    AddHandler NorthwindCustomers.RowChanged, _
            AddressOf NorthwindChangesMade
    AddHandler NorthwindCustomers.RowDeleted, _
            AddressOf NorthwindChangesMade
End Sub

Private Sub NorthwindChangesMade( _
     ByVal sender As Object, _
     ByVal e As DataRowChangeEventArgs)
    btnSave.Enabled = True
    btnCancel.Enabled = True
End Sub

Private Sub btnSave_Click(ByVal sender As Object, _
                        ByVal e As System.EventArgs) Handles btnSave.Click

    Try
        NorthwindCustomersAdapter.Update(NorthwindCustomers)
        LoadData()
        btnSave.Enabled = False
        btnCancel.Enabled = False
    Catch Ex As Exception
        MessageBox.Show(Ex.Message, "Error", _
        MessageBoxButtons.OK, MessageBoxIcon.Error)
    End Try
End Sub

Private Sub btnCancel_Click(ByVal sender As Object, _
                        ByVal e As System.EventArgs) Handles btnCancel.Click
    NorthwindCustomers.RejectChanges()
    btnSave.Enabled = False
```

**LISTING 6.6**   Continued

```
        btnCancel.Enabled = False
    End Sub

    Private Sub SetupDataObjects()
        Dim NorthwindConnection As New _
        SqlConnection(ConfigurationSettings.AppSettings( _
                    "Northwind.ConnectionString"))
        NorthwindCustomers = New DataTable("Customers")
        NorthwindCustomersAdapter = New SqlDataAdapter( _
                    "SELECT * FROM Customers " & _
                    "ORDER BY ContactName", _
                    NorthwindConnection)

        With NorthwindCustomersAdapter
            .InsertCommand = New SqlCommand("INSERT INTO Customers " & _
            "(CustomerID, CompanyName, ContactName, " & _
            "ContactTitle, Address, City, " & _
            "Region, PostalCode, Country, Phone, Fax) VALUES " & _
            "(@CustomerID, "@CompanyName, @ContactName, @ContactTitle, " & _
            "@Address, @City, @Region, " & _
            "@PostalCode, @Country, @Phone, @Fax)", NorthwindConnection)
            With .InsertCommand
                .Parameters.Add("@CustomerID", _
                    SqlDbType.NChar).SourceColumn = "CustomerID"
                .Parameters.Add("@CompanyName", _
                    SqlDbType.NVarChar).SourceColumn = "CompanyName"
                .Parameters.Add("@ContactName", _
                    SqlDbType.NVarChar).SourceColumn = "ContactName"
                .Parameters.Add("@ContactTitle", _
                    SqlDbType.NVarChar).SourceColumn = "ContactTitle"
                .Parameters.Add("@Address", _
                    SqlDbType.NVarChar).SourceColumn = "Address"
                .Parameters.Add("@City", _
                    SqlDbType.NVarChar).SourceColumn = "City"
                .Parameters.Add("@Region", _
                    SqlDbType.NVarChar).SourceColumn = "Region"
                .Parameters.Add("@PostalCode", _
                    SqlDbType.NVarChar).SourceColumn = "PostalCode"
                .Parameters.Add("@Country", _
                    SqlDbType.NVarChar).SourceColumn = "Country"
                .Parameters.Add("@Phone", _
```

**LISTING 6.6**   Continued

```
                           SqlDbType.NVarChar).SourceColumn = "Phone"
                  .Parameters.Add("@Fax", _
                           SqlDbType.NVarChar).SourceColumn = "Fax"
          End With

          .UpdateCommand = New SqlCommand("UPDATE Customers SET " & _
            "CompanyName = @CompanyName, ContactName = @ContactName, " & _
            "ContactTitle = @ContactTitle, Address = @Address, City = @City, " & _
            "Region = @Region, PostalCode = @PostalCode, Country = @Country, " & _
            "Phone = @Phone, Fax = @Fax WHERE CustomerID = @CustomerID", _
            NorthwindConnection)
          With .UpdateCommand
              .Parameters.Add("@CustomerID", _
                  SqlDbType.NChar).SourceColumn = "CustomerID"
              .Parameters.Add("@CompanyName", _
                  SqlDbType.NVarChar).SourceColumn = "CompanyName"
              .Parameters.Add("@ContactName", _
                  SqlDbType.NVarChar).SourceColumn = "ContactName"
              .Parameters.Add("@ContactTitle", _
                  SqlDbType.NVarChar).SourceColumn = "ContactTitle"
              .Parameters.Add("@Address", _
                  SqlDbType.NVarChar).SourceColumn = "Address"
              .Parameters.Add("@City", _
                  SqlDbType.NVarChar).SourceColumn = "City"
              .Parameters.Add("@Region", _
                  SqlDbType.NVarChar).SourceColumn = "Region"
              .Parameters.Add("@PostalCode", _
                  SqlDbType.NVarChar).SourceColumn = "PostalCode"
              .Parameters.Add("@Country", _
                  SqlDbType.NVarChar).SourceColumn = "Country"
              .Parameters.Add("@Phone", _
                  SqlDbType.NVarChar).SourceColumn = "Phone"
              .Parameters.Add("@Fax", _
                  SqlDbType.NVarChar).SourceColumn = "Fax"
          End With

          .DeleteCommand = New SqlCommand("DELETE FROM Customers " & _
          "WHERE CustomerID = @CustomerID", NorthwindConnection)
          With .DeleteCommand
              .Parameters.Add("@CustomerID", _
                  SqlDbType.NChar).SourceColumn = "CustomerID"
```

**LISTING 6.6** Continued

```
            End With
        End With
    End Sub

    Private Sub LoadData()
        NorthwindCustomers.Rows.Clear()
        NorthwindCustomersAdapter.Fill(NorthwindCustomers)
    End Sub
```

First, you can see that the code declared a DataTable to store the data and a SqlDataAdapter to retrieve and send back the data. Make sure that these are declared in the scope of your form, so all methods that you write to work with them and call them will have access to them. You might be asking yourself why this example didn't specify these variables as new instantiated objects. I recommend never using the New keyword when declaring member variables in a class, which is what you're doing in this case. Doing so allows you to take advantage of objects overloaded constructors while still being able to properly handle errors that occur; this also helps keep your code clean.

Next, you need to initialize these objects and set up all of their properties. The SetupDataObjects method in Listing 6.6 does this. The first bit of code in this method instantiates and initializes the objects so you can use them later. You should note that when instantiating the DataTable, you pass in the name of the table as it exists in the Northwind database—Customers. This sets the TableName property of the DataTable, which will be important later. The DataAdapter is then instantiated, along with setting up the SelectCommand and its connection using the overloaded constructor. As mentioned before, this is so when you call the Fill method, it will know what data to retrieve.

The rest of the code in SetupDataObjects will set up the other Command objects needed to update data back to the database. The code sets up three different properties of the DataAdapter—InsertCommand, UpdateCommand, and DeleteCommand. All three are set up in the same way, just with different values. Each is instantiated, passing in the SQL statement to do the necessary task and a reference to the connection to execute it against. The SQL statements are just standard INSERT, UPDATE, and DELETE statements, but with parameters instead of hard-coded values.

Then, after you have the new command, you set up the parameters as discussed earlier in this chapter, but with one major difference. Because the Command.Parameters.Add method returns the instance of the newly created parameter, you can do anything you want with it, such as set a property value on it. In this case, you need to set the SourceColumn property to the name of the column that this parameter maps to in the Customers table in the database. This helps the DataAdapter understand how to map the various "updates" to the actual table.

Next, this code includes a method called LoadData to take care of actually getting the data. This is really easy with the DataAdapter now set up, because all you have to do is call the Fill method and pass in the DataTable. You'll notice though that there's a line of code before that to clear out all the rows in the DataTable. This allows you to call the LoadData method more than once. It's possible that the DataTable might already have rows in it. If you have not specified the primary key for the DataTable, the Fill method will just dump in all the rows again from the database. If a primary key has been specified, it won't put in any duplicates. Because this example doesn't specify one, you should clear out all rows to be sure.

## DATAADAPTER CONFIGURATION WIZARD

If you have created a DataAdapter at design time, your DataAdapter is visible in the component tray of your form. You can select the DataAdapter, and go to the Property window. At the bottom of the window, you will see a few hyperlinks. Click Configure Data Adapter. A wizard will appear to help you configure your data adapter. Some of the great features include writing the stored procedures for INSERT, UPDATE, and DELETE for you, automatically retrieving key fields after inserts, setting up optimistic concurrency, and using a query designer to help you come up with your SELECT SQL statement. Use the tools that are available to you whenever applicable.

With these two methods, you can now bring it all together in the form's load event handler by calling them, and then setting the DataGrid's DataSource to the now filled DataTable. You will notice two more lines in the load event that are dynamically adding event handlers to the NorthwindChangesMade method, so when the DataTable's RowChanged or RowDeleted events are fired, it will be called.

Taking a look at this method, you can see that all it's doing is setting the Enabled property for the two buttons on the form to True. The application could display the Customers table in the DataGrid and if changes are made in the DataGrid, such as editing a field of one of the rows, adding a new row, or deleting a row completely. The Save and Cancel buttons will be enabled. You can save the changes that have been made to the data in the DataTable or cancel any of the changes that have been made.

The code for btnCancel's Click event calls the RejectChanges method of the DataTable. This reverts all the data back to the way it was originally. Because you are data binding to the DataGrid, it is aware of the changes and refreshes its view of the data. Then you clean up your UI by disabling the two buttons again, because now there are no changes to save or cancel.

Finally, the code executed when btnSave is clicked will send all of the changes back to the table in the database from calling the Update method of the DataAdapter. Because you've set each of the commands in the DataAdapter properly, in theory this will execute without a hitch. Technically speaking, there is no such thing as a true batch update in ADO.NET. You do get a batch-like update using the DataAdapter though. When you call the Update method, it is actually iterating through all the changes that have been made to the data and calling the appropriate command to update the data back. The DataRow class has a RowState property that lets the DataAdapter know what sort of action is required to update the current row it's looking at. After the update to the database, the UI is updated, to signify there are no longer any changes to be saved or cancelled.

Two last things that are in the btnSave event handler code is the call to the LoadData method after updating and the fact that all the code is in a Try Catch block. These two issues are actually partially related. One reason to use a Try Catch block is because it's possible the update will fail. If you were to enter incorrect data, for example, you'll find that after the code displays the message in a message box, the DataGrid will also catch on to the error and display a red exclamation point next to the rows that contain errors, along with a tooltip of the actual error when you roll over the red exclamation point.

Another exception that might be returned is the DBConcurrencyException. This exception will be thrown whenever the DataAdapter realizes that after making the updates, no rows were actually affected in the table in the database, which leads you into the next section on concurrency violations.

## Handling Concurrency Violations

Picture two employees sitting down to your application, plugging away, changing records at the same time on the data that is currently in memory on their machine. They both select the first record in the system and start editing. Person 1 makes her changes to that first row and then presses the Save button so that her changes are saved to the database. Person 2 has also been working on that first row, but tries to save his changes after Person 1 has done so. The DataAdapter will attempt to call the Update command on the first row, but the Update command will update a row only if it hasn't been changed since it was first retrieved. The Update will return zero rows affected and a DBConcurrencyException is thrown.

ADO.NET does not contain any methods for automatically handling concurrency violations. Using a Try Catch block will allow you to catch the DBConcurrencyException and do the necessary processing to help the user in making a decision about what to do next. In the previous example of Person 1 and Person 2, a possible fix for this might be to ask Person 2 if he would like to discard his changes or overwrite Person 1's changes with his own.

This is also the reason why LoadData is called in the code from Listing 6.6. (Check in the btnSave Click event handler, after the call to Update on the DataAdapter.) This will ensure that the user has the "freshest" copy of the data to work with. If any rows were changed since they last got the data, they would now have the changes.

# Advanced Data Topics

There are many other ways to use ADO.NET to work with data and process updates. Earlier in this chapter, you learned how to use the DataReader to read through a result set. The chapter also covered retrieving data into a `DataTable`, but if you want to find a subset of data in the `DataTable`, you have to write some looping code. The `DataView` class is designed to take care of this.

## DataView

The `DataView` is exactly what it sounds like. It is a view of data, specifically a view of the data in a `DataTable`. You can have any number of views against the same `DataTable`, and each one can have its own filter and sort specified. When you specify a `DataTable` as the source for data binding, you are actually binding to the `DataView`, the `DataTable`'s `DefaultDataView` to be precise.

A quick-and-dirty example of a scenario where you could use a `DataView` is to filter on a table based on the currently selected row of another table. Using the Northwind database as an example again, say you have a `DataSet` that contains two `DataTables`—the `Customers` and `Orders` tables. Now in your user interface, you select a customer and you want to see how many orders that customer has placed. This can be accomplished by attaching a `DataView` onto the `Orders` `DataTable` and setting the `RowFilter` property.

```
Dim OrdersView As New DataView(dsNorthwind.Tables("Orders"))
```

Notice the DataView's constructor can take the `DataTable` you want to have a view of. Now, you can use the `CustomerID` retrieved from the UI to filter the rows in the view.

```
OrdersView.RowFilter = "CustomerID = '" & SelectedCustomerID & "'"
```

When the `RowFilter` is set, the `DataView` is reduced down to only the rows that match. You can use the `AND` and `OR` keywords when constructing your `RowFilter`, almost anything that could appear in the `WHERE` clause of a SQL statement. Now you can display how many orders the currently selected customer has placed.

```
MessageBox.Show(OrdersView.Count.ToString & "(s) have been placed")
```

You could re-query the database every time you wanted to know how many orders a customer has placed, but by keeping the data local to the application and querying it locally, you save the extra hits back to the SQL Server. This method of setting the `RowFilter` is quite a bit faster too.

## SqlTransaction

The `SqlClient` namespace provides an additional class for working with transactions called `SqlTransaction`. It is very straight-forward to use and aids in data integrity. If you're not familiar with the idea of a transaction, think of it like this. You walk up to a vending machine and determine what you want to purchase. The item you want to buy takes three coins. You enter the first two coins into the slot. All of a sudden the power goes out. Your money is more than likely gone forever. Even if the power comes back on, the machine will probably not be so kind as to remember the money you gave it. Now imagine when you first walked up to the vending machine, and instead you had three coins that had strings attached to them. You slide the first two coins down the slot and the power goes off. Shortly after, the power comes back on. You still have the ends of the strings that are attached to first two coins you gave to the vending machine. Give them a yank and pull them back out. Now you have your money back. This is how transactions work.

Let's get the scenario a little closer to home now. Say you have three actions you'd like to perform on different tables in your database. For your data integrity level to stay high, you need all three of these actions to be executed successfully. Now what if after executing two of them successfully, the third action fails? You now have invalid data, because the first two items have already been executed on your database, but the third did not. By including all three actions on your database in the same transaction, you can have any changes that succeeded before the item that failed, undone. This "all-or-nothing" idea is what transactions are all about. Take a look now at a SqlTransaction in action.

Start a new Windows Forms project. On Form1, place two link labels. Name one of them lnkSuccess and one lnkFailure. Now place the code from Listing 6.7 in Form1's code.

**LISTING 6.7**    Using a Transaction to Ensure an All-or-Nothing Command-Execution Series

```
Private Connection As SqlConnection
Private Command1, Command2, Command3 As SqlCommand

Private Sub lnkSuccess_LinkClicked(ByVal sender As System.Object, _
                               ByVal e As LinkLabelLinkClickedEventArgs) _
                               Handles lnkSuccess.LinkClicked

    Command2 = Nothing
    SetupDataObjects()
    ExecuteCommands()
End Sub


Private Sub lnkFailure_LinkClicked(ByVal sender As System.Object, _
                               ByVal e As LinkLabelLinkClickedEventArgs) _
                               Handles lnkFailure.LinkClicked

    SetupDataObjects()
    Command2.CommandText = _
        "INSERT INTO Customers" & _
        " (CustomerID, ContactName)" & _
        "VALUES ('USER2', 'User 2')"
    ExecuteCommands()
End Sub
```

**LISTING 6.7**   Continued

```
Private Sub SetupDataObjects()
    If Connection Is Nothing Then
        Connection = New _
        SqlConnection( _
            ConfigurationSettings.AppSettings( _
        "Northwind.ConnectionString"))
    End If

    If Command1 Is Nothing Then
        Command1 = New SqlCommand("INSERT INTO Customers " & _
        "(CustomerID, CompanyName, ContactName) VALUES " & _
        "('USER1', 'User Company 1', 'User 1')", Connection)
    End If

    If Command2 Is Nothing Then
        Command2 = New SqlCommand("INSERT INTO Customers " & _
        "(CustomerID, CompanyName, ContactName) VALUES " & _
        "('USER2', 'User Company 2', 'User 2')", Connection)
    End If

    If Command3 Is Nothing Then
        Command3 = New SqlCommand("INSERT INTO Customers " & _
        "(CustomerID, CompanyName, ContactName) VALUES " & _
        "('USER3', 'User Company 3', 'User 3')", Connection)
    End If
End Sub

Private Sub ExecuteCommands()
    Dim MyTransaction As SqlTransaction

    Connection.Open()
    MyTransaction = Connection.BeginTransaction()

    Command1.Transaction = MyTransaction
    Command2.Transaction = MyTransaction
    Command3.Transaction = MyTransaction

    Try
        MessageBox.Show("Executing Command1...")
        Command1.ExecuteNonQuery()
        MessageBox.Show("Executing Command2...")
```

**LISTING 6.7** Continued

```
        Command2.ExecuteNonQuery()
        MessageBox.Show("Executing Command3...")
        Command3.ExecuteNonQuery()
        MyTransaction.Commit()
        MessageBox.Show("All Commands executed successfully!")
    Catch
        MyTransaction.Rollback()
        MessageBox.Show("There was an error!" & vbCrLf & _
        "All changes have been rolled back")
    Finally
        Connection.Close()
    End Try
End Sub
```

The details of this code aren't very important, but you can put this in the form to see how it works. The important part to focus on is the ExecuteCommands method. It opens a connection and starts a new transaction on that connection and stores it in a variable. You can then add each of the pre-setup commands that will simply add records to that transaction. Inside the Try Catch block, a message box is displayed and a command is executed. You do this three times—once for each command in this example. After all three have executed, you can then call the Commit method on the transaction, to commit all of the changes to the database, because they were all successful. However, the Catch section will catch if any of them fail and call the RollBack method of the transaction, so any rows that have been added in this case will be removed. It then finally closes the connection. In case of an error, no changes are made to the database, even though you had already performed actions on it. In Listing 6.7, the click event handler for lnkFailure is calling the same SQL statements as lnkSuccess, except that Command2 doesn't include all fields required to add a record to the Customers table, which will produce an error. This will cause the data changes to be rolled back.

Because of the nature of transactions and how they are used, you can include anything as a condition for rolling back or committing data, such as making a file system change or calling a Web Service. Include whatever code you want in the Try section of the Try Catch block and you're good to go.

# In Brief

This chapter presented advanced features of ADO.NET you can use to more easily work with your data dynamically, as well as explained the details of some of the "magic" that Visual Studio .NET does for you:

- ADO.NET provides lots of flexibility and power, such as attaching a `ConnectionString` to an attribute in an XML file.

- The `command` class allows you to call SQL statements directly as well as stored procedures. You can also set up parameters to make your queries more manageable and secure.

- Sending data back to your database is easy and flexible using the `Command` and `DataAdapter` classes.

- You can accomplish many tasks with some of the extra classes like `DataView` and `Transaction`, while saving queries and helping data integrity.

# Object-Oriented Programming in Visual Basic .NET

## What Is Object-Oriented Programming and Why Is it Important?

Ask almost any .NET guru what skills a Visual Basic 6.0 programmer needs to succeed with .NET and they will list Object-Oriented Programming (OOP) near the top of the list. Often they will even comment that it is the hardest part of .NET for Visual Basic developers to understand, because it is new to them. Well, I agree with the first of these comments, but not the second. Visual Basic programmers have been working with objects, properties, methods, and even interfaces for quite a long time; it certainly isn't new to them. What has changed though is that OOP has gained a higher profile for the Visual Basic programmer; the .NET Framework takes full advantage of OOP concepts such as interfaces (which Visual Basic has enjoyed for some time) and inheritance (which is new to Visual Basic .NET) and forces you to understand those concepts even if you don't use them in your own applications. This chapter briefly explains the basic concepts of objects, shows you the syntax for defining your own objects in Visual Basic .NET, and then digs into the new OOP concepts (such as inheritance) that have been added to Visual Basic.

The basic concepts of OOP might be just a refresher for most of you, because these concepts existed in Visual Basic 6.0, but please read through this material anyway to ensure that you understand the terms and concepts used in this book. The chapter begins with the basic definition of objects and all the terms and concepts that they bring along with them.

## Understanding Objects

To define the term "object," the simplest definition starts with just the word "thing." An object is a generic description of anything you might want to discuss or work with. In regular conversation, object is usually intended to describe only material objects, but in programming, where very little is truly material, this definition is expanded to include any entity. We can refer to a car, person, or building as an object, but it is also acceptable to use this term to describe something less tangible like an interest rate or a rule that will be applied to incoming email.

The use of objects allows your programs to be focused on the entities you are working with, the end goal of which is to produce systems that are easier to understand and to enhance. Instead of a program where all the information and code related to a single entity are scattered throughout the entire application, an object-based approach consolidates this information by bringing it into the definition of the object.

## Classes and Instances

To understand objects requires you to quickly move to the concept of a class. Classes, as in classifications, describe a group or type of entity, and all objects are one member of a certain class. Classes are the description of an object, providing details that define its behavior and telling what types of information are available about an object. You could, for instance, have a Car class. This class would tell you that the following information is available about a car: its color, speed, weight, make, model, and year. All these things are attributes of the object, descriptive pieces of information referred to as the object's properties. In addition to these properties, the class also describes what the object can do, and how it does it. These behaviors are often called the object's methods, and a car object might have methods such as TurnLeft, GoForward, BackUp, and so on. Using this class, which provides information on the object's properties and methods, along with some other details, as a template, actual objects are then created.

Returning to the car example, the class would be the specification of the car, the blueprint that describes how it works and looks. That class is then used to create many cars, each of which exists on its own, but all of which are based on that same specification. Each individual car has the same properties because those come from the specification, such as color, but each one might have a different value for those properties (blue car, red car, yellow car, and so on). All the cars would also share the same behaviors or actions (the methods of the class), such as GoForward, and all the cars built to the same specification would perform this action in the same way.

177

What Is Object-Oriented Programming and Why Is it Important?

When you create a car based on the specification, it is equivalent to creating an object based on a class. So, whereas the Ford Thunderbird would be a class, Bob's blue T-Bird would be an object. Each of those individual objects is an *instance* of the class, and there is no limit to the number of these instances you can create. Every instance shares the template, or description, provided by its class. This means that every single instance of the Car class will have the same properties and methods and will behave in the same general fashion. Each individual instance has its own values for its properties, though; all cars have a color property, but each car might be a different color.

## Understanding and Using Properties

Properties are attributes about an object you can retrieve and set, and can be added to a class in one of two ways. The first, and the simplest, method is to declare a variable as Public. In the case of a class, anything that is declared as Public is available to anyone using that class. Including the line Dim Year As Integer in a class would not create an exposed property because Year would only be available internally. If you were to declare Year as Public Year As Integer, suddenly it is exposed through every instance of this object. Technically, a public variable isn't the same as a property (it is called a *field*, and the difference is slight but important) but the result is quite similar.

### Property Statements

Just declaring a public variable doesn't create a property, it creates a field. Real properties are declared using a special Property syntax:

```
Dim myVar as <Property Data Type>
Public Property <Property Name>() As <Property Data Type>
    Get
        Return myVar
    End Get
    Set(ByVal Value As <Property Data Type>)
        myVar = value
    End Set
End Property
```

The two parts of the property definition, Get and Set, represent the retrieval of the property value, and the setting of that value. Generally, the Get code simply returns the value of an internal variable (a class-level variable that represents the property, sometimes prefixed with m to indicate a member value), and the Set code places a value (which is provided through the special parameter value) into that same internal variable. Overall, although public variables (fields) produce similar results, properties are much more flexible because they allow you to define whatever code is required to properly control the setting and retrieval of the property value.

### ReadOnly and WriteOnly Properties

It is not unusual to have a property that you want to be read-only, such as a version property, or perhaps a creation date. It is much less common, though not impossible, that you might have a property that can be changed but cannot be read, such as a password field. In previous versions of Visual Basic, you could create these read-only or write-only properties simply by choosing not to implement either the Set or the Get portion of the property definition. That is partially what you do in Visual Basic .NET. If you are creating a read-only property, you do not create the Set portion of the property definition, but you must also specify ReadOnly as an additional keyword. This is shown in the following code with the Description property, which is a computed value and therefore it wouldn't make much sense to have it be write-able. You wouldn't want to set a property like Description because it is really just the result of a calculation.

```
Dim m_Color As String
Dim m_Make As String
Dim m_Model As String
Public ReadOnly Property Description() As String
    Get
        Return m_Color & " " & m_Make & " " & m_Model
    End Get
End Property
```

For a write-only property, the keyword used is WriteOnly, and you supply only the Set portion of the property definition:

```
Dim m_Password As String
Public WriteOnly Property Password() As String
    Set(ByVal Value As String)
        m_Password = Value
    End Set
End Property
```

## Turning Concept into Code

Let's turn some of these concepts into code. First, to create objects, you must have a class. Many classes are available that have been created by other people; in fact, the entire .NET Framework is really a "class library," a set of preexisting classes that you can use in your programs. This example, though, uses the Car class, because it is really not that complex to make a simple class.

Open Visual Studio .NET, and create a new Windows Application from under the Visual Basic Projects folder (see Figure 7.1).

179

What Is Object-Oriented Programming and Why Is it Important?

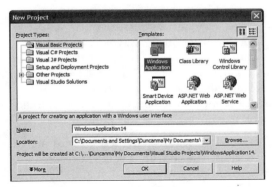

**Figure 7.1** A Windows application is a good choice for playing around with code because it is easy to display message boxes and set up a sample interface.

This project contains a single form and a code file holding the assembly information, so you will add a new file for the sample code. Choose Project, Add Class from the menu. This adds a new, empty class to the project (name it Car.vb), a great starting point for this exercise. The shell of a class has been created into this file now, providing the following code:

```
Public Class Car

End Class
```

At this point, a class has been created, but it is completely blank. Now, within this shell of code, you can begin to describe the properties and methods of the Car objects. Whatever you place in this class will be part of every object instance created from it. For now, let's add Make, Model, and Color properties.

To implement the color property in Car, you could use code like Listing 7.1.

**LISTING 7.1** Creating Properties in Classes

```
Public Class Car
    Dim m_Color As String
    Public Property Color() As String
        Get
            Return m_Color
        End Get
        Set(ByVal Value As String)
            m_Color = value
        End Set
    End Property
End Class
```

Now, add property code for each of Make and Model, remembering to add two additional internal variables as well (both of these properties should use String as their data type).

## REFERENCE TYPES

In programming, an additional concept is introduced, that of *referencing* an object. An object variable, any variable declared as an object of some type (Dim myCar As Car), does not hold the object itself, but merely a reference (also known as a pointer) to that object. This is different from value variable types, such as integers or doubles, where the variable directly holds the value. This means that more than one object variable can refer, or point, to the same object. Generally, this isn't the case. You create one object and use it with one variable, but it is important to understand the difference between objects and other variable types in this regard.

## Creating an Object Instance

After you have this class, you can create an instance of it in another part of the project. Add a button to Form1 (named Button1 by default) and double-click it to go into the Click event for the button. Your code should look like Listing 7.2 at this point.

This new procedure is the test area for the new class. The code in it will be executed when you run this application and then click that button, so this is where you will start writing the code to work with your new class. To get started using the new class, you have to first create a variable of the appropriate type:

```
Dim firstCar As Car
```

**LISTING 7.2**   Creating a Button Click Event for Testing

```
Private Sub Button1_Click( _
    ByVal sender As System.Object, _
    ByVal e As System.EventArgs) Handles Button1.Click

End Sub
```

This declaration looks like declaring a regular variable, such as a String or Integer, but it is very different. At this point, you have a variable that could hold a reference to an object of type Car, but that is currently holding nothing. When you declare a String variable, the string itself has been created. Although it might not have any data in it, it does exist. In this case, you do not have anything in firstCar at all. So, the next step is to create an instance of the class, which you can do with the New keyword:

```
firstCar = New Car
```

Dim first CAr AS CAr = New CAr()
Dim firstCar As New Car()

181

What Is Object-Oriented Programming and Why Is it Important?

## SHOP TALK

### OVERZEALOUS INTELLISENSE CREATES BAD PROGRAMMING PRACTICE

Writing a simple object declaration in Visual Studio .NET 2003 exposes a small flaw in the text editor for Visual Basic. This flaw is relatively benign, but it can be quite annoying if you are used to stricter languages. When you declare a new instance of a class in Visual Basic .NET, the parentheses around the constructor arguments are optional if there are no arguments being passed. So, both of the following statements are perfectly legal in terms of the Visual Basic language specification:

```
X = New System.Random
```

```
X = New System.Random()
```

If you need to pass in one or more arguments to the constructor, the parentheses are required.

```
X = New System.Random(325)
```

Because they are required sometimes, and sometimes not, some consistency-minded developers choose to always include the parentheses, at least until they started using Visual Studio .NET 2003. Inside Visual Studio, the text editor will automatically remove your parentheses unless you have constructor arguments, so consistency is not an option.

As I mentioned earlier, this is quite annoying to some developers, but there is actually quite a good reason for this behavior. In various tests and usability studies, the Visual Basic team found that developers would often declare arrays by accident due to these empty parentheses. Developers would start with a declaration that created a new instance of the object (Dim X As New System.Random()), and then decide to remove the New keyword. In the Visual Studio .NET 2002 editor, because an empty pair of parentheses was automatically added, they ended up declaring an array of the specified type instead of a single variable.

```
Dim X As System.Random()
```

In the Visual Studio .NET 2003 release, the Visual Basic editor was modified to help prevent this confusion. The editor no longer adds the empty parentheses when creating a new instance of an object, but they took it too far. Instead of just removing the automatic add, the editor also removes empty parentheses if you add them yourself. The result is that you cannot choose to use empty parentheses when creating a new instance, unless you want to use a different IDE.

So, you now have created an instance of Car and assigned a reference to that new object to the firstCar variable. You can now, through firstCar, access the properties of the new object:

```
firstCar.Color = "Red"
firstCar.Make = "Ford"
firstCar.Model = "Escort"
```

These properties can be retrieved just as easily:

```
Public Function GetDescription() As String
    Return String.Format("{0} {1} {2}", Year, Make, Model)
End Function
```

Because objects work by reference, you can create additional variables, all pointing at the same location:

```
Dim firstCar As Car
Dim secondCar As Car
firstCar = New Car()
secondCar = firstCar
firstCar.Make = "Ford"
secondCar.Make = "Chevy"
'secondCar.Make is equal to firstCar.Make
```

Contrast this with a non-object variable, such as an Integer, where the actual value is moving between locations:

```
Dim firstValue As Integer
Dim secondValue As Integer

firstValue = 32
secondValue = firstValue
secondValue = 56
' firstValue <> secondValue
```

Normally, when dealing with variables, as soon as the variable goes out of scope, it ceases to exist. Because multiple variables can point at a single object, the rules controlling object destruction are a little different. When all the variables that reference the object are gone, the object becomes inaccessible and is eventually destroyed by the background services of .NET. This process, which is called *garbage collection*, allows the program to freely create and release objects knowing that the system is following along behind cleaning up any mess. In this way, .NET cleans up on behalf of your program, providing another underlying service so that individual programs do not have to worry about such issues.

## Encapsulating Code into Your Classes

Now you have seen, in code, the creation of a class, the instantiation of objects based on that class, and the manipulation of those object properties. Moving along, consider the idea that a class, unlike a UDT (User-Defined Type or Struct), describes more than just a set of values. A class can include behavior and programming logic, in addition to being capable of storing data. To provide this implementation of behavior, a class includes more than just

183

What Is Object-Oriented Programming and Why Is it Important?

code to set and retrieve property values; it can also include code to perform property validation and other actions. With the Car class, you can see this feature by adding some validation code to its properties. Currently, you could set the property Color to any string value, even if it isn't a color at all (firstCar.Color = "John"). To make the representation of a Car object a little bit smarter, you can add a bit of code that checks any value submitted against a list of colors and rejects anything that does not match. This involves rewriting the routine for the Color property as shown in Listing 7.3.

**LISTING 7.3**    Adding Validation to the Color Property

```
Public Class Car
    Dim m_Color As String

    Public Property Color() As String
        Get
            Return m_Color
        End Get
        Set(ByVal Value As String)
            Select Case Value.ToUpper()
                Case "RED"
                    m_Color = Value
                Case "YELLOW"
                    m_Color = Value
                Case "BLUE"
                    m_Color = Value
                Case Else
                    Dim objException As _
                        New System.ArgumentOutOfRangeException()
                    Throw objException
            End Select
        End Set
    End Property
End Class
```

Now, an attempt to set the property to an invalid color (invalid by the code's internal list, which considers the popular color "mauve," for instance, to be invalid) results in an exception being raised. For more information on exceptions and exception-based error handling, see Chapter 4, "Working with Files." As described in that chapter, you can correctly deal with this exception by rewriting the test code (contained in the click event handler of a button) to include a Try...Catch structure. This modified code is shown in Listing 7.4.

**LISTING 7.4**   Including Error Handling in the Test Code

```vb
Private Sub Button1_Click( _
    ByVal sender As System.Object, _
    ByVal e As System.EventArgs) Handles Button1.Click

    Dim firstCar As Car
    Dim carColor As String
    firstCar = New Car
    firstCar.Year = 1999
    Try
        firstCar.Color = "Green"
    Catch ex As System.ArgumentOutOfRangeException
        'whoops! Handle the error!
        MsgBox("Whoops!" & vbCrLf & ex.Message)
    End Try
    carColor = firstCar.Color
    firstCar.Make = "Ford"
    firstCar.Model = "Escort"
    MsgBox(firstCar.GetDescription)
End Sub
```

## PICKING THE RIGHT SCOPE

If you created this property procedure as `Private`, it would still be usable from inside this class but would not be available from any other code. Alternatively, you can also declare elements of the class (properties, functions, subroutines) as `Friend`. This declaration ensures that code within the same assembly can access these portions of the class as if they were `Public`, but that they would be hidden (`Private`) to any code external to the assembly (project) containing the class. `Protected` is yet another scope modifier available to you, and it is specifically designed for use in an inheritance situation. A class member designated with `Protected` can be accessed from only its own class or from an inherited class. `Protected` can also be combined with `Friend` (producing `Protected Friend`) to specify that a member should be available only within the same assembly and from within the same class or from an inherited class.

Other than property validation, which is powerful itself, a class can contain a code function or subroutine that is not part of any of the property retrieval or setting code, commonly referred to as a *method*. Methods are designed to provide related functionality to an object and often act based on property information (because it is available). For the Car class, a useful method might be to produce an age of the car by comparing the current date and time to a property of the car representing its manufacturing date. Creating the manufacturing date property is relatively straightforward. It is just like the earlier properties you created except that it is a date, and adding this method is actually as easy as creating a public function inside the class definition.

185

What Is Object-Oriented Programming and Why Is it Important?

First, the new property:

```
Dim m_Manufactured As Date
Public Property Manufactured() As Date
    Get
        Return m_Manufactured
    End Get
    Set(ByVal Value As Date)
        m_Manufactured = value
    End Set
End Property
```

Listing 7.5 shows the new method.

**LISTING 7.5** The GetAge Method

```
Public Function GetAge() As Integer
    Dim days As Integer
    Dim currentDate As Date
    currentDate = System.DateTime.Today
    days = currentDate.Subtract(m_Manufactured).Days
    Return days
End Function
```

After you have added that code to the class, you can call it through any instance, (myCar.GetAge()), as in Listing 7.6.

**LISTING 7.6** Using the New Method

```
Dim myCar As New Car
myCar.Manufactured = #1/30/2002#
MsgBox(myCar.GetAge())
```

For the Car class, a better method example might be something action-related, such as DisplayInfo, a sample implementation of which is provided in Listing 7.7.

**LISTING 7.7** The New Action-Oriented Method

```
Public Sub DisplayInfo( _
    ByVal windowHeading As String)
    MsgBox(Me.GetDescription)
End Sub
```

Although the class example is quite small, objects are not usually so simple. Through a combination of properties (some with code, some without) and methods, it is possible to create complex objects. Keep in mind that the objects that make up the .NET Framework (such as System.Console and others) are built according to these same rules and have all the same characteristics as objects that you can create. The only real difference between the .NET Framework and your objects is that you didn't have to write the ones in the Framework!

## SHOP TALK

### PROPERTY OR METHOD?

Deciding what should be a property and what should be a method is not always easy, and many developers make the wrong choice. There is no "rule" that tells you what to do, but I can offer you the guideline I use and the logic behind it. I use a simple test as I design my objects: properties shouldn't cause anything to happen. I like to write classes so that setting a property three times has the same end result as setting it once.

This single guideline avoids situations whereby the order of setting an object's properties can affect the outcome. In a class for calculating mortgages, for example, you could write the code so that setting the Principal property caused the payment amount to be recalculated. If that was the case, you would want to make sure that you had set all the other properties (AnnualInterestRate and NumberOfYears) before Principal. I avoid putting any code into a property routine that changes other internal parts of my class, other than changing its corresponding internal variable. A class member that calculates and returns the PaymentAmount for your mortgage could reasonably be a property or a method because it doesn't change anything about the class when it does its calculation. I am not completely consistent in this type of situation, but I am more likely to implement a calculated value as a function instead of a property. In addition to the property rule, I also subscribe to a rule that says that properties should represent the setting and retrieving of values. With the possible exception of validation, I try to avoid calculated values in my property routines.

# New OOP Features in Visual Basic .NET

Although properties and methods allow you to create powerful and complex objects, the object support in .NET has many more features beyond those basics. These advanced features make it easier for you to represent concepts and entities in your code, producing a system that is easier to use, maintain, and extend. Although the object support in .NET is extensive, this section provides a brief overview of five main areas: overloading, inheritance, constructors, namespaces, and static class members.

# Overloading

Overloading allows a single function or subroutine to be called with a variety of different parameters. This allows a single method, for instance, to accept parameters in different combinations or using different data types. So, returning to the Car example, you could design the GetAge method so that it could work in any one of several different ways. The existing implementation takes no parameters and returns the difference in days between the current date and the manufactured date, but perhaps you would also like to allow a user of the object to request the difference between the manufactured date and any arbitrary date, and also to allow the user to specify the unit of time to measure the difference in. To do this without this concept of overloading, you would have to create a different function for each possible call, as in Listing 7.8.

**LISTING 7.8**   Building Many Variations on a Single Method

```
Public Function GetAge() As Integer
    Dim days As Integer
    Dim currentDate As Date
    currentDate = System.DateTime.Today
    days = currentDate.Subtract(m_Manufactured).TotalDays
    Return days
End Function


Public Function GetAgeAtDate(ByVal pointInTime As Date) As Integer
    Dim days As Integer
    days = pointInTime.Subtract(m_Manufactured).TotalDays
    Return days
End Function


Public Function GetAgeInUnits(ByVal unit As String) As Integer
    Dim units As Integer
    Dim current As Date
    Dim difference As System.TimeSpan
    current = System.DateTime.Today
    difference = current.Subtract(m_Manufactured)
    Select Case unit
        Case "Hours"
            units = difference.TotalHours
        Case "Days"
            units = difference.TotalDays
        Case "Minutes"
            units = difference.TotalMinutes
```

## LISTING 7.8   Continued

```
        Case "Years"
            units = difference.TotalDays \ 365
    End Select
    Return units
End Function
```

All these functions are really just variations of GetAge, but each different parameter list and different corresponding code needs its own function name. With overloading, you remove this restriction and can create all these functions using the same name (GetAge). To use this feature, all you need to do is add the Overloads keyword in front of each (including the original) function declaration (before the Public) and change each function name to be the same:

```
Public Overloads Function GetAge() As Integer
End Function
```

```
Public Overloads Function GetAge(ByVal pointInTime As Date) As Integer
End Function
```

```
Public Overloads Function GetAge(ByVal unit As String) As Integer
End Function
```

In the code example that uses this function, you can now choose between any one of the three possible declarations for this function (see Figure 7.2).

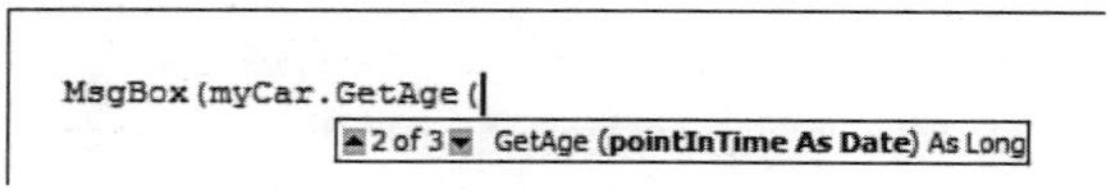

```
MsgBox(myCar.GetAge (|
         2 of 3   GetAge (pointInTime As Date) As Long
```

**Figure 7.2**   All the available versions of a function are shown through IntelliSense when you are using Visual Studio .NET to create a client.

Each function declaration must be different in some way—number of parameters, data type of parameters, or the data type of the return value—or it will not be allowed. Merely changing the *name* of your parameters does not count as a different procedure declaration.

Overloading represents the concept that the same action or request can be used in a variety of ways and allows you to model that in your object without having to resort to creating multiple distinct methods (GetAge, GetAgeFromDate, and so on). This technique is used throughout the .NET Framework to allow you to call functions with a variety of different parameter sets. Consider, for instance, the System.Console.WriteLine method, which can be called using any one of 18 parameter lists. As the Framework demonstrates, this is a useful way to simplify objects and provide the most options to programs using them.

# Using Inheritance

To some people, this is one of the most exciting features of Visual Basic .NET—a feature that is considered fundamental to the creation of object-based systems and that has been missing from Visual Basic until this version. I am not going to argue with this opinion, but somehow I managed to build systems for many years before .NET arrived, without inheritance. Regardless, the addition of inheritance to the Visual Basic language is an important feature and worth a little discussion.

As discussed earlier in this chapter, objects are a way for you to represent concepts or entities in code, and each of the object features of Visual Basic is designed to help you make the most useful representation possible. In many situations, one entity or concept is really a sub-object of a more basic entity or concept. Many examples of this are used in programming books, and sadly I am not going to come up with anything too revolutionary. Consider the class of objects designed to represent cars, such as a Ford Mustang, Toyota Celica, or Chevy Cavalier. The class would have various properties, such as Doors (number of doors the car has), MaxSpeed, Color, and others.

## IS OVERLOADING BETTER THAN LOOSE DATA TYPING?

In Visual Basic 6.0, you could combine all of these functions into one by declaring the parameters as "Variants" (or by using ParamArrays, which are still available in Visual Basic .NET), but the resulting code would be quite complex as you would have to test the data type and determine which code path to use for each possible form of input. In Visual Basic .NET, overloading allows you to support multiple sets of parameters while still retaining strongly typed (and easier to write) procedures. In each overloaded procedure, you can trust the compiler to validate the data-type of your inputs, which is a critical piece of code you don't have to write. The general problem with a loosely typed parameter list, as opposed to the strongly typed procedures you can create with overloading, is that they are too flexible. If you have a procedure that can accept a string or a date, and you declare the parameter as variant, you are allowing it to be called with any data type at all. Suddenly you need to add a block of code to confirm that you've been passed the right type of data, and the variant data type does nothing to help guide any programmer(s) who are trying to determine what type of input a particular procedure needs.

This general Car class really contains several subclasses of objects, such as Hatchbacks and Convertibles. Those classes would, of course, have all the properties of their parent class, Car, such as Doors, MaxSpeed, and Color, but they could also have unique properties of their own. A hatchback could have properties that described the size and behavior of its rear door. This relationship, between Car and its subclasses of Hatchback and Convertible, would be considered a parent-child relationship, and the method for representing this relationship is called *inheritance*. The class Hatchback is said to inherit from its base class Car. This relationship means that, in addition to any properties and methods created in the child class, the child will also possess all the properties and methods of the parent.

The previous example started with the Car class and headed downwards. Let's take the same starting point of Car and head upwards for a more detailed example of inheritance. To start, you could have a base class of Vehicle, which could represent any type of vehicle (boat, car, truck, plane) and has the properties of MaxSpeed, NumberOfPassengers, Color, and Description. You could easily represent this class in Visual Basic code, as shown in Listing 7.9.

**LISTING 7.9**    The Vehicle Class

```
Public Class Vehicle
    Public Property MaxSpeed() As Long
        Get
        End Get
        Set(ByVal Value As Long)
        End Set
    End Property

    Public Property NumberOfPassengers() As Long
        Get
        End Get
        Set(ByVal Value As Long)
        End Set
    End Property

    Public Property Color() As String
        Get        End Get
        Set(ByVal Value As String)
        End Set
    End Property

    Public Function GetDescription() As String
    End Function
End Class
```

The code that goes within the various procedures in that class is not really relevant to this example, so you can leave it blank for now. If you were to jump to some code to try using the object (for instance, in a button click event, as in an earlier examples), you would see that you can create objects of type Vehicle and work with their properties, as in Listing 7.10.

**LISTING 7.10**    Working with the Vehicle Class

```
Private Sub Button2_Click(ByVal sender As System.Object, _
        ByVal e As System.EventArgs) Handles Button2.Click
    Dim objVehicle As Vehicle
    objVehicle = New Vehicle

    objVehicle.Color = "Red"
    objVehicle.MaxSpeed = 100
End Sub
```

Now, by adding an additional class to the project (see Listing 7.11), you can create a class (Car) that inherits from Vehicle, just like the real class of object Car is a subclass or child of the Vehicle class of objects. Because you are creating a class designed to deal with just cars, you can add a couple of properties (NumberOfDoors and NumberOfTires) specific to this subclass of Vehicle.

**LISTING 7.11**   Creating a Child Class

```
Public Class Car
    Inherits Vehicle
    Public Property NumberOfTires() As Integer
        Get
        End Get
        Set(ByVal Value As Integer)
        End Set
    End Property

    Public Property NumberOfDoors() As Integer
        Get
        End Get
        Set(ByVal Value As Integer)
        End Set
    End Property
End Class
```

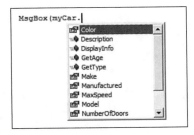

**Figure 7.3**   Classes expose all their public properties and methods, along with the public properties and methods of the class they are based on.

The key to this code is the line Inherits Vehicle, which tells Visual Basic that this class is a child of the Vehicle class and therefore should inherit of all that class's properties and methods. Once again, no code is actually placed into any of these property definitions because they are not really relevant at this time. After that code is in place, without having to do anything else, you can see the effect of the Inherits statement.

Returning to the button click procedure, you can create an object of type Car, and you'll quickly see that it exposes both its own properties and those of the parent class (see Figure 7.3).

## Overrides and Shadows

When an inherited class adds new methods or properties, it is said to be *extending* the base class. In addition to extending, it is also possible for a child class to *override* some or all of the functionality of the base class. This is done when the child implements a method or property that is already defined in the parent or base class (or anywhere along the inheritance chain). In such a case, the code in the child will be executed instead of the code in the parent, allowing you to create specialized versions of the base method or property.

For a child class to override some part of the base class, that portion must be marked Overridable in the base class definition. For instance, in the version of Vehicle listed earlier, none of its properties had the keyword Overridable and therefore child classes would be unable to provide their own implementations. As an example of how overriding is set up in the base and child classes, the code in Listing 7.12 marks the GetDescription() function as being overridable, and then overrides it in the Car child class. Note that unrelated portions of the two classes have been removed for clarity.

LISTING 7.12   Using the Overridable and Overrides Keywords

```
Public Class Vehicle
    'Code removed for simplicity....

    Public Overridable Function GetDescription() As String
        Return "This is my generic vehicle description!"
    End Function
End Class

Public Class Car
    Inherits Vehicle
    'Code removed for simplicity....

    Public Overrides Function GetDescription() As String
        Return "This is my Car Description"
    End Function
End Class
```

When overriding a method or property, as done in Listing 7.12, you can refer back to the original member of the base class by using the built-in object MyBase. For example, to refer to the existing GetDescription() method of the Vehicle class, you could call MyBase.GetDescription() from within the GetDescription method of Car. This functionality allows you to provide additional functionality through overriding without having to redo all the original code as well.

If you create a new class member with the same name as a member from an inherited class (without specifying overrides) you will get an error, unless you add the Shadows keyword.

Shadows is an interesting feature that allows you to hide a base class's declaration of a member, essentially replacing it with your own. In general, I consider this to be bad practice, as it is breaking the inheritance relationship. It is good to know that it exists, in case you need it to work around some particular bad class design, but try to avoid its use whenever possible as the results can be quite confusing.

## Abstract Classes and the MustOverride Keyword

In addition to marking code as Overridable, it is also possible to mark a method or property as MustOverride and a class as MustInherit. The MustOverride keyword indicates that any child of this class must provide its own version of this property or method, and the MustInherit keyword means that this class cannot be used on its own (you must base other classes off of it). If a class contains a method marked MustOverride, the class itself must be marked as MustInherit. Listing 7.13 illustrates this by creating two classes, one marked as MustInherit and one that inherits from that class and overrides one of its methods. You cannot create an instance of a class marked as MustInherit, but you can create an instance of a class that inherits from it.

**LISTING 7.13**   Two Classes: One Called MustInherit and One That Inherits from That Class

```
Public MustInherit Class Animal
    Public MustOverride Function GetName() As String
End Class


Public Class Dog
    Inherits Animal

    Public Overrides Function GetName() As String
        Return "Dog"
    End Function
End Class


Public Class TestMustInherit
    Sub Main()
        'Dim spot As New Animal 'invalid, will not compile
        Dim spot As New Dog
        Dim myPet As Animal
        'nothing wrong with assigning a non-abstract child
        'to a variable of the parent type
        myPet = spot

        MsgBox(myPet.GetName) 'displays "Dog"
    End Sub
End Class
```

It is worth noting that a common name for a class that cannot be instantiated (marked as MustInherit in Visual Basic .NET) is *an abstract class*.

### The Base of All Base Classes

If you look at the list of what is exposed by this new instance of the Car class, you will see more than simply the properties of Vehicle and of Car. The methods ToString() and GetType() are exposed by this object, but are not part of its class or its parent class. These methods are actually another result of inheritance. Whereas Car inherits from Vehicle, both Vehicle and Car (and every other class in .NET) inherit from the base class System.Object. This ultimate base class provides a few methods that are automatically part of every class you create.

One additional result of inheritance, one that is certainly worth mentioning, is in the area of data types. As discussed back in Chapter 2, every variable is of a certain data type, and objects are no exception. Declaring a variable to be of type Car is just as strict data typing as with integers and strings. If you make a function parameter of that type, only that type of object can be passed to that function. In an inheritance situation, the child class can act as if it was an instance of the parent class. This means, in this example, that you can put the Car objects into variables and procedure arguments that are of type Vehicle. Listing 7.14 shows an example of this.

**LISTING 7.14**    A Child Class Acting as an Instance of the Parent Class

```
Dim objVehicle As Vehicle

Dim objCar As Car
objCar = New Car
objCar.Year = 1993
objCar.Model = "CarModel"

objVehicle = objCar

objVehicle.Color = "Red"
objVehicle.MaxSpeed = 100
```

The instance of Car represented by objCar was easily placed into the variable objVehicle, and from that point on could be treated just like a Vehicle object. This fact, that a child object can be used as if it was an instance of the parent class, allows for the creation of generic code that will work with a class or any of its subclasses.

This is just one way that inheritance can be used to create better solutions, but there are many others. This has been a rapid overview of the subject of inheritance, but the custom control development in Chapter 8, "Building Custom Controls," will include a more practical example of using inheritance in your code.

# Defining and Using Interfaces

One of the more powerful features of object-oriented programming (OOP) is the capability to treat an object as if it was an instance of another class. When you are dealing with inheritance, this means that you can treat any derived class as if it was any one of its ancestors. This is useful and is often a key motivator of creating base classes, but it is limited to use with classes with an inheritance relationship.

Another way to produce a similar result, classes that can be treated as if they were other classes, is to use interfaces. An *interface* is a special type of class that contains no code but is used instead as a way of describing the appearance of an object. Other classes then can implement one or more of these interfaces, allowing them to be treated as if they were objects of one of those types.

Interfaces are used throughout the .NET Framework, allowing any number of classes to state that they all provide a specific set of functionality. One of the interfaces defined in the .NET Framework is IComparable (interface names often are prefixed by a capital I), which provides a single method (CompareTo) that is used to compare the current object to another instance of the same class. Any class that implements the IComparable interface is essentially stating that two instances of that class can be compared and a greater than, less than, or equal to relationship can be determined.

To implement an interface, a class usually has to provide its own version of one or more methods. Classes that want to implement IComparable just have to write their own version of the method CompareTo. Listing 7.15 shows a class that has decided to implement IComparable and the custom version of CompareTo that it has provided.

**LISTING 7.15**   Implementing an Interface

```
Public Class Person
    Implements IComparable

    Private m_name As String
    Private m_firstName As String
    Private m_lastName As String

    Public ReadOnly Property DisplayName() As String
        Get
            Return String.Format("{0} {1}", _
                m_firstName, m_lastName)
        End Get
    End Property

    Public Property FirstName() As String
        Get
            Return m_firstName
```

**LISTING 7.15**   Continued

```vb
        End Get
        Set(ByVal Value As String)
            m_firstName = Value
        End Set
    End Property


    Public Property LastName() As String
        Get
            Return m_lastName
        End Get
        Set(ByVal Value As String)
            m_lastName = Value
        End Set
    End Property


    Public Function CompareTo(ByVal obj As Object) As Integer _
            Implements System.IComparable.CompareTo
        'Compare this instance to obj, return a number
        'less than zero to indicate obj < me, 0 to indicate
        'obj = me, and greater than zero to indicate obj > me
        Dim objOtherPerson As Person
        If TypeOf obj Is Person Then
            objOtherPerson = DirectCast(obj, Person)
            If objOtherPerson.LastName < Me.LastName Then
                Return -1
            ElseIf objOtherPerson.LastName > Me.LastName Then
                Return 1
            Else
                If objOtherPerson.FirstName < Me.FirstName Then
                    Return -1
                ElseIf objOtherPerson.FirstName > Me.FirstName Then
                    Return 1
                Else
                    Return 0
                End If
            End If
        Else
            Throw New ArgumentException( _
                "CompareTo requires another Person object", "obj")
        End If
    End Function
End Class
```

By implementing IComparable, the Person class can now be passed into functions as if it were an object of type IComparable and used with other objects that require this interface to be implemented. An example of how this could be useful can be found in the .NET Framework class SortedList. This class allows you to build a list of objects, each with an associated key, and it keeps the list sorted by the key values. The catch is that the objects you supply as keys must support IComparable because the SortedList depends on the CompareTo method exposed by that interface to perform its sorts. This requirement is not a problem if your key is a simple data type, such as a String, Integer, or Date, because all these support the IComparable interface. But if you want to use a class of your own as the key, it will not work unless that class implements IComparable. Listing 7.16 shows how you could now build a sorted list using instances of the Person class as key values.

**LISTING 7.16**    Implementing IComparable Allows a Class to Work in a Sorted List

```
Dim objPerson1 As New Person
Dim objPerson2 As New Person
Dim objPerson3 As New Person
Dim Val1, Val2, Val3 As Integer

Val1 = 234
Val2 = 13
Val3 = 500

objPerson1.FirstName = "John"
objPerson1.LastName = "Adams"
objPerson2.FirstName = "Quincy"
objPerson2.LastName = "Wallace"
objPerson3.FirstName = "Arlene"
objPerson3.LastName = "Ratuski"

Dim slPeople As New SortedList
slPeople.Add(objPerson1, Val1)
slPeople.Add(objPerson2, Val2)
slPeople.Add(objPerson3, Val3)

For Each objDE As DictionaryEntry _
        In slPeople
    Console.WriteLine("{0} {1}", _
    DirectCast(objDE.Key, Person).DisplayName, _
        DirectCast(objDE.Value, Integer))
Next
```

Interfaces should be used instead of inheritance when your intention is to indicate that a class provides some form of common functionality (such as the capability to be compared). The Person class from the previous examples has a purpose completely unrelated to its support for being compared, so that support is best indicated using an interface.

The .NET Framework provides a wide variety of interfaces, but you can also create your own in a manner similar to defining a new class. The definition of an interface starts with Public Interface <*interface name*>, ends with End Interface, and contains declarations for methods, properties, and events between the start and end. No code goes into an interface no matter what you are doing, so the method and property declarations consist of only the first line of a regular declaration. Listing 7.17 defines a simple interface, IDebugInfo, to provide some general information about the class for the purposes of debugging.

**LISTING 7.17**   Interfaces Look Like Empty Classes

```
Option Explicit On
Option Strict On

Public Interface IDebugInfo
    ReadOnly Property ClassName() As String
    ReadOnly Property Author() As String
    ReadOnly Property SourceFile() As String
    ReadOnly Property Description() As String
End Interface
```

Interfaces are similar in some ways to classes, but as you can see from Listing 7.17, quite different in others. Inside the Interface declaration, the members are defined with their declarations only, and no implementation code is provided. Scope also is not included as part of these declarations, but Public is the default when you implement this interface in one of your classes. Regardless of the scope you choose in your class, these members will be available through the IDebugInfo interface. In the case of this interface, these properties will be the same for each instance of a single class, and they are intended to describe that particular class. The nature of these properties allows for read-only values, but interfaces can include any form of property needed.

Interfaces and Inheritance both provide the capability to have many different objects share common attributes, but two key differences make them suitable for different roles. Interfaces do not include any implementation along with those attributes; the Interface definition contains no code, and the classes that implement that interface must provide all the functionality themselves. That is certainly an advantage of Inheritance, the sharing of implemented functionality from the base to the derived classes, but interfaces make up for that difference by greatly increased flexibility, allowing a single class to implement as many interfaces as desired.

In the end, the two technologies have some similarities, but they are intended for different purposes. Use interfaces when you want to indicate that a class has certain (often more than one) capabilities, equating to a relationship such as "myClass supports the IDebugInfo interface." Inheritance, on the other hand, indicates an "is a" relationship. Phrases such as "Customer is a Person" and "Employee is a Person" could describe the relationship between two derived classes and their base class.

## Initializing Objects with Constructors

When you want to use an object, you have to either work with an existing instance or create your own. Creating an object instance is done through the New keyword, which takes the specified class and establishes an area in memory for this instance of that class. *Constructors* are a way to provide information to the class at this creation time to allow it to initialize itself or perform other configuration tasks at this point. If a class has a constructor, and many of the .NET Framework classes do, you can usually supply parameters at creation time, as part of the call to New. The following code shows this working with the creation of a new exception object (see Chapter 4 for more information on exceptions and other error-handling topics), supplying an error message as a parameter to its constructor. This error message will be used automatically by the new object to populate one of its properties.

```
Dim ex As System.Exception
Dim message As String
message = "This will be the error message."
ex = New System.Exception(sMessage)
```

The creation of a constructor for the Vehicle class is relatively easy. You first have to create a method named New that is public and has no parameters.

```
Public Sub New()
End Sub
```

With this completed constructor (that doesn't do anything yet) in place, you will see little difference in your code, and until you add some functionality into this New() subroutine, nothing different happens. The constructor, even without parameters, can be used as a place to initialize internal variables, such as the Manufactured Date in the Vehicle class (see Listing 7.18).

**LISTING 7.18**   Using a Constructor to Initialize the Members of a Class

```
Public Sub New()
    m_Manufactured = System.Date.Today()
End Sub
```

Just like any other method of an object, it is possible to overload that method and provide more than one way to call it. As long as none of the overloaded versions uses the Overload keyword, that keyword can be skipped altogether when declaring these variations on the new procedure. In this case, you could quickly create a few useful constructors (shown in Listing 7.19) just by thinking of the different ways in which someone might want to initialize your object.

**LISTING 7.19**   Overloading a Class's Constructor to Provide Ways to Initialize Objects

```
Public Sub New()
    m_Manufactured = System.DateTime.Today()
End Sub

Public Sub New(ByVal newColor As String)
    m_Manufactured = System.DateTime.Today()
    m_Color = newColor
End Sub

Public Sub New(ByVal newColor As String, _
    ByVal dateManufactured As Date)
    m_Manufactured = dateManufactured
    m_Color = newColor
End Sub
```

In the case of a child class, one that inherits from another class, you might want to call the base class's constructor from your New procedure. You can accomplish this easily using the special object MyBase, using code such as MyBase.New().

If you are used to writing classes in Visual Basic 6.0, the constructor is very similar to the Class_Initialize event handler, but with the added capability to take parameters.

## Namespaces

A *namespace* is an abstract concept used to group a number of classes or modules together, allowing you to logically categorize all these objects within a single higher-level object. The .NET Framework makes extensive use of namespaces, allowing it to have the multi-level classifications of System, System.Data, and System.Data.SqlClient. Your code can include the same type of namespaces by wrapping your code in Namespace <*name*> and End Namespace statements. By having Namespace Chapter7 at the top of the classes and a corresponding End Namespace at the bottom, you effectively create a grouping called Chapter7 that contains all the classes within it. After this namespace exists, it is used by default for object references made in code within the same namespace, but can also be explicitly stated (Dim myCar as Chapter7.Car).

There are many reasons why you might want to create and use namespaces, not the least of which is the basis for the moniker "namespace," as a way to create a private area to ensure that your class names are unique. By defining a namespace, the class Car becomes Chapter7.Car, and therefore will no longer conflict with any other class created with the name Car.

Another, subtler, reason to use namespaces is because they produce easier code to maintain. The grouping of classes under higher-level namespaces leads to code that is clearly defined by some categorization scheme and is therefore more readable and easy to maintain.

For the examples throughout this book, you could have created namespaces based on the chapter (for instance, all the code from this chapter would be placed under the Chapter7 namespace), all of which could then be located under a book-wide namespace of KickstartVB. The classes could be created as simply Chapter7.Car, but to ensure no ambiguity, you could also refer to them as their fully qualified name (KickstartVB.Day7.Car, for instance).

This method of grouping classes is similar to the concept of variable scope; a class only has to be unique within its particular namespace. If you do happen to make a class that shares its name with a class that exists in another namespace, you will need to make sure that you are specifying the full name of the class whenever you reference it from outside its own namespace.

Namespaces are hierarchical, which allows you to create a multiple level scheme for grouping your classes and objects, just like within the .NET Framework itself. There are two ways to create a lower-level namespace: define the namespace using the fully qualified name (see Listing 7.20) or nest namespace definitions (see Listing 7.21).

**LISTING 7.20**   Declaring a Multipart Namespace

```
Namespace MyApp.Info
    Module Main
        Sub Main()
            Dim objHW As New MyApp.Info.Utilities
            objHW.DisplayData()
        End Sub
    End Module

    Public Class Utilities
        'Run the application
        Public Sub DisplayData()
            MsgBox(Environment.MachineName)
            MsgBox(Environment.SystemDirectory)
            MsgBox(Environment.GetLogicalDrives())
            MsgBox(Environment.Version.ToString())
        End Sub
    End Class
End Namespace
```

**LISTING 7.21**   Using Nested Namespaces to Create Object Hierarchies

```vb
Namespace MyApp
    Namespace Info
        Module Main
            Sub Main()
                Dim objHW As New MyApp.Info.Utilities
                objHW.DisplayData()
            End Sub
        End Module

        Public Class Utilities
            'Run the application
            Public Sub DisplayData()
                MsgBox(Environment.MachineName)
                MsgBox(Environment.SystemDirectory)
                MsgBox(Environment.GetLogicalDrives())
                MsgBox(Environment.Version.ToString())
            End Sub
        End Class
    End Namespace
End Namespace
```

Within your applications, you can use namespaces as a way to group conceptually related code together, but other than their effect on the scope of classes, namespaces are not really required for building a system.

## Shared Objects and Members

Earlier in this chapter, when the relationship between classes and objects was described, you learned that to use any method or property described in a class you would have to obtain or create an instance of that class. In general, this is the case; you cannot work directly with a class, only with instances of the class that you create. There is a way to expose certain functionality through the class itself, though, independently of any particular instance of that class. In Visual Basic 6.0, the Global keyword was used to make a class (or module) member available throughout an application, but Visual Basic .NET accomplishes a similar result through the use of the Shared keyword. Shared, like the other access descriptors you have seen (such as Public, Private, and Friend), denotes that part of a class is available without the creation of an instance. The .NET Framework uses this feature in its classes, such as the exposed property Today of the System.DateTime class. An example of defining and then using a Shared class member is shown in Listing 7.22.

**LISTING 7.22**  Shared Class Members Can Be Accessed Without Using an Instance of the Class in Question

```
Public Class DisplayInfo
    Shared Function GetUserName() As String
        Return System.Environment.UserDomainName & "\" _
            & System.Environment.UserName
    End Function
End Class

Public Class ClientApplication
    Public Sub DisplayUserName()
        MsgBox(DisplayInfo.GetUserName())
    End Sub
End Class
```

These Shared members can be created in your own code when you want a particular property or method to be accessible at all times without the overhead of object creation. In general, though, avoid using this unless you really require it because having many shared members is almost the same as simply creating a module full of procedures and reduces the meaning of your objects. Note that modules are a special type of class; all members of a module are considered Shared by default. My general guideline for determining whether a particular class member should be a Shared member or an instance member is based around the concept and existence of state. If the member is dependent on any form of state, such as an internal variable inside the class, it should be an instance member. Of course, this is just a simple guideline that I use and you are free to use Shared members however you want within your applications.

Note that in VB you can access Shared members of a class through any instance of the class, as well as through the class's name. This is different than other languages, such as C#, where only the class name can be used to access Shared (static in C#) members. Listing 7.23 illustrates this, showing that you can access a Shared function using either the class name or any instance of that class.

**LISTING 7.23**  In Visual Basic .NET, Shared Members Can Be Accessed Through the Class Name or Through an Instance of the Class

```
Public Class DisplayInfo
    Shared Function GetUserName() As String
        Return System.Environment.UserDomainName & "\" _
            & System.Environment.UserName
    End Function
End Class
```

**LISTING 7.23**   Continued

```
Public Class ClientApplication
    Public Sub DisplayUserName()
        'all three calls to GetUserName are
        'exactly the same
        MsgBox(DisplayInfo.GetUserName())
        Dim di As DisplayInfo
        MsgBox(di.GetUserName())
        Dim myDI As New DisplayInfo
        MsgBox(myDI.GetUserName)
    End Sub
End Class
```

Note that the two methods (accessing a shared member through an instance or through the type name) produce the same results but accessing through the instance can be confusing to many programmers.

# In Brief

This chapter presented the object-oriented programming (OOP) features in Visual Basic .NET, some of which are new and some of which have existed in Visual Basic 6.0 or earlier. Among the important points of the chapter were:

- Objects are everywhere in .NET; you will need to understand OOP concepts even if you are not making extensive use of them in your own code.

- Inheritance indicates relationships between entities in your systems and it can be used to save you from writing redundant code.

- Namespaces provide a useful way to avoid naming conflicts as well as organize your code.

- Shared members of classes can be accessed without creating an instance of the class in question.

# Building Custom Controls

## Control Development Changes in .NET

Developing your own user interface controls, or using custom controls you bought or pulled down off the Web, is at the very core of Visual Basic's success. For quite some time, it has been relatively easy to create a custom UI control and share it with other programmers, and the result is that a huge number of both commercial and free controls are available for use in your Visual Basic applications. The growth of this type of reusable component was given even more of a boost when Visual Basic 5.0 came out with the capability to create your own controls right inside Visual Basic. Suddenly, every Visual Basic developer had the tools necessary to build their own controls; this has become one of the most common ways to create reusable code.

Visual Basic .NET does not take away any of the control development features that were available in previous versions, but it adds quite a few more options due to the availability of inheritance. In the past, creating your own version of an existing control was a matter of placing that control onto a design surface, wrapping all of its properties and methods with your own code, and then adding whatever custom functionality you needed. Creating a new control that added a simple validation check to a text box required hundreds of lines of code just to wrap the existing set of functionality exposed by that control. The code you were really interested in, that adds the validation check, would likely end up being only a fraction of the total amount of work you had to do.

In Visual Basic .NET, that type of control development is still available (and still has its place, the "user control" model allows you to place more than one existing control onto the surface of your new control), but because of inheritance you can also add functionality simply by creating your own version of any existing control.

This chapter shows you how to extend the existing DateTimePicker through inheritance as well as creating a "traditional" user control. It also shows you how to create a control that handles all of its own drawing and how to create a control with no UI.

# Extending Through Inheritance

Inheriting from an existing control provides a new control with all of the functionality (methods, properties, and events) of the existing class without writing a single line of code. The only code you have to write is for the functionality you are adding; the base class provides everything else for you.

## Making a Simple Example

To create your own inherited control, start by adding a new class to an existing project, or by creating a "Class Library" project. Then, in the new class file, go through the following steps to build your very own custom text box that only allows numeric input.

First, you can save yourself a bunch of time by inheriting from System.Windows.Forms.Textbox. You do this by adding Inherits System.Windows.Forms.Textbox under the class name. Listing 8.1 illustrates how little code is required to create your own class that inherits from the existing TextBox.

LISTING 8.1    The Inherits Statement Is All You Need to Give Your New Control All of the Functionality of an Existing Windows Forms Control

```
Public Class NumericTextBox
    Inherits System.Windows.Forms.TextBox


End Class
```

Before that line will work, you might have to add a reference to System.Windows.Forms.dll into your project, otherwise the Inherits statement will have a red squiggle under it and your code will not compile.

If you were to stop right there, and not add a single line of additional code, you already have a completely functional text box. Although it would work, there is little point to creating a version that does not add anything beyond the base control. Instead, you will put a bit of code into the new class to ensure that it will only accept numeric values. There are a few ways you can handle this, but the simplest is to add some code into the KeyPress event on the control. You will not actually add an event handler though; you will override an internal method (called OnKeyPress) of the text box instead. The base class calls these internal methods whenever the corresponding external event will be raised, and they can be overridden in a derived control. Handling the KeyPress event would produce similar results, but event handlers are more "expensive" in terms of memory use and performance, so it is a better idea to override OnKeyPress.

Listing 8.2 shows the override, where you check the key pressed against all manner of values to determine whether it could be part of a number (or a special key like a backspace).

**LISTING 8.2** Overriding an On <event name> Procedure Is Better Coding Practice than Handling an Event Raised by Your Own Class

```
Protected Overrides Sub OnKeyPress( _
        ByVal e As KeyPressEventArgs)
    If Char.IsDigit(e.KeyChar) _
        OrElse e.KeyChar = ","c _
        OrElse e.KeyChar = "."c OrElse _
        Char.GetUnicodeCategory(e.KeyChar) _
            = Globalization.UnicodeCategory.Control OrElse _
        Char.GetUnicodeCategory(e.KeyChar) _
            = Globalization.UnicodeCategory.CurrencySymbol _
        OrElse Char.GetUnicodeCategory(e.KeyChar) _
            = Globalization.UnicodeCategory.Format Then
        e.Handled = False
    Else
        e.Handled = True
    End If
End Sub
```

To try out this new text box control, you need a test project. Add a new Windows Application project to the current solution and make it the start-up project (right-click the new project and choose Set as StartUp Project from the menu). Now, build the entire project so that you turn your new custom text box into a DLL on disk.

Once you've built the project, you can add your new text box to the Toolbox by right-clicking the toolbox and choosing Add/Remove Items. Browse to the newly created DLL from your control project (it should be in the /bin directory under the project that contains your new NumericTextBox class) and then select it (see Figure 8.1).

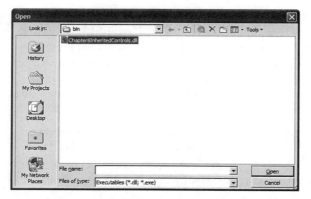

**Figure 8.1**    Use the Customize toolbox dialog box to add your new control.

Once you've added the control to your toolbox, you can open the design view of the Form in your new test project and drag your text box (from the toolbox) onto it. Run the solution (press F5) and you can try out your new numeric-only text box.

## Adding Support for DBNull to the Existing DateTimePicker

Visual Basic .NET includes a great control for selecting and viewing dates, the DateTimePicker (see Figure 8.2), but it has a big problem if you are planning to bind it to a column of a database table. It is possible, depending on the settings of your table, for a date-time field to have a value of NULL, instead of any form of the date. When you have bound a date column to a DateTimePicker control though, and you navigate to a record containing a null value, it will cause an error in the control and the binding will be lost (meaning that it will not display the correct value even if you navigate to a different record). Using the power of inheritance, you can create your own version of the DateTimePicker that does not have this problem. You need to add a new property that you can bind to instead of the existing Value property. This new property will be able to handle Null values and so binding will work just fine.

To create this new control, just go back to the same class file you were already using for NumericTextBox and add a new class declaration (the new control in this example is called NullableDateTimePicker). Add a new property (called NullableValue) and enter the code showing in Listing 8.3.

**LISTING 8.3**    Adding a New Property to an Existing Control Is a Great Example of the Benefit of Inheritance

```
Public Class NullableDateTimePicker
    Inherits System.Windows.Forms.DateTimePicker
    Public Property NullableValue() As Object
        Get
            If MyBase.Checked Then
                Return DBNull.Value
            Else
                Return MyBase.Value
            End If
        End Get
```

**LISTING 8.3** Continued

```
        Set(ByVal Value As Object)
            If IsDBNull(Value) Then
                MyBase.Checked = True
            Else
                MyBase.Value = CDate(Value)
            End If
        End Set
    End Property
End Class
```

This chapter does not go into the details of using this control, but the sample code for this chapter includes a form that demonstrates this control against a table with null date values.

# Combining Controls

Before Visual Basic .NET, the only type of control you could create in VB was a user control. When you created a new control, you ended up with an empty "design surface" just like a form. You placed controls (buttons, text boxes, and so on) onto that surface and the combined result could be used like a single control on other forms. An example is shown in Figure 8.2.

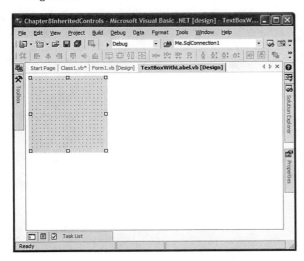

**Figure 8.2** User controls are similar in many ways to forms.

This form of control works well for some things, like combining a text box with a label for ease of arrangement, but it is difficult to use when all you want to do is wrap an existing control. The chapter already covered the concept of extending an existing control in the section entitled "Extending Through Inheritance," but user controls still exist in Visual Basic .NET and can be a great way to "pre-package" several controls for common situations. To create a new user control, add a new item to your existing project by right-clicking your project in the Solution Explorer and choosing Add User Control from the menu, or create a new Windows Control Library project. The example shown here adds a new class to the same project as the NumericTextBox and NullableDateTimePicker classes.

Regardless of how you create it, you will end up with a new user control open in the Designer. As an example, you will create a new control that combines a text box with a label because those two controls are often placed together. The control is called TextBoxWithLabel. Add a text box and label to your new control, and then change their names to itemCaption for the label and itemContents for the text box. Dock the label to the left side (set the Dock property to Left) and then dock the text box as Fill. This combination of dock settings will allow the relative width of the two controls to be modified just by changing the label width.

Now, unlike an inherited control, the user control does not automatically expose any of the properties of the two controls it contains. You will have to add properties and methods to the user control and then link them to the appropriate members of the label and text box (an example of which is shown in Listing 8.4). To use this control in your real applications, you would likely need to map a huge number of the internal control properties. For now, concern yourself with the label's text, the label's width, and the text box's text.

**LISTING 8.4**    At Least These Three Properties Will Need to Be Mapped from the Internal Controls

```
Public Property Contents() As String
    Get
        Return Me.itemContents.Text
    End Get
    Set(ByVal Value As String)
        Me.itemContents.Text = Value
    End Set
End Property


Public Property Caption() As String
    Get
        Return Me.itemCaption.Text
    End Get
    Set(ByVal Value As String)
        Me.itemCaption.Text = Value
    End Set
End Property


Public Property CaptionWidth() As Integer
    Get
        Return Me.itemCaption.Width
    End Get
    Set(ByVal Value As Integer)
        Me.itemCaption.Width = Value
    End Set
End Property
```

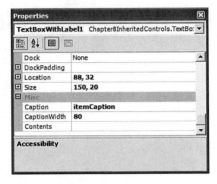

**Figure 8.3** If you don't specify a category for new properties, they will appear under Misc.

If you try this control on a test application, by building your control class and then adding it to the toolbox as you did with the NumericTextBox earlier in this chapter, these three new properties will be visible in the property window (see Figure 8.3).

These are all grouped under Misc, which is what happens when you don't specify a category for each property. By using an attribute, you can indicate that you want the two String properties placed under Appearance and the caption width grouped under Layout. There are several other useful attributes that can be applied to members of your controls, including the Bindable attribute (which indicates that the property is a common one for binding, even though all properties can be bound to). Listing 8.5 shows the same properties as in Listing 8.4, but with attributes for specifying the category and a Bindable attribute have been added to the Contents property.

**LISTING 8.5**  Attributes

```
<System.ComponentModel.Category("Appearance"), _
 System.ComponentModel.Bindable(True)> _
Public Property Contents() As String
    Get
        Return Me.itemContents.Text
    End Get
    Set(ByVal Value As String)
        Me.itemContents.Text = Value
    End Set
End Property

<System.ComponentModel.Category("Appearance")> _
Public Property Caption() As String
    Get
        Return Me.itemCaption.Text
    End Get
    Set(ByVal Value As String)
        Me.itemCaption.Text = Value
    End Set
End Property
```

**LISTING 8.5**  Continued

```
<System.ComponentModel.Category("Layout")> _
Public Property CaptionWidth() As Integer
    Get
        Return Me.itemCaption.Width
    End Get
    Set(ByVal Value As Integer)
        Me.itemCaption.Width = Value
    End Set
End Property
```

Always try to use the right type of control for the job. I often run into developers who want to just add a property to a text box, or perform some other simple type of extension to an existing control, but they started by creating a blank user control. At least 90% of their code is often unnecessary if they have followed this path, instead of just inheriting from the desired control in the first place. Whenever you come up with the need for a control, take the time to write out all of your requirements and to determine what type of control development is necessary.

# Drawing Your Own Interface

If you need to create an interface that is different from any of the controls you currently have access to, you can always turn to drawing your own interface. When developing business applications, the standard set of controls are usually sufficient. Sometimes though, doing your own graphics is the only way to get the results you want. Consider the following control; I wanted to draw a series of messages into a window (tip-of-the-day type of information) and have each new message slowly fade-in over the top of the previous one. I could have implemented this using a label that I slowly changed the ForeColor on, but I plan on adding images and other aspects to the message in the future, so drawing my own control gives me the most flexibility.

To get started on any custom drawn control, create a new class that inherits from System.Windows.Forms.Control, and then override OnPaint to add your own graphics code. There's a bit more code needed in order to track the current message and to track the current stage in the animation. The result is a message block that fades in and fades out as it moves through a list of messages to display. Listing 8.6 shows the OnPaint routine where the drawing occurs. This routine handles drawing each phase of the animation from stop to go.

**LISTING 8.6**   Writing Your Own OnPaint Routine Is the Key to Drawing Your Own Control

```
Public Enum AnimationStage
    fadingIn
    stayingPut
    fadingOut
End Enum

Public Class MessageDisplayer
    Inherits System.Windows.Forms.Control
Const ANIMATION_STEPS As Integer = 10
Dim currentStage As AnimationStage _
    = AnimationStage.fadingIn
Dim m_Messages As String() _
    = {"No Messages", "No Really"}
Dim m_currentMessage As Integer = 0
Dim m_previousMessage As Integer = 0
Dim m_interval As Integer = 1
Dim m_currentStep As Integer = 0
Dim WithEvents m_timer As Timer

Private Sub m_timer_Tick( _
        ByVal sender As Object, _
        ByVal e As System.EventArgs) _
        Handles m_timer.Tick
    If Me.m_currentStep < Me.ANIMATION_STEPS Then
        Me.m_currentStep += 1
        Me.Invalidate()
    Else
        Me.m_currentStep = 0
        Select Case Me.currentStage
            Case AnimationStage.fadingIn
                Me.currentStage = AnimationStage.stayingPut

            Case AnimationStage.fadingOut
                If Me.m_currentMessage < _
                        Me.m_Messages.Length - 1 Then
                    Me.m_currentMessage += 1
                Else
                    Me.m_currentMessage = 0
                End If
                Me.currentStage = AnimationStage.fadingIn
```

**LISTING 8.6**  Continued

```
            Case AnimationStage.stayingPut
                Me.currentStage = AnimationStage.fadingOut
        End Select
        Me.Invalidate()
    End If
End Sub


Protected Overrides Sub OnPaint( _
        ByVal e As PaintEventArgs)

    Dim alpha As Integer
    Select Case Me.currentStage

        Case AnimationStage.stayingPut
            e.Graphics.Clear(Me.BackColor)
            alpha = 255

        Case AnimationStage.fadingIn
            e.Graphics.Clear(Me.BackColor)
            alpha = (256 \ ANIMATION_STEPS) _
                        * Me.m_currentStep

        Case AnimationStage.fadingOut
            e.Graphics.Clear(Me.BackColor)
            alpha = 255 - ((256 \ ANIMATION_STEPS) _
                        * Me.m_currentStep)

    End Select
    Debug.WriteLine(alpha)

    Dim fColor As Color _
        = Color.FromArgb(alpha, Me.ForeColor)
    Dim message As String = Me.m_Messages( _
        m_currentMessage)
    Dim layoutRect As Drawing.RectangleF
    layoutRect = New Drawing.RectangleF( _
        0, 0, Me.Width, Me.Height)
    layoutRect.Inflate(-10, -10)
    Dim messageBrush As Brush _
```

**LISTING 8.6**   Continued

```
    = New SolidBrush(fColor)

Dim myFormat As New _
    StringFormat(StringFormatFlags.LineLimit)
myFormat.Trimming = _
    StringTrimming.EllipsisWord
myFormat.Alignment = _
    StringAlignment.Center

e.Graphics.SmoothingMode = _
    Drawing2D.SmoothingMode.AntiAlias
e.Graphics.DrawString( _
    message, Me.Font, _
    messageBrush, layoutRect, myFormat)
End Sub
End Class
```

To reduce flicker when handling your own graphics, there are some useful control level settings you can configure. The first three settings (shown in Listing 8.7) produce the least amount of flicker possible. Because this text is being wrapped and sized to fit the available space, it will need to be redrawn whenever the size of the control changes, which is handled by the fourth setting ResizeRedraw.

**LISTING 8.7**   These Control-Level Settings Can Help to Prevent Flicker and to Ensure that the Control Redraws as Needed

```
Public Sub New()
    Me.SetStyle(ControlStyles.AllPaintingInWmPaint, True)
    Me.SetStyle(ControlStyles.UserPaint, True)
    Me.SetStyle(ControlStyles.DoubleBuffer, True)

    Me.SetStyle(ControlStyles.ResizeRedraw, True)
    SetupTimer()
End Sub
```

The call to SetupTimer in Listing 8.7 is one of the many small details of this sample code that is not shown in the in-book listings. Download this chapter's code to see the full set of code for this and all the other controls covered here.

# Creating Non-Visual Controls

In Visual Basic 6.0, some controls (such as Timer) were non-visual, meaning they had no user-interface aspect. Although these controls were placed directly onto the form, just like any other control, they were only visible at design time. In Visual Basic .NET, non-visual controls are still common (the Timer is still around, for example), but they are referred to as components. Instead of going directly onto the form, they sit in a special area (commonly known as the *component tray*) below the main design window (see Figure 8.4).

**Figure 8.4**    Non-visual controls, or components, appear in their own special area of the Windows Forms designer.

To create a non-visual control yourself, you need to inherit from System.ComponentModel.Component, as shown in Listing 8.8.

By inheriting from Component, your class has gained all the code necessary to be added to the toolbox and dragged out onto any design surface. Even if you are creating a regular class library without any user-interface aspects, marking classes as Components provides the user of your code with an easy drag-and-drop experience. As a sample of a non-visual component, let's walk through creating a component that will perform a few simple Web-related tasks. This component will:

- Retrieve the HTML text of a Web page

- Return the current IP address of your machine

- Watch a specified Web URL and let you know if it becomes unavailable

**LISTING 8.8**    Inheriting from Component Allows Your New Class to Be Dragged onto a Design Surface as a Non-Visual Control

```
Public Class nonvisual
    Inherits System.ComponentModel.Component
End Class
```

That is quite a range of functions, but it will illustrate a few useful concepts, including raising events from a component, and it has the side-effect when interacting with the Web from your .NET programs. The most complicated of these functions is ensuring the URL is available, so let's discuss the other two first.

## Getting Your Current IP Address(es)

The DNS (Domain Name Service) turns the names into addresses, thus allowing you to type `http://msdn.microsoft.com` and have it resolve to the external IP Address of that server. Luckily, your local machine has a bit of DNS-related smarts too; you can use the `System.Net.Dns` class to determine the hostname as well as any associated IP addresses. Listing 8.9 shows the full code to retrieve a string array of the local machine's current addresses.

**LISTING 8.9**  The System.Net.Dns Class Makes it Easy to Retrieve IP Information About a Machine Using the Hostname

```
<DnsPermission( _
    Security.Permissions.SecurityAction.Demand)> _
Public Function MyIPAddresses() As String()
    Dim host As IPHostEntry = _
        Dns.GetHostByName(Dns.GetHostName())

    Dim ipList As IPAddress()
    ipList = host.AddressList

    Dim output As New ArrayList
    For Each ip As IPAddress In ipList
        output.Add(ip.ToString)
    Next
    Return output.ToArray(GetType(String))
End Function
```

The first thing you might notice about this listing is the `DnsPermission` attribute attached to the function declaration. This attribute forces a check of the entire code path that has led to this function call, and will raise an error if any part of that path lacks the permission to access DNS information. Similar checks have been added to the other methods of this component. For more details on permissions and other code security topics, check out my Web site for a set of related links (`http://www.duncanmackenzie.net/kickstartvb/chapter8`).

The rest of the code follows this path: you retrieve the local machine's hostname using `Dns.GetHostName()`, and then retrieve the `IPHostEntry` for that machine name using `Dns.GetHostByName`. Once you have the `IPHostEntry` (which represents the available DNS information on a specific host), retrieving the list of addresses is easy (`host.AddressList`). You simply have to convert the list into an array of strings for ease of use.

## Retrieving the Contents of a Web Page

Pulling back the HTML contents of a Web page might not be an everyday activity, but it does seem to come up often, so it is a useful bit of code to have around. Listing 8.10 shows one way you can code this function, but you can also use the HttpWebRequest and HttpWebResponse classes to pull back the information.

**LISTING 8.10**    The WebClient Class Makes Retrieving a Web Page Almost Too Easy

```
<WebPermission( _
    Security.Permissions.SecurityAction.Demand)> _
Public Function RetrieveHTML(ByVal URL As String) As String
    Dim wc As New WebClient
    Dim reader As New IO.StreamReader(wc.OpenRead(URL))
    Return reader.ReadToEnd
End Function
```

The OpenRead function of System.Net.WebClient opens a stream from which you can read the response. The ReadToEnd function of the new IO.StreamReader then grabs the contents of the server response and stuffs it into a string.

## Monitoring a URL

As mentioned earlier, monitoring the availability of a specific URL was the most complicated of the three functions of this component, so it requires a relatively lengthy explanation.

Checking the URL itself is the first issue; how do you determine whether a URL is available? The network utility PING comes to mind, but PING verifies that you can get a response from a specified IP address, not a URL. It is possible to have a server that is responding to a ping, but isn't functioning in some other way, and conversely it is possible to have a perfectly functioning Web site that won't respond to a ping at all (try pinging www.microsoft.com for example).

If you can't use ping, the alternative is to try to retrieve the URL using the HTTP protocol. Both the System.Net.WebClient and System.Net.HttpWebRequest classes are capable of making a request against a URL, but HttpWebRequest is used here because it allows you to specify the method of the request. In HTTP, the method indicates what type of request you are sending to the Web server and must be one of GET, HEAD, POST, PUT, DELETE, TRACE, or OPTIONS. GET is the default and indicates that you want to retrieve the specified resource, but this example uses HEAD for the sake of efficiency. Specifying HEAD indicates that all you want back are the headers, which are sufficient to determine the availability of a Web page, and might mean less data transferred than retrieving the entire resource. Even once you have the headers back, there is still the matter of determining which response indicates that the resource is "available." Should you say that a resource is available if you get back a 404 (not found) status code? Should only a 200 (OK) code count? In the HTTP protocol, all of the various status codes in the 200's are some form of successful response, so this example takes any of those values as indication that the URL was available. A private CheckURL function (shown in Listing 8.11) handles making the request and interpreting the results.

**LISTING 8.11**    Any Exception in the CheckURL Function Is Taken to Mean that the URL Is not Available

```
<WebPermission( _
    Security.Permissions.SecurityAction.Demand)> _
Private Sub CheckURL(ByVal url As String)
    Dim e As New WatchedURLEventArgs
    e.URLBeingWatched = url
    Me.m_lastCheck = Now
    e.CheckedTime = Me.m_lastCheck

    Try
        Dim wr As WebRequest = WebRequest.Create(url)
        If TypeOf wr Is HttpWebRequest Then
            Dim httpWR As HttpWebRequest
            httpWR = DirectCast(wr, HttpWebRequest)
            httpWR.Method = "HEAD"
            httpWR.AllowAutoRedirect = False
            Dim wResponse As WebResponse
            wResponse = httpWR.GetResponse()
            If TypeOf wResponse Is HttpWebResponse Then
                Dim httpResponse As HttpWebResponse
                httpResponse = DirectCast( _
                    wResponse, HttpWebResponse)
                Dim response As Integer
                response = CInt(httpResponse.StatusCode)
                Me.m_lastResponse = _
                    httpResponse.StatusDescription

                e.Status = response
                e.StatusDescription = Me.lastResponse

                If response >= 200 And response < 300 Then
                    e.URLAvailable = True
                    Me.m_WatchedURLAvailable = True
                Else
                    Me.m_WatchedURLAvailable = False
```

## LISTING 8.11    Continued

```
                e.URLAvailable = False
            End If
        Else
            Me.m_WatchedURLAvailable = False
            Me.m_lastResponse = "Check Failed"

            e.Status = 0
            e.StatusDescription = Me.lastResponse
        End If
    Else
        Me.m_WatchedURLAvailable = False
        Me.m_lastResponse = "Invalid URL Type"

        e.Status = 0
        e.StatusDescription = Me.lastResponse
    End If
Catch ex As Exception
    Me.m_WatchedURLAvailable = False
    Me.m_lastResponse = _
        "Error Checking: " & ex.Message

    e.Status = 0
    e.StatusDescription = Me.lastResponse
Finally
    Me.OnWatchedURLChecked(e)
    RaiseEvent WatchedURLChecked(Me, e)
    If Not Me.WatchedURLAvailable Then
        Me.OnWatchedURLUnavailable(e)
        RaiseEvent WatchedURLUnavailable(Me, e)
    End If
End Try
End Sub
```

Regardless of the availability of the resource, you must raise the WatchedURLChecked event and call the internal routine OnWatchedURLChecked. If you determine that the resource is not available, you raise the WatchedURLUnavailable event and call the corresponding internal routine. For both events, you populate an instance of the WatchedURLEventArgs class to send the status information along with the event.

Now that the code to check whether a URL is available is in place, you still have to know when to call it. The example creates an instance of a Timer class, which is set up to fire an event every second when it is active. At those one-second intervals (see Listing 8.12), the code checks to see whether the total number of seconds since the last check of the URL has exceeded the desired interval and, if so, performs the check of the URL.

**LISTING 8.12**   The Timer Stops During the Elapsed Event Handler So That the Next Event Won't Fire Before the First One Has Completed

```
Private Sub m_internalTimer_Elapsed( _
    ByVal sender As Object, _
    ByVal e As System.Timers.ElapsedEventArgs) _
    Handles m_internalTimer.Elapsed
    Me.m_internalTimer.Stop()
    If Now.Subtract(Me.m_lastCheck).TotalSeconds _
            >= Me.m_SecondsBetweenCheck Then
        If (Not Me.m_WatchedURL Is Nothing) _
            AndAlso (Not Me.m_WatchedURL = String.Empty) Then
            CheckURL(Me.m_WatchedURL)
        End If
    End If
    Me.m_internalTimer.Start()
End Sub
```

Overall, a fair bit of code, but if you download the code sample for this chapter, you will find it easier to understand when it is open inside Visual Studio.

# In Brief

This chapter has quickly covered the complicated world of control development in .NET. Among the important points of the chapter were:

- Inheritance provides a quicker and easier way to add functionality to an existing control.

- User controls are still available and useful in Visual Basic .NET.

- Drawing your own control is easy to get started with, and very hard to get right.

- Non-visual controls can also be created and used in your applications, extending the world of control development outside of the proposed UI.

# Integrating with COM

## COM and .NET Interoperability

Regardless of what people may say, the Component Object Model (COM) is not dead. Let's face it; we've been developing COM objects with previous versions of Microsoft Visual Basic for too long to just throw away these painful and valuable investments. In previous versions of Visual Basic, developers relied on COM to segment their applications into physical chunks. More importantly, Visual Basic applications could consume the many COM objects provided by other applications and vendors. This allowed developers to assemble solutions from reusable components. A good example of this is the use of Visual Basic to automate Microsoft Excel through the COM interfaces provided by Excel. In the big picture, COM definitely has its place in application development. COM does have its shortcomings, some of which can lead to "DLL hell!"

COM evolved from the ashes of OLE 1.0 and ActiveX into a technology that allowed applications blocks (EXEs and DLLs) to communicate with each other regardless of their implementation through a structured set of interfaces. COM is a binary-compatible way of reusing code as opposed to source-compatible, meaning that a COM object is a COM object regardless of the language or tool that was used to create it. COM works on the premise that applications that consume COM objects don't need to know anything about the implementation of the object except for its interface, that is, the exact way the object exposes its properties and methods. These interfaces act as contracts between the COM object and those who want to consume it. In essence, the COM object states: "These are my methods and properties and this is how you can use them." Consumers of this interface rely on this contract and it must always hold true. If the COM object changes the way it exposes its methods and properties, existing client applications would break.

COM relies heavily on the operating system and the system Registry for tracking and defining COM objects. Every COM object (and its interfaces) is registered in the system Registry. In fact, all classes that are exposed as a COM object must have their own unique identifier, called a CLSID. This CLSID uniquely identifies the object to the operating system. The operating system not only helps to represent COM objects but also plays a fairly significant role in instantiation of COM objects. The system Registry will store additional information about the COM class such as the location and name of the binary file that implements the class, the type of class (in-process or out-of-process), versions, and in some cases a Programmatic Identifier (ProgID). When a program wants to use a COM class, it provides the operating system with either the CLSID or ProgID of the COM class. The operating system is responsible for locating its implementation and allowing the calling application to use the methods and properties provided by COM class.

## SOME DEFINITIONS FROM THE COM WORLD

A CLSID is a Globally Unique Identifier (GUID). It looks similar to `{00000514-0000-0010-8000-00AA006D2EA4}`, which happens to represent the `ADODB.Connection` class that is implemented in `C:\Program Files\Common Files\System\ado\msado15.dll`.

## IN-PROCESS COM CLASSES

In-process COM classes are implemented as DLLs. They are called in-process because at runtime all DLLs map into the caller's process space. Out-of-process COM classes are implemented as EXEs that execute in their own process space.

Despite the good things that COM provides, its implementation causes some problems in the real world. First, as I just stated, every COM class needs to be registered with the system Registry. This means that when deploying COM components, you must also register the COM classes in the system Registry using utilities like regsvr32.exe or with custom installation packages. Additionally, COM made it virtually impossible to have two different versions of the same COM class in different locations active at the same time. The system Registry allows only one location to be specified for every CLSID and only a single CLSID can be specified for every ProgID. Also, in some occasions the replacement of COM classes with newer versions break applications that relied on the previous version. In essence, the contracts that COM interfaces establish between the client application and the COM classes are relatively easy to break. For this reason, you might have heard the term "DLL hell" in reference to distribution issues associated with COM classes.

Again, however, COM isn't just going to go away with .NET—well, not right away. In fact, integration between .NET applications and COM is essential for the immediate future. For example, Microsoft Office still only exposes COM interfaces, so if you require any form of Microsoft Office automation, such as using Excel for calculations, analysis, and graphing, you need to be able to call, instantiate, and execute these COM objects from your Visual Basic. NET applications. Additionally, the opposite scenario might exist where you want COM clients to call your managed applications. Either case demonstrates the importance of finding some way of communicating between the COM and .NET worlds.

# Important COM Interop Concepts

Conceptually, developers have two problems to solve. First, they must be able to consume COM objects in their applications, including their Active-X custom controls. Second, they must be able to allow unmanaged COM clients to use the managed .NET objects. Although these steps do not sound all that complicated, it turns out that the COM and .NET worlds are quite different; in order for them to communication with one another, there needs to be some sort of interoperability layer between them. *Wrapper* is the common term to describe these interop layers. The communication process between the .NET runtime and COM is commonly referred to as *COM Interop*.

In COM Interop, there are two types of wrappers that you need to deal with—a Runtime Callable Wrapper (RCW) and a COM Callable Wrapper (CCW). The RCW is a wrapper that is callable from the .NET runtime. In essence, the RCW allows applications built on the .NET Framework to consume COM objects. The second type of wrapper, the CCW, enables classes built on the .NET Framework to be available to COM clients through a traditional COM interface. Figure 9.1 shows where these wrappers exist architecturally.

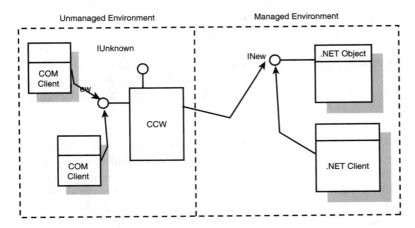

**FIGURE 9.1** Runtime Callable Wrappers and COM Callable Wrappers are the heart of COM Interop, allowing managed and unmanaged applications to seamlessly co-exist.

It helps to review a few definitions before digging into the work of the Runtime Callable Wrapper; remember that applications and components that are built on top of the .NET runtime are commonly called *managed applications*, whereas all other applications (including anything built with Visual Basic 6.0) are referred to as *unmanaged*. The job of the RCW is to act as a proxy between managed and unmanaged classes by continually marshalling calls between the two environments. The runtime will use one copy of the RCW for every COM object your .NET classes invoke and is responsible for the actual COM object invocation, adding and releasing COM reference counters as required. When your application creates the RCW, it in turn instantiates the appropriate COM object that it manages. When your application releases the RCW, it will decrease the reference count of the COM object. The COM object will be destroyed once its reference count is equal to zero, signaling that no other application is using it.

The RCW, on the other hand, is managed. This means that even though your COM object may have been physically destroyed, the RCW is subject to garbage collection and can hang around until such a time when it's cleaned up.

COM Callable Wrappers (CCW) allow unmanaged code to call managed code through a COM interface. In essence, CCWs allow you to expose a COM interface for your .NET object, thus providing a proxy between the COM client and your .NET object. The runtime automatically creates one CCW for exactly one managed object regardless of the number of COM clients that request it. The CCW, in turn, holds a single reference to the managed object that implements the interface and is garbage collected. This will allow COM and .NET clients to make requests on the same managed object simultaneously.

CCWs act like traditional COM objects in many important ways:

- CCWs are reference-counted like other COM objects, which means they release their references whenever the last client stops using them.

- CCWs also have CLSIDs and IIDs just like traditional COM objects.

- CCWs, like most COM objects and not like RCWs, are not managed in the same manner as most code you will create from Visual Basic .NET. In order for other COM clients to consume CCWs, these wrapper objects must be created from a non-collected heap and are not subject to garbage collection.

CCWs and RCWs don't quite solve the problem of COM Interop, however. There is still a little problem with data types. One of the great things about applications built on .NET is that they share a common set of data types regardless of the programming language used. For example, the definition of an integer is the same everywhere in the managed environment. This breaks down many barriers when it comes to interacting with other managed objects. In most cases, COM parameters and return values share common data type representations with the managed environment. However, in some cases, COM can present types that are either ambiguous or do not have any equivalent in the managed environment. Because of this, you need something that will help ensure type translations between the COM and .NET applications. The process of packaging parameters and return values into equivalent data types as they move to and from COM objects is called *interop marshalling* and is no small problem.

The .NET Framework and Visual Studio .NET provide you with a lot of support when it comes to COM Interop. In fact, much of what's described here is implicit in many cases, allowing you to focus on your application's functionality and not on the details of COM Interop. The rest of this chapter shows you how to create RCWs and CCWs and discusses some important considerations for someone about to use COM Interop in their application.

# Accessing COM Objects from Visual Basic .NET

By far, one of the most common and important forms of COM interop is the consumption of COM objects from inside of managed applications. Runtime Callable Wrappers enable such consumption. The following sections describe how to create and consume Runtime Callable Wrappers from your managed applications.

## Creating a Runtime Callable Wrapper Automatically

In order to access COM objects from managed code, you need to have a Runtime Callable Wrapper. You can obtain RCWs for COM objects in two ways. The first is to create them yourself, and the second is to use the vendor's PIAs (Primary Interoperability Assemblies). In this section, you will see how you can create RCWs for virtually any COM object, leaving a discussion on PIAs for later in this chapter.

You might expect that Microsoft would make it easy to reference COM objects from your .NET applications and, in fact, they have. There are two ways for you to create an RCW—using the command-line utility TBLImp or automatically using Visual Studio .NET. Let's start with using Visual Studio .NET, the more traditional method. Perform the following steps to refer to the Microsoft CDO 1.21 library:

1. Create or open a VB.NET project.

2. Select Add Reference from the Project menu in Visual Studio.NET to display the Add References dialog box.

3. Click the COM tab of the Add Reference dialog box.

4. Select Microsoft CDO 1.21 Library from the list of registered COM objects and click the Select button, and then click OK.

If you are familiar with adding COM references in Visual Basic 6.0, you should see that this process is virtually identical. After performing the previous steps, you will see a new entry under the References section of your project named MAPI, which refers to the name of the COM object you just made a reference to.

## MAILING FROM .NET

CDO stands for Collaborative Data Objects. This library allows you to access data programmatically on any MAPI-compliant provider such as Microsoft Exchange. In fact, CDO is a COM wrapper around Microsoft's Messaging API called MAPI. You can use CDO to access and send email, examine the contents of folders, and refer to the Exchange Address Book. In general, if your users are using a Microsoft email solution, CDO is a fairly simple way to send mail and interact with your mail server.

If you can't count on CDO being installed and working on a user's machine, your next best bet is to use the basic SMTP protocols. Sending email through SMTP is even provided in the .NET Framework through the `System.Web.Mail` namespace. The Framework email code requires CDOSYS (a scaled down, SMTP-based set of messaging code similar to CDO), which must be installed for the `System.Web.Mail` code to work.

If you are looking for a dependency free method for sending email messages, don't despair! There are many good samples of sending SMTP email messages using just the networking classes in the .NET Framework, and links to several are provided on the Chapter 9 section of `http://www.duncanmackenzie.net/kickstartvb`.

Let's take a closer look at what Visual Studio .NET just did for you. The COM DLL that you referred to is normally installed in `C:\Program Files\Common Files\System\MSMAPI\1033\CDO.dll` on most systems. As stated, Visual Studio needed to bridge the gap between the CDO COM object and your .NET application. To do this, it automatically created an RCW for you to consume from your Visual Studio project. Right-click and view the properties of the MAPI in the References section of your project. The first thing that you should notice is that the Copy Local property is set to TRUE. Note also that the path listed for the selected COM reference is pointing to a DLL in your project's OBJ directory called Interop.CDO.DLL, which isn't the COM library just referenced. It's instead the Runtime Callable Wrapper that Visual Studio automatically created for you. The Copy Local property simply instructs Visual Studio to copy the new RCW into a local directory. When you want to work with CDO from Visual Studio .NET, you will actually be working directly with the RCW, and the wrapper in turn is responsible for the instantiation and ongoing communication with the underlying CDO COM library. It is important to note that if you are to distribute your application to other computers, you must also ship the wrapper that Visual Studio .NET created for you.

Listing 9.1 demonstrates some code that will consume the CDO object through the RCW.

**LISTING 9.1**  Declare and Use the RCW Just as You Would the COM Object Directly

```vb
Dim oMAPISession As New MAPI.Session
Try
    oMAPISession.Logon()
    MessageBox.Show("Logon Successful for " _
        & oMAPISession.CurrentUser, _
        "Logon Result")
Catch
    MessageBox.Show("Logon Failed", "Logon Results")
End Try
```

For readers familiar with the programming of CDO from Visual Basic 6.0, much of the code in Listing 9.1 should be familiar if not identical to what you are used to. Notice that the code calls the RCW as if you were calling the COM object directly, because the RCW proxies all of your calls to the specific COM object it was built to wrap. As you can see on the first line, you instantiate the RCW in the same way you do the COM object. Calling methods of your RCW is identical to calling the methods of the CDO object as you can see in the calls to Logon and CurrentUser. In fact, you can also use the Object Browser in Visual Studio .NET to view the classes and interfaces automatically created for you in the RCW that map to COM interfaces, methods, and properties of the COM object it wraps, as depicted in Figure 9.2. You can now use the COM object as if you were calling it directly from your code.

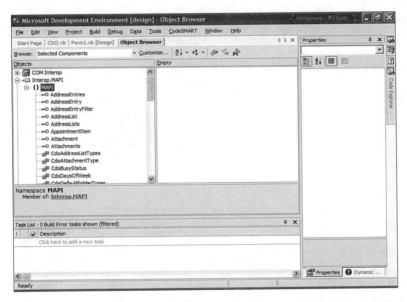

**FIGURE 9.2**    Use the Object Browser to view the properties, methods, and events of the RCW that wraps an underlying COM object.

## Creating a Runtime Callable Wrapper with TLBImp

You just used Visual Studio .NET to do all the dirty work to create an RCW. However, what happens if the underlying COM object changes its CLSID (Class ID) or adds new interfaces? The short answer is that the wrapper will break. It knows about your COM object by its CLSID; the CLSID determines where the COM object is physically located and how it can be used.

*SHOP TALK*

**KEEPING IT COMPATIBLE**

As a long-time Visual Basic developer, and therefore a long-time COM developer, talking about the Class ID (CLSID) of a component brings up a lot of frustrating memories. A COM object is defined by its interfaces, which are represented in a structure called a COM type library. Type libraries can either be included with the binary of the object or stored in a separate file with a .TLB extension. CLSIDs and IIDs are GUIDs (128-bit values, designed to be unique across all systems) that help to uniquely identify a COM object and the interfaces that it exposes. When a type library is created, a CLSID is created for that library, which is how other applications reference your library (using early binding). If, at some point in the future, you change the Class ID of your library, any application that was referencing your component will break. You can help prevent this in Visual Basic 6.0 by configuring your projects to be Binary Compatible. This setting forces Visual Basic to reuse the CLSID of an existing reference library (usually an earlier version of your own code) reference object that you can choose. There are other techniques to reduce the impact of changing an already referenced COM library, but this is more of a Visual Basic 6.0 and COM topic. I am bringing this topic up here, in a Visual Basic .NET book, for two reasons. The first reason is to make you appreciate that many of these issues (such as registering type libraries on the user's machine) go away when you are dealing with managed code. The second reason is to ensure that you keep these COM issues in mind when adding COM references to your .NET code; the Runtime Callable Wrapper is performing early binding and is just as susceptible to its target COM library changing its CLSID.

The quick and dirty answer to this problem is to regenerate the RCW. In order to do this using Visual Studio .NET, you need to delete the existing RCW on the file system, and re-add the reference to the COM object. If you find yourself doing this often, you might want to use the command-line utility called TLBImp.exe, which ships with the .NET Framework. The TLBimp.exe utility creates RCWs for most COM objects in the same way that Visual Studio did for you automatically. It does this by reading meta information stored about the COM object from a type library. Type libraries can be stored in a separate file (a .TLB file), or can be embedded directly into the COM object binary.

```
Tlbimp.exe CDO.dll
```

Using TLBImp to create RCWs is straightforward. The command line shown previously generates an RCW DLL with the same name as the type library found in CDO.dll (as opposed to the name of the physical filename) with a .DLL extension. In this case, TLBImp will create a new assembly called MAPI.DLL in the same directory as CDO.DLL. You can now move this assembly to a location in your project directory where you can reference it directly from your project. This time, however, when you are setting up the references you must refer to it like a normal .NET assembly instead of a COM object as you did when you made a reference to the CDO.DLL COM library directly. Perform the following steps to refer to RCW that you generated with TLBImp.exe in your project:

1. Copy the MAPI.DLL assembly to some location in your project, such as the bin directory from the location it was created in. Optionally, you can use the /Out command-line parameter of TLBImp to specify the location of the resulting RCW. Refer to Table 9.1, which contains the common command-line parameters, for more information.

2. Add a new reference to your project by choosing Add Reference from the Project menu in Visual Studio .NET.

3. From the Add References dialog box, select Browse to choose the RCW that you just placed in the project directory.

4. Select the MAPI.DLL file from the location you placed it in step 1, and then click OK.

As you would expect, using TLBImp.exe from the command line to create your RCWs does give you more options than having Visual Studio create them for you. For example, you can use some of the following command-line switches in Table 9.1 to customize how you can generate an RCW.

**TABLE 9.1**

**Command-Line Options for TLBImp.exe**

| COMMAND-LINE SWITCH | DESCRIPTION |
| --- | --- |
| /asmversion:*versionNumber* | Allows you to specify the version number of the assembly to produce using the format *major.minor.build.revision*. |
| /help or /? | Displays command syntax and options for TLBImp. |
| /keyfile:*filename* | Signs the resulting assembly with a strong name using the publisher's official public/private keypair found in *filename*. |
| /namespace:namespace | Specifies the namespace in which to produce the assembly. |
| /out:filename | Specifies the name of the output file, assembly, and namespace in which to write the metadata definitions. |
| /primary | Produces a primary interop assembly for the specified type library. Additional information is added to this assembly detailing the publisher of the type library produced the assembly. You should use the /primary option only if you are the publisher of the type library that you are importing with Tlbimp.exe. Note that you must also sign a primary interop assembly with a strong name. |
| /silent | Suppresses the display of success messages. |
| /strictref | Does not import a type library if the tool cannot resolve all references within the current assembly or the assemblies specified with the /reference option. |
| /verbose | Specifies verbose mode; displays additional information about the imported type library. |

In fact, using TLBImpl.exe is extremely useful if you want to produce your own primary interop assemblies or RCWs that have a strong name such that they can be placed in the Global Assembly Cache (GAC).

# Inheriting from COM Objects

Once you have successfully created your RCW, you can use it almost exactly as you do other classes. In fact, you can even create classes that inherit from a COM object's RCW. Perform the following steps to create a class that inherits from the CDO object you just wrapped:

1. Add a new class to your project by selecting the Project menu and selecting Add Class. Name the file CDO.vb and click Open.

2. Instruct your new class to inherit from the MAPI.Session class, which is denied by the CDO COM object and wrapped through the RCW, as shown in Listing 9.2.

**LISTING 9.2**   Writing Code that Inherits from a COM Object

```
Public Class CDO
    Inherits MAPI.SessionClass


End Class
```

Once you have inherited the class, you can begin by providing implementations for the public functions you can override. To view these methods, choose (Overrides) from the left code window drop-down box. Then use the right code window drop-down box to view the methods that can be overridden. For example, Listing 9.3 demonstrates how you can override the CDO Logon method with custom code that will first require confirmation to continue the logon operation from the users.

**LISTING 9.3**   Provide an Implementation for the Overridden Logon Method

```
Public Overrides Function Logon( _
        Optional ByVal ProfileName As Object = Nothing, _
    Optional ByVal ProfilePassword As Object = Nothing, _
    Optional ByVal ShowDialog As Object = Nothing, _
    Optional ByVal NewSession As Object = Nothing, _
    Optional ByVal ParentWindow As Object = Nothing, _
    Optional ByVal NoMail As Object = Nothing, _
    Optional ByVal ProfileInfo As Object = Nothing) As Object

    Dim result As DialogResult _
            = MessageBox.Show("Are you sure you want to logon?", _
                "Please Confirm", _
                MessageBoxButtons.YesNo, _
                MessageBoxIcon.Question, _
                MessageBoxDefaultButton.Button1)
```

**LISTING 9.3**   Continued

```
    If result = vbYes Then
        Try
            MyBase.Logon()
            MessageBox.Show("Successful Logon", _
                "Success", _
                MessageBoxButtons.OK, _
                MessageBoxIcon.Information)
        Catch
            MessageBox.Show("Logon Failed", _
                "Error", _
                MessageBoxButtons.OK, _
                MessageBoxIcon.Asterisk, _
                MessageBoxDefaultButton.Button1)
        End Try
    End If

End Function
```

Note that when you create classes that inherit from your COM object, it works like implementing an interface; you must provide complete implementation for all methods of the COM object.

## Capturing COM Events

It's important to know that the RCW that you created will also propagate events generated by the underlying COM object, provided you want to receive them. Capture COM events as you would events from other classes using WithEvents in the declaration and Handles for the event handler. As an example, Listing 9.4 demonstrates how to catch the NewMail event from Microsoft Outlook.

**LISTING 9.4**   You Handle a COM-Generated Event as You Would Any Other Event

```
Public Class Form1
    Inherits System.Windows.Forms.Form
...
    Private WithEvents oOutlook As New Outlook.Application

    Private Sub oOutlook_NewMail() Handles oOutlook.NewMail
➥       MessageBox.Show("You have new mail")
    End Sub
End Class
```

## COM Interop Late Binding

All of the examples given so far have demonstrated how to use a COM object through early binding. That is, at compile time you already know the type of the object you are calling. In many cases, you might not have that luxury and must use late binding. Late binding forces your applications to wait until runtime to determine the type of object called. Listings 9.5 and 9.6 demonstrate how to perform late binding in both Visual Basic 6.0 and Visual Basic .NET. As you can see, the code is virtually identical.

**LISTING 9.5**   Visual Basic 6.0 Code for Late Binding

```
Dim oMAPI as Object Set oMAPI = CreateObject("MAPI.Session") oMAPI.Logon
```

For those of you who might be confused about language choice, should you use C# or Visual Basic .NET, I consider late binding to be a clear example of how Visual Basic .NET's heritage works in your favor. As an existing Visual Basic/COM developer, interoperability with COM objects will be a major part of your development tasks, and Visual Basic .NET makes interoperability easier than it is in C#. The simplicity of late binding is one such example, and the other example would be the difference between C# and Visual Basic .NET in their support for calling COM functions with optional parameters. In Visual Basic .NET, you can just omit optional parameters when you are calling a procedure, without any special code required. In general, if you have to work with a great deal of legacy Visual Basic code or other COM objects, you will find it easier to do this work in Visual Basic .NET.

**LISTING 9.6**   Visual Basic .NET Code for Late Binding Dim

```
oMAPI as Object oMAPI = CreateObject("MAPI.Session") oMAPI.Logon
```

In the previous example, oMAPI is declared as an object and the CreateObject method creates an object of the type specified in its string literal parameter, in this case a MAPI session object. MAPI.Session is referred to as the ProgID and is associated with the object's CLSID in the system Registry. At runtime, this application will dynamically determine the CLSID of the COM object and bind the results to the oMAPI variable.

Optionally, you can use reflection to perform late binding to COM objects in Visual Basic. NET. Reflection is the .NET way to late-bind to objects and is not limited to COM objects. Listing 9.7 uses reflection to late-bind to CDO and call the Logon method.

**LISTING 9.7**   Use Reflection to Late-Bind to a COM Object and Call its Methods and Properties

```
Dim oCDO As Object
Dim oCDOType As Type

Try
```

**LISTING 9.7** Continued

```
        oCDOType = Type.GetTypeFromProgID("mapi.session")
        oCDO = Activator.CreateInstance(oCDOType)    oCDOType.InvokeMember("Logon", _
                Reflection.BindingFlags.Default _
                Or Reflection.BindingFlags.InvokeMethod, _
                Nothing, _
                oCDO, _
                Nothing)
Catch
        MessageBox.Show("Can not call CDO")
End Try
```

As you can see, CreateObject is a much cleaner implementation of late binding and without a doubt you should use it whenever possible. Reflection, however, is a very powerful feature of .NET; I encourage you to leverage it within your applications.

## Using and Creating Primary Interop Assemblies

If you develop software that uses COM objects supplied by third-party vendors, you should make every attempt to use the Primary Interop Assembly (PIA) for those COM objects. A Primary Interop Assembly is a unique, vendor-supplied, RCW for a specific COM type library. It's important to use these RCWs because Visual Studio .NET and TLBImp do not always create the optimum wrapper for the underlying COM object. For example, if you attempt to automatically generate the RCWs for the Microsoft Office COM type libraries, such as Microsoft Office XP, you will find that the RCW you create does not work quite right.

Microsoft provides the PIAs for Microsoft Office XP that have been specifically generated and tested for use by those who want to automate Microsoft products from .NET. In addition, if different developers generate and sign their own interop assemblies for the same COM type library, they create a set of unique types that are incompatible. For that reason there can be exactly one vendor-supplied PIA for any COM type library, which must be signed with a strong name. PIAs are generally installed into the Global Assembly Cache so that they are readily accessible by any .NET application that wants to use the COM type libraries these PIAs represent.

Of course, you can create PIAs for your own COM objects, as demonstrated in Listing 9.8. Typically, you use the TLBImp utility with the /primary command-line switch to create PIAs. You will need to provide a strong name for the PIA, which essentially means you need to provide a cryptographic key to digitally sign the assembly.

**LISTING 9.8**   Using TLBimp to Generate Primary Interop Assemblies

```
tlbimp MyCOMObj.dll /primary ➡
       /keyfile:MyCompany.snk /namespace:MyCompany.MyCOMObj ➡
       /out:MyCompany.MyCOMObj.dll
```

Notice the use of the /keyfile switch; it references a .SNK file that contains the cryptographic information required to provide a strong name for the resulting assembly, MyCompany.MyCOMObj.dll, as specified with the /out switch. By using the /namespace switch, you can provide a .NET namespace that can be used to reference this object.

In order for other developers to use the PIA you just created, you must install and register your PIA. Typically, vendors provide a setup program to install and register the PIAs they provide. Note that PIAs do not need to be registered if you do not plan to use them with Visual Studio .NET. To register a PIA, use the Assembly Registration Tool (Regasm.exe) utility provided with the .NET Framework. The syntax for registration will look similar to the following command line.

```
Regasm MyCompany.MyCOMObj.dll
```

If you are simply distributing your PIAs to computers that will not be using them for development, you need to install the PIAs only in the Global Assembly Cache of the computer using the GACUtil command-line utility provided with the framework.

# Using ActiveX Controls on VB .NET Forms

ActiveX controls are also COM objects and you must rely on COM interop to continue using these controls on your Visual Basic .NET forms. As with other COM objects, an RCW is required to work with ActiveX controls. Again, you have two ways of creating RCWs for ActiveX controls—using Visual Studio .NET or using a command-line utility that ships with the .NET Framework called AxImp.exe.

Let's start with using Visual Studio.NET to create an RCW for an ActiveX control, which in this case is the Microsoft MAPI Session control. This control allows you to perform MAPI operations through a form control versus using CDO's object model. Perform the following steps to add the MAPI Session ActiveX control to your project's toolbox.

1. Open or create a new Visual Basic. NET program and select Add/Remove Toolbox items from the Tools menu. This will display the Customize Toolbox dialog box, as shown in Figure 9.3.

2. Click the COM Components tab in the Customize Toolbox dialog box to display a list of all of the ActiveX controls registered on your computer.

3. From the list of ActiveX controls, click the check box next to the Microsoft MAPI Session Control, version 6.0.

4. Click OK to add the control to your toolbox.

5. Drag the control to a form.

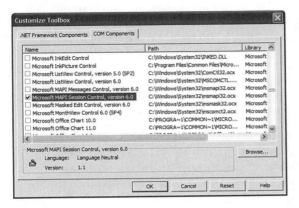

**FIGURE 9.3** Adding an ActiveX control to the Visual Studio .NET control toolbox.

Once you have dragged the control to the form, you can set its properties and call its methods as you normally would any control.

Just as when you added a COM object reference to your project, an RCW was created to help facilitate communication between your managed application and the ActiveX control. If you look under References in your Solution Explorer, you should see two new entries—AxMSMAPI and MSMAPI. Windows forms can be a host only to Windows Forms controls, which are derived from `System.Windows.Forms.Control`. The AxMSMAPI assembly is a Windows Forms proxy for ActiveX controls and allows the underlying ActiveX control to act as a Windows Forms control in a .NET application. The MSMAPI reference is the RCW for the underlying ActiveX control and is responsible for calling the ActiveX control directly. Visual Studio .NET also copies these files into your project's directory, thus making them local to your project.

The AxImp utility, shipped in the .NET Framework SDK, is another method you can use to create wrappers for you ActiveX controls so that they can be consumed by your .NET forms. Just like TLBImp, AxImp is a command-line utility that is considerably more functional than Visual Studio when it comes to the creation of the wrapper assemblies. With AxImp, you can specify the name and location of the output files as well as provide a strong name for your wrapper assemblies, as shown below. In the example, the AxMSMAPI and MSMAPI assemblies are created in `C:\Windows\System32` directory and the assemblies are given a strong name using the cryptographic information provided in the keyfile called MyCompany.snk. Similar to RCW created with TLBImp, if you want to have these assemblies made available to many different .NET applications, you can install the assemblies into the GAC.

```
aximp c:\windows\system32\msmapi32.ocx /keyfile:MyCompany.snk
```

# Exposing VB .NET Objects to COM Clients

The majority of this chapter has dealt with the most common use of COM Interop—consuming COM objects from managed applications. There will be times, however, when the opposite will be true—unmanaged applications want to call managed code as they would any other COM object. Exposing .NET classes as COM objects enables any unmanaged COM client to use managed classes as COM servers. This type of functionality is useful on many levels, such as during the conversion of large, complex Windows DNA-based applications comprised of many COM objects running on one or more computers. Having the capability for .NET classes to present themselves as COM objects might allow you to re-implement parts of your application one component at a time. To the clients of the COM object you are migrating, the implementation appears to have changed. However, the interfaces would stay the same and thus be transparent.

At the heart of this is the COM Callable Wrapper (CCW). The job of the CCW is to create the COM interfaces that clients expect to find—IUnknown (which every COM object must have) and IDispatch (which allows clients to be late bound and accessible through scripting languages such as VBScript). Not only does the CCW expose IUnknown and IDispatch, it also exposes some additional COM interfaces such as ISupportErrorInfo, IProvideClassInfo, IDispatchEx, IconnectionPointContainer, and IObjectSafety.

Each of these interfaces has specific uses by COM clients. The CLR will only create one instance of a CCW for a .NET class. Like all COM objects, the CCW will maintain a reference count to track the clients who have established references to it. When the reference count on the CCW reaches zero, it will be terminated. Because it is allocated from an unmanaged heap, the CCW will be terminated immediately. When the CCW is released, the reference to the .NET object will also be released. If no other managed applications are using this instance of the .NET object, it will be collected during garbage collection.

Similar to an RCW, one of the biggest responsibilities of the CCR is to marshal arguments between unmanaged and managed environments. This is especially true for return values because COM clients expect to receive HRESULT codes from method calls. To solve this problem, the CCW passes return values into an additional argument passed to the method. It must, however, convert runtime exceptions to HRESULT codes, so it must catch all exceptions generated by the runtime and map them against negative HRESULT values for COM clients to understand.

The process of exposing a .NET component to COM clients is quite simple but involves a number of steps. Instead of showing you the easy way first, let's start by showing how you would accomplish this manually. First, create a new class that looks similar to the class in Listing 9.9.

**LISTING 9.9**   A Simple Class with Public Members that Will Be Exposed to COM Clients

```
Public Class COMClass
    ' A public variable
    Public PublicField As Double
    ' A private variable
    Private PrivateField As String

    ' A read-write property
    Property ReadWriteProperty() As String
        Get

        End Get
        Set(ByVal Value As String)

        End Set
    End Property

    ' A read-only property with one argument
    ReadOnly Property ReadOnlyProperty(ByVal Index As Integer) As Boolean
        Get

        End Get
    End Property
End Class
```

This class really doesn't do much, but it demonstrates how you can make it accessible to COM clients.

In order for COM components to consume your .NET component, you need to specify some additional attributes of your class. Use the COMClass attribute to specify the CLSID, InterfaceID (IID), and EventsID for your class. Each of these IDs is represented with a GUID or Globally Unique Identifier (a 128-bit number that is intended to be unique for every component). Next, add public constants to your code to assign GUIDs to each of the required COM IDs, as demonstrated in Listing 9.10.

**LISTING 9.10**   Using the COMClass Attribute to Assign Necessary GUIDs for the Exposed COM Interface.

```
<ComClass(COMClass.ClassId, COMClass.InterfaceId, COMClass.EventsId)> _
Public Class COMClass
    Public Const ClassId As String = "39696648-9058-441d-88C4-52E9A04C8A5B"
    Public Const InterfaceId As String = "57E40850-B6C6-4786-954D-402A0A43D0D6"
    Public Const EventsId As String = "E5580E61-8497-4523-AB47-E1C37E2C92F2"
```

The compiler will then automatically include metadata required to expose your .NET class to COM clients using the information provided to the COMClass attribute. These values are actually defined within the class and are string representations of GUIDs. Although I've provided some GUIDs already in my sample code, you should use the Create GUID utility launched from Visual Studio's Tools menu to create GUIDs for the ClassID, InterfaceID, and EventsID constants.

Next, ensure that the "Register for COM Interop" option is selected in the Project Properties dialog box (see Figure 9.4).

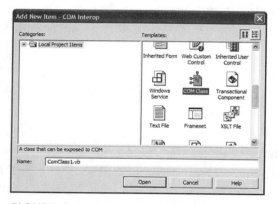

**FIGURE 9.4**    Setting the properties of a project to automatically register for COM Interop.

This setting will cause Visual Studio .NET to create a type library (.tlb file) and register your new COM component when you build your .NET component.  To register your .NET assembly with COM on other machines, you can manually use the RegAsm tool (Register Assembly) that is included with the .NET Framework install. RegAsm takes the name of a DLL containing an assembly and registers all the classes that the DLL contains. This is similar to using the RegSvr32 on COM objects, but for .NET components instead of COM components.

You can also use RegAsm to automatically create a .REG file (a Registry import file) that contains all of the Registry entries that RegAsm would create to register the DLL using the /regfile option. This switch, however, cannot be used in conjunction with the /tlb switch. For example, the following command line will generate a file called ccwproject.reg.

```
regasm ccwproject.dll /regfile
```

The resulting .REG file can then be used with installation routines to help distribute your COM enabled assemblies.

Once you have completed all of these steps, you can now consume your .NET object from any COM client as you would any other COM object. You can unregister your .NET component by using RegAsm with the /u switch.

Of course, there are a few additional shortcuts you can take to make this a bit less painful. First, instead of adding all of the additional attributes required to instruct the compiler to add COM relevant metadata to the assembly by hand, you can use the COM class template when adding a class you want to be available to COM clients. Perform the following steps to use the COM Class template:

1. Create or open a project.

2. From the Project menu in Visual Studio, select Add Class to display the Add New Item dialog box.

3. From the Add New Item dialog box, select the COM Class template from the list of templates (as depicted in Figure 9.5), and provide a name for the new class.

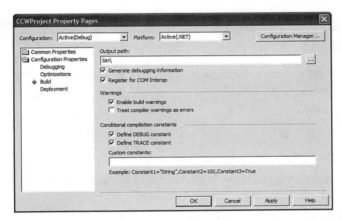

**FIGURE 9.5** Using the COM Class template that comes with Visual Studio .NET.

You will notice that the template automatically adds the appropriate attributes and provides default values for the GUID-based IDs used by the COMClass attribute.

With the "Register for COM Interop" option set, every time you build your assembly, Visual Studio will do all of the dirty work for you. Of course, RegAsm does have more advanced options you can use from the command line so don't be surprised if you still have to use this tool in your projects.

# Some Additional Considerations

The most common problems you will encounter with COM Interop typically surround type conversion. Occasionally, the only way to fix some of these problems is by messing around with the Intermediate Language (IL) directly using a utility called ildasm.exe. In fact, many Primary Interop Assemblies shipped by vendors of COM objects will have probably tweaked the IL of an RCW to either fix slight issues with conversion or to make the RCW easier to consume. This is a non-trivial operation, and I recommend against doing this yourself.

Also, remember that obtaining PIAs for any third-party COM object or ActiveX control is essential. The PIAs for Microsoft Office XP are good examples of essential vendor provided wrappers. Without these, you will find numerous issues with trying to automate Microsoft Office XP from a .NET application. The good news is that COM objects created with Visual Basic 6.0 interact very well with .NET applications, making the migration of your old applications a scenario you should not fear. It is recommended, however, that you take the time to create and distribute PIAs for these objects as vendors would theirs.

# In Brief

This chapter laid the foundation required to begin writing Visual Basic .NET applications that interoperate with COM based applications, which included:

- Defining key concepts and definitions

- Explaining how to access COM objects from Visual Basic. NET applications

- Explaining how to re-use ActiveX controls

- Describing how to make your Visual Basic. NET objects available to unmanaged COM clients

- Underscoring the importance of Primary Interop Assemblies

# Advanced Topics

## What Makes These Topics Advanced?

I placed these topics together in this chapter for two reasons: Visual Basic 6.0 developers use them less frequently, and covering them in detail would take more room than is available. Regardless, a quick introduction now will save you a lot of trouble if you need to work within any of these areas in your Visual Basic .NET code. As with all of the chapters in this book, if you go to `http://www.duncanmackenzie.net/kickstartvb`, you will find a detailed listing of additional resources related to each specific chapter.

## Introducing ASP.NET and Web Forms

Web development was not a big part of Visual Basic 6.0, although there were a few Web-focused features such as DHTML applications. The Microsoft technology of choice for Web development prior to the release of .NET was Active Server Pages (ASP). You might have written some VB6 COM DLLs to use from an ASP application, but the actual code for the Web pages was usually written using other tools (such as Notepad, Visual Interdev, or even FrontPage). With the arrival of .NET, the situation has really changed, making Web development just another type of project in the set of available applications that you can build with Visual Basic .NET.

ASP.NET, the new version of Microsoft's server-side Web development technology, more closely resembles the Windows development model used in Visual Basic. Now, you can create full Web applications written in Visual Basic .NET built inside of the Visual Studio .NET development environment.

Although building Web applications is an important topic, the world of ASP.NET is still different enough from "regular" Windows development that it would take an entire book to cover properly. In fact, several books dedicated to nothing but ASP.NET already exist, including one in this same "Kick Start" series. For this chapter I am just going to walk you through a simple example, just enough to get you started into the new Web development model.

## SETTING UP AND REPAIRING THE ASP.NET INSTALL

If you install IIS after you have installed Visual Studio .NET 2003, IIS will not be properly set up to work with ASP.NET. Before you uninstall Visual Studio .NET 2003 and start over, there is help. Locate the file aspnet_regiis.exe. It should be located in the directory `\Windows\Microsoft.NET\Framework\v1.1.4322`. Open a command prompt in that directory, and run:

```
aspnet_regiis.exe /i
aspnet_regiis.exe /r
```

The first command line installs the ASP.NET handlers into IIS. The second call likely isn't required, but couldn't hurt. It is used to register ASP.NET with the IIS Metabase (the internal directory IIS uses for configuration). This should be done with the `/i` parameter, but I have seen situations where both calls were required, likely because I have too many versions of .NET on my machine, and I never clean up properly (read: reformat my hard drive) after moving between internal builds of Visual Studio .NET 2003.

Once you have run those commands, ASP.NET should be properly registered, and you should be able to use Visual Basic .NET to create Web applications.

The first step is to make sure you have a Web server that can run an ASP.NET application. In order to create a Web application with Visual Basic .NET, you need access to a computer running IIS 5.0 or above, meaning one of Windows 2000, Windows XP (Professional), or Windows Server 2003. In addition, you need sufficient permissions on the computer hosting the Web site to create new virtual roots (VRoots), because Visual Studio creates a virtual root on the Web server when you create a Web application.

When you create a Web application with Visual Basic .NET, you will have created a number of files in a VRoot. These files are:

- Webform1.aspx—This is the first page created in the Web site. ASP.NET pages, or Web Forms, have the extension .ASPX. You will create your application by adding controls and code to this and future .ASPX pages.

- Web.config—ASP.NET uses a hierarchical configuration system. There are settings defined at the machine level, and each VRoot can override these settings in its own web.config file.

- Global.asax—If you worked with ASP, you know of the global.asa file. This file is used to store event handlers for the VRoot, as well as code you want to access throughout your Web application. For example, when a user first visits a page on your Web site, ASP.NET creates an application and a session to track the user. You can have an event handler inside this file that is called when that happens. Table 10.1 shows some of the events that can be handled in this file.

## TABLE 10.1

**Global.asax Events**

| EVENT | DESCRIPTION |
|---|---|
| OnStart | Occurs when the first user accesses your Web site. |
| OnEnd | Occurs as the application is ending. By default, this occurs 20 minutes after the last user request for any page. |
| BeginRequest | Occurs at the beginning of each user request. |
| AuthenticateRequest | Occurs after BeginRequest; allows the application to identify the user. |
| AuthorizeRequest | Occurs after AuthenticateRequest; allows the application to determine whether the user has permissions for the request. |
| EndRequest | Occurs when all processing for the request is complete. |
| Error | Occurs when an unhandled error occurs somewhere in the application. This is a good event to handle if you want a global error handler for your application. |

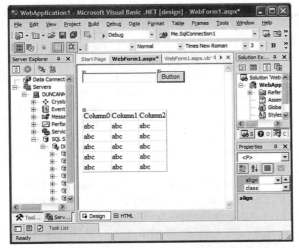

**Figure 10.1** The design experience for Web Form development is much closer to Windows development than ever before.

- Styles.css—Cascading Stylesheet that may be used by the application.

- vsdisco file—Named for the project, this file is rarely used by Web pages, but is more important for XML Web Services. XML Web Services are discussed later in this chapter.

Once the VRoot and project have been created, you will see Webform1.aspx in the Designer. (See Figure 10.1.) Notice that it looks remarkably like a Windows Form. In fact, you build a Web application in the same manner that you build Windows applications: drop controls on the form, double-click to add code, and press F5 to run the application in the Debugger.

When an ASP.NET application runs, you end up viewing the site in a Web browser, whereas all the code executes on the server. Behind the scenes, HTML is generated, some magic happens, and voila! You end up with a Web site (some design skills required).

In my experience, most applications, whether they are Web or Windows based, involve some form of database. The simple ASP.NET sample here displays a listing of data retrieved from a SQL Server database (see Figure 10.2).

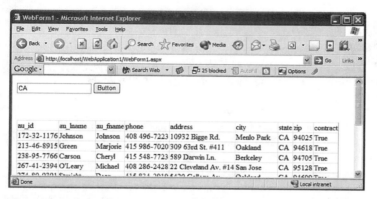

**Figure 10.2**  The standard data example, pulling records out of the Pubs database, is recreated for the Web in this sample.

## DATA BINDING FOR WEB APPLICATIONS

Web Applications in Visual Basic .NET support data binding, but it works in a slightly different way than Windows Forms applications. Data binding for the Web is one-way; the information is pulled out of the data source and used for display, but you have to write your own code to handle putting any user edits back into the database. This style of data binding certainly has its drawbacks, but it does allow you to use a data reader (see Chapter 6 for more info on data readers) as a data source, even though data readers are read-only and forward-only.

To build this Web page for yourself, select the Web Form (page) created when you created your Web Form project. Change the pageLayout to FlowLayout; it will behave more like a regular Web page when you have that setting chosen. Next, add a textbox, a button, and a data grid (all from the toolbox), producing results similar to Figure 10.1. Don't change any of the default names (TextBox1, Button1, and DataGrid1) and double-click the button to enter code view right inside the button's click event handler. Enter the code shown in Listing 10.1 to connect to a database, execute a query, pull the results back into a data reader and bind that reader to the data grid.

**LISTING 10.1**  Retrieving and Displaying Data

```
If Me.TextBox1.Text.Trim.Length = 2 Then
    Dim conn As New SqlClient.SqlConnection( _
        "Integrated Security=SSPI;" & _
        "Data Source=(local);" & _
        "Initial Catalog=pubs;")

    Dim cmdAuthors As _
        New SqlClient.SqlCommand( _
        "SELECT * FROM authors WHERE state = @state", _
        conn)
    cmdAuthors.Parameters.Add("@state", _
        SqlDbType.Char, 2).Value = _
        Me.TextBox1.Text
    conn.Open()
    Dim authorsDR As SqlClient.SqlDataReader
    authorsDR = cmdAuthors.ExecuteReader
    Me.DataGrid1.DataSource = authorsDR
    Me.DataGrid1.DataBind()
    conn.Close()
End If
```

Now, run the Web Form by pressing F5. A browser window will open, pointing at
http://localhost/webapplication1/webform1.aspx; your application is now running. Enter a
valid state code (2 characters only), CA or OR for example, and click Button1. Clicking that
button sends the page back to the server where the Button1_Click code is executed. The database information is retrieved, the data grid is filled, and then the page is returned to the
browser.

Obviously, this is only the tip of the iceberg. For more on ASP.NET, you should check out
*ASP.NET KickStart*; or the Developer Center on MSDN at http://msdn.microsoft.com/asp.net/.

# Using XML in Visual Basic .NET

XML is not new to Visual Basic programmers; it has been available through a variety of
methods in Visual Basic 6.0 and earlier, but it is quite a bit more prominent within the .NET
Framework. Although you might already have some experience with XML, this section starts
with a brief explanation of the format before getting into the .NET methods for working
with it.

## What Is XML?

Extensible Markup Language (XML) is a way of adding information to text. XML is the current popular term in software—entire companies and product lines have been created or modified just to add XML to the product brochures—and there are many myths and misconceptions about what it can do and is intended to do.

XML is similar to HTML; in fact, they are related. One (overly simplified) way of thinking about XML is that XML is to data (and databases) what HTML is to text. Another way of thinking about XML is that it is like HTML, but you can define your own tags. There are some differences, however. XML is much stricter about what you put into it. Table 10.2 describes some of the more important components of XML files, whereas Table 10.3 describes a few of the rules that apply to an XML file. (Refer to the sample XML file in Listing 10.2 as you go along.)

### TABLE 10.2

**XML File Components**

| ITEM | DISCUSSION |
| --- | --- |
| XML declaration | XML files should start with a line similar to the first line of the sample XML file. This is the XML declaration that identifies the version, and optionally the formatting of the XML document. |
| Element | Elements are the most important part of an XML document. They are composed of a start tag and an end tag. There may be text, or other elements between the two. There are many elements in the sample XML file; for example, book, title, authors, and author are all elements, as are chapters and chapter. |
| Attributes | An attribute is some characteristic of an Element. It is written within an Element's start tag. All attributes must be surrounded in quotes, even if they are numbers. In the sample document, ISBN, count, Id, and name are all attributes. |
| Comments | XML files can include comments. The way you mark a comment is just as with HTML files, you wrap the comment in the characters: <! — and —>. |

### TABLE 10.3

**Rules for XML Documents**

| RULE | DISCUSSION |
| --- | --- |
| There can only be one root element | There must be one, and only one root element for an XML document. For example this is not valid XML:<br>`<author>Duncan Mackenzie`<br>`    <title>Visual Basic .NET KickStart</title>`<br>`</author>`<br>`<author>Erik Porter`<br>`    <title>Visual Basic .NET KickStart</title>`<br>`</author>`<br><br>In the sample XML, the root element is book. |

**TABLE 10.3**

**Continued**

| | |
|---|---|
| Empty elements | If an Element does not contain another element or text, it is empty. Empty elements may be written in one of two forms:<br>`<chapter></chapter>`<br>or<br>`<chapter />`<br><br>This second form is a handy shortcut. Notice that the chapter elements in the XML file use this form. (Even though they include Attributes, they are still considered empty.)<br><br>This is one of the major differences between HTML and XML. If you have worked with HTML, you know that there is a `<br>` element that defines a line break. To use this properly in an XML document, this should be written `<br />`. |
| All elements must be properly nested | Both the start and end tag of an element must be contained by the start and end tag of its parent. So, `<book><title>Visual Basic .NET KickStart</book></title>` is not proper as the close tag for `title` is not within the start and end tags for `book`.<br><br>This type of sloppy coding is acceptable in HTML, however, as you could write something like `<font face="Arial"><b>Some Text</font></b>` and most browsers would interpret it correctly. |
| Well-formed | XML is well-formed if it follows all of these rules. Generally, you will need well-formed XML to use the tools in Visual Basic .NET. |
| Validated | Rather than use any tags in a document, it is often preferred to use a definition of the document. For XML, these are either DTDs (Document Type Definition) or XML Schema (the preferred form of defining documents) documents. These definitions describe the valid tags for a document, ordering of tags, and similar information about what the document should look like. In "real-world" systems, you will likely want to create one or more XML Schemas, defining the types of XML documents your application will process. This allows the various parts of your application to ensure compliance with those Schemas. |

One thing to keep in mind as you work with XML: it is case-sensitive. When you are searching for, or using a particular Element or Attribute, the case must match the version in the document. So, Book, book, and BOOK are three different items as far as XML is concerned.

**LISTING 10.2**   Sample XML File

```xml
<?xml version="1.0" encoding="utf-8"?>
<!—information about this book—>
<book isbn="0-672-32549-7">
    <title>Microsoft Visual Basic .NET 2003 Kick Start</title>
    <authors>
        <author>Duncan Mackenzie</author>
        <author>Andy Baron</author>
        <author>Erik Porter</author>
        <author>Joel Semeniuk</author>
    </authors>
    <chapters>
        <chapter id="1" topic="Introducing Visual Basic .NET" />
        <chapter id="2" topic="Language Changes" />
        <chapter id="3" topic="Building Windows Applications" />
        <chapter id="4" topic="Working with Files" />
        <chapter id="5" topic="Data Binding" />
        <chapter id="6" topic="Data, without the binding" />
        <chapter id="7" topic=" Object-Oriented Programming " />
        <chapter id="8" topic="Custom Controls" />
        <chapter id="9" topic="COM Interop" />
        <chapter id="10" topic="Advanced Topics" />
        <chapter id="Appendix" topic="Upgrade Tools" />
    </chapters>
</book>
```

# How to Use XML in Your Applications

How does XML fit into your applications? Essentially, you can use it in almost any way you want; it is just a file format for storing information. XML can be used for data, configuration, and as a format for moving information between layers of a distributed application. For example, the configuration files used by both ASP.NET and Windows Forms applications are XML files. XML Web Services (as you will see later this chapter) uses XML as the format for moving information to the clients of the Web Service.

Visual Basic .NET provides several ways of directly working with XML, although many other activities (such as Web Services and Configuration files) also handle XML. This section takes a look at only one of the more common methods, using the DOM (Document Object Model) method. It is worth noting that there are also the reader/writer and serialize/deserialize methods.

For a Visual Basic 6 developer who has used MSXML before, using the DOM will seem quite natural. This is because both MSXML's DOMDocument, and Visual Basic .NET's System.Xml.DomDocument are both based on the recommended model for dealing with XML, as defined by the W3 organization (see http://www.w3.org).

For the DOM (either MSXML's DOMDocument object or System.Xml.DomDocument), an XML document is a collection of nodes. These nodes form a tree, with a single root node at the base. Each node is of a certain type; such as element, attribute, text, or comment. When writing, you create nodes, and add them to the tree. Reading works by walking the list of child nodes of the root, and then their child nodes, and so on, very similar to the way one would work with a directory tree on a hard drive.

## Using DOM to Write Out XML

In order to demonstrate the use of the XMLDocument to read and write an XML file, Listing 10.3 shows the code used to write out the Book XML file shown earlier (in Listing 10.2).

**LISTING 10.3**   XMLDocument Exposes the Node Hierarchy of an XML File

```
Dim myDoc As New Xml.XmlDocument

myDoc.AppendChild( _
    myDoc.CreateXmlDeclaration( _
    "1.0", "UTF-8", String.Empty))


myDoc.AppendChild( _
    myDoc.CreateComment( _
    "information about this book"))

Dim rootBook As Xml.XmlNode = _
myDoc.AppendChild( _
myDoc.CreateElement("book"))
rootBook.Attributes.Append( _
    myDoc.CreateAttribute("isbn"))
rootBook.Attributes( _
    "isbn").Value = "0-672-32549-7"
```

**LISTING 10.3**   Continued

```vb
Dim title As Xml.XmlNode
title = rootBook.AppendChild( _
    myDoc.CreateElement("title"))
title.InnerText = _
    "Microsoft Visual Basic .NET 2003 Kick Start"
Dim authors As Xml.XmlNode _
    = rootBook.AppendChild( _
    myDoc.CreateElement("authors"))
Dim Duncan, Andy, _
    Erik, Joel As Xml.XmlNode

Duncan = authors.AppendChild( _
    myDoc.CreateElement("author"))
Andy = authors.AppendChild( _
    myDoc.CreateElement("author"))
Erik = authors.AppendChild( _
    myDoc.CreateElement("author"))
Joel = authors.AppendChild( _
    myDoc.CreateElement("author"))

Duncan.InnerText = "Duncan Mackenzie"
Andy.InnerText = "Andy Baron"
Erik.InnerText = "Erik Porter"
Joel.InnerText = "Joel Semeniuk"

Dim chapters As Xml.XmlNode _
= myDoc.CreateElement("chapters")

rootBook.AppendChild(chapters)

Dim chapterElements(10) As Xml.XmlElement

For i As Integer = 0 To 10
    chapterElements(i) = _
        myDoc.CreateElement("chapter")
    With chapterElements(i)
        .Attributes.Append( _
            myDoc.CreateAttribute("id"))
        .Attributes("id").Value = _
            CStr(i + 1)
        .Attributes.Append( _
```

**LISTING 10.3**  Continued

```
            myDoc.CreateAttribute("topic"))
    End With
    chapters.AppendChild( _
        chapterElements(i))
Next


chapterElements(0).Attributes( _
    "topic").Value = _
    "Introducing Visual Basic .NET"
chapterElements(1).Attributes( _
    "topic").Value = _
    "Language Changes"
chapterElements(2).Attributes( _
    "topic").Value = _
    "Building Windows Applications"
chapterElements(3).Attributes( _
    "topic").Value = _
    "Working with Files"
chapterElements(4).Attributes( _
    "topic").Value = _
    "Data Binding"
chapterElements(5).Attributes( _
    "topic").Value = _
    "Data without the Binding"
chapterElements(6).Attributes( _
    "topic").Value = _
    "Object-Oriented Programming"
chapterElements(7).Attributes( _
    "topic").Value = _
    "Custom Controls"
chapterElements(8).Attributes( _
    "topic").Value = _
    "COM Interop"
chapterElements(9).Attributes( _
    "topic").Value = _
    "Advanced Topics"

chapterElements(10).Attributes( _
    "id").Value = _
    "Appendix"
```

## LISTING 10.3   Continued

```
chapterElements(10).Attributes( _
    "topic").Value = _
    "Upgrade Tools"

Dim myWriter As New _
    Xml.XmlTextWriter( _
    "C:\thisbook.xml", _
    System.Text.Encoding.UTF8)

myWriter.Formatting = _
    Xml.Formatting.Indented
myDoc.Save(myWriter)
myWriter.Close()
```

The code in Listing 10.3 creates an XML document one piece at a time, creating each element and then assigning attributes and text values as required. It takes quite a bit of code to work with XML files using the DOM, but none of that code is very complicated.

## Reading XML Back In

Reading the sample book XML in using the XMLDocument is a bit easier than writing it out, mostly because you can do your reading in a few simple loops, but the general concept for reading is the same as for writing. Listing 10.4 shows how to use the XMLDocument class to read values out of an XML file.

## LISTING 10.4   Reading in XML Using XMLDocument Requires Traversing the Hierarchy of Nodes

```
Dim myDoc As New Xml.XmlDocument
myDoc.Load("c:\thisbook.xml")

Dim book As Xml.XmlElement
book = myDoc.DocumentElement()
Debug.WriteLine("ISBN: " _
    & book.Attributes("isbn").Value)

Dim title As Xml.XmlElement
title = book.Item("title")
Debug.WriteLine(title.InnerText)

Debug.WriteLine("Authors:")
Dim authors As Xml.XmlElement
authors = book.Item("authors")
```

**LISTING 10.4**  Continued

```
For Each node As Xml.XmlNode _
    In authors.ChildNodes
    If node.Name = "author" Then
        Debug.WriteLine(node.InnerText)
    End If
Next

Debug.WriteLine("Chapters:")
Dim chapters As Xml.XmlElement
chapters = book.Item("chapters")

For Each node As Xml.XmlNode _
    In chapters.ChildNodes
    If node.Name = "chapter" Then
        Debug.WriteLine( _
            node.Attributes("id").Value)
        Debug.WriteLine( _
            node.Attributes("topic").Value)
    End If
Next
```

# XPath and XSLT

This section barely scratched the surface of working with XML with Visual Basic .NET. As you scan the documentation, you will also hear of two other major XML standards—XPath and XSLT.

XPath is a way of querying XML documents. It is similar to querying a hard drive with a path in that it allows you to describe the navigation to a particular node in a document. Listing 10.5 shows how an XPath query could be used to retrieve all of the chapter numbers from the sample XML file.

**LISTING 10.5**  XPath Is Somewhat Like SQL for XML, it Allows You to Query for the Portion of the XML Hierarchy You Are Interested In

```
Dim myDoc As New Xml.XmlDocument
myDoc.Load("c:\thisbook.xml")

Dim chpts As Xml.XmlNodeList = _
    myDoc.SelectNodes( _
    "/book/chapters/chapter")
For Each nd As Xml.XmlNode In chpts
```

**LISTING 10.5**   Continued

```
      Debug.WriteLine( _
          nd.Attributes("id").Value)
  Next
```

XSLT, or Extensible Stylesheet Language Transformations, is a means of converting an XML document to something else (different XML, HTML, text, and so on). In one sense, it is a programming language, just a rather different looking one. With XSLT, you define a number of templates that describe what to look for, and what to do once that is detected. When transforming, each of these templates replace the searched for text, and produce their output. Often used to transform XML into other formats of XML or into HTML for display, XSLT is a powerful, albeit slightly opaque tool in your XML workbench. You can either ignore it, or spend the time to learn it, as you choose.

# Learning About Web Services

Web Services are applications that exist on a network. They communicate using standard Internet communication protocols (HTTP) via XML (rather, one particular dialect of XML called SOAP). The main benefit of Web Services over other means of distributing applications is that Web Services are not exclusive to any one platform or toolset. Web Services enable communication between different platforms, operating systems and/or programming languages. They are a simple, but powerful concept that allows developers to interconnect systems, even systems written using different tools and technologies.

## Using a Web Service

Before you create a Web Service, you will use one first, in this case one of the Web Services made available at http://www.gotdotnet.com. In this case, you will use simple Math Web Service at http://samples.gotdotnet.com/quickstart/aspplus/samples/services/MathService/VB/MathService.asmx.

Open the URL in a browser, and you will see the page shown in Figure 10.3. This is a page generated automatically by the Web Service; you will see later how little you will need to do to make it work.

Click one of the methods to view a Web Form allowing you to test the method. Again, this page is automatically generated by .NET, no effort on your part. Notice that in addition to the form, there is documentation illustrating how to program against this Web Service. This will enable people to call your service, showing them what a correct call and return look like. To try the service, enter some values for the selected method and click Invoke. You should end up with XML, similar to the contents of Listing 10.6, containing the result.

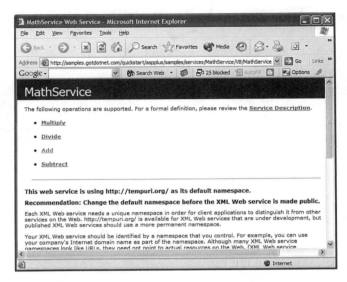

**Figure 10.3** When you create a Web Service using .NET, the test page is created for you.

**LISTING 10.6** XML Result from Calling the Add Function

```
<?xml version="1.0" encoding="utf-8"?>
<float xmlns="http://tempuri.org/">7</float>
```

Although the page created for the ASMX file is useful for testing, your users will not be using it to access your service. Instead, you will create a client (either a Windows Form or Web Form) that will communicate with the Web Service. Communication between this client and the Web Service works through an intermediate class, also known as a proxy. The proxy class, which Visual Studio generates for you when you add a Web Reference to your project, enables your code to call a Web Service as if it were just a regular object.

To try a Web Service from your own code, follow these steps:

1. Create a new Windows Application called MathClient. You will use this application to test the Web Service.

2. Add a Web reference by right-clicking the MathClient project and selecting Add Web Reference. You should see the dialog box in Figure 10.4.

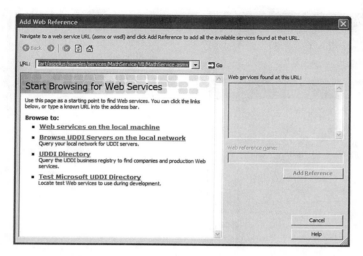

**Figure 10.4**    Use the Add Web Reference dialog box to add Web Services into your projects.

3. Enter the URL for the Math Service into the Address field, and click the Goto button (the green arrow). On the left side of the dialog box, you should see the initial form you saw earlier, followed by an item in the right side, and the Add Reference button should become enabled.

4. Click the Add Reference button to add a reference to this service to your project.

Although the Add Web Reference dialog box shows you nothing but pretty Web pages, it is really working with something a bit more complicated. To see the "real" information being used when you added this Web Service reference, enter the URL for the math service into a Web browser, but this time append ?wsdl to the end of it. The result (see Figure 10.5) will be the XML specification for the Web Service, which is not quite as pretty as the normal display but it is very informative.

This is the WSDL for the Math service (see the sidebar, "More Acronyms Than You Can Shake a Stick At") and it defines the properties and methods available from a Web Service.

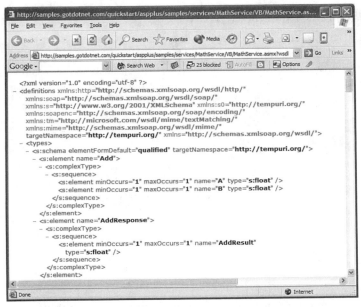

**Figure 10.5** The Web Service Description Language (WSDL) view of a Web Service is used by Visual Studio to create a local proxy of all of the Web Service's methods.

## SHOP TALK

### MORE ACRONYMS THAN YOU CAN SHAKE A STICK AT (MATYCSASA)

One thing XML has plenty of is acronyms. Once you start reading anything on XML, you might begin to doubt that such things as vowels exist. XML, SOAP, WSDL, and UDDI are just a few of the letters you may become familiar with as you drill into Web Services. For most Visual Basic .NET developers, though, these acronyms are optional reading. Visual Studio .NET 2003 makes working with Web Services as easy as dealing with any other component, and the XML fades into the background as an implementation detail. If, however, you like to know what you are playing with, here is a quick primer on these acronyms, and a few non-acronyms you will be hearing in the near future.

- XML—See the previous section. Extensible Markup Language is a means of encoding data, to include information about the data. It looks like, and is related to, HTML.

- SOAP—A dialect of XML. That is, SOAP (not actually an acronym as it doesn't stand for anything anymore, but it used to mean Simple Object Access Protocol) is XML that complies with a specific Schema. SOAP is a means of providing a standard means of communicating between calls. You can think of it as a way of calling objects and their methods remotely, conceptually similar to DCOM.

- WSDL—Another dialect of XML. WSDL (Web Services Description Language) is a means of describing the functionality provided by a Web Service. In one sense it is very similar to the idea of IDL (Interface Definition Language) used by COM in their type libraries. WSDL describes the available methods, and their parameters. As Visual Studio .NET 2003 generates WSDL documents based on a Web Service, you may never need to generate a WSDL document. However, you should have some knowledge of the information in a WSDL document.

- UDDI—Universal Definition, Discovery, and Integration is (ready for this?) yet another XML dialect. In this case, UDDI is a query mechanism, and a directory of Web Services. A number of companies have together created the UDDI organization (http://www.uddi.org). Some of these companies offer directories of Web Services, some using XML Web Services, but also including other, non-SOAP-based services. Using UDDI, you can query these directories to find providers of Web Services.

Once you add the Web Reference to the Math Web Service, you can use it just like any other .NET class.

5. On your Windows Form (Form1), add a pair of text boxes and a button. Using those controls, the newly added Web Service, and the code from Listing 10.7, you can add the contents of the two text boxes together and display the result in a message box.

**LISTING 10.7**   Once You've Added a Reference to a Web Service, Using it Isn't Any Different than Any Other .NET Class

```
Private Sub Button1_Click( _
        ByVal sender As System.Object, _
        ByVal e As System.EventArgs) _
        Handles Button1.Click

    Dim myMath As New _
        com.gotdotnet.samples.MathService
    MsgBox(myMath.Add( _
            CSng(TextBox1.Text), _
            CSng(TextBox2.Text)))
End Sub
```

Note that the namespace for your newly added Web Service defaults to the reverse of its Internet domain, although you can specify a different name in the Add Web Reference dialog box. Reversing the Internet domain is a pretty good way to name your Web Services though, as namespaces are generally listed in order from most general to most specific, which is what you get when you reverse an Internet domain name as well.

If you want, you can write additional code to try out the other functions available through the Math Web Service, but the general concept is the same no matter which service or function you are using.

## Creating a Web Service

You create a Web Service by creating a Web Service project in Visual Basic .NET, which is really just a variation on a Web Application and requires the same things (creates a new VRoot on a Web server, and so on). When you create a new Web Service project, you will start out with a single .ASMX file, which represents your new service. Within that file you can add new methods just like a regular class, but with one exception; if you add a <WebMethod()> attribute to a method in this class, it will be exposed as a Web Service.

To try this out for yourself, create a new method that returns the current date and time and mark it with the WebMethod() attribute (as shown in Listing 10.8).

**LISTING 10.8**   Creating a Web Service Is a Simple Task When You Are Using Visual Basic .NET

```
<WebMethod()> _
Public Function GetCurrentTime() As Date
    Return Date.Now
End Function
```

Once you have created that method, if you press F5 to run your code, you will see the test page of your new Web Service. As with the Math service from GotDotNet, even with only a few lines of code the underlying functionality in ASP.NET has provided you with a working "home page" for your Web Service and a test page for each method you have created.

## SHOP TALK

### SHOULD I USE WEB SERVICES EVERYWHERE?

When developers hear the noise coming out of Redmond, and see just how easy it is to create and use Web Services, they want to use Web Services everywhere in their applications. In fact, I have seen some applications where all communication between the components is via Web Services. The argument these people use is that it gives the benefit of having a single method of creating, discovering, and calling the various parts of their application. Although this is undeniable, it is also undeniable that they are adding a huge amount of overhead to their application. Each time a Web Service is called:

- The parameters must be converted to XML
- The XML must be moved to the other component

- The XML must be converted into .NET types
- The function is called
- The result must be converted to XML
- The XML must be moved to the other component
- The XML must be converted to .NET types
- The original function now has its result

A lot happens when you call a Web Service!

So, when should you use a Web Service? I find it easiest if you think of Web Services as another user interface. Just as you might have a Web user interface that people can browse to, or a Windows interface people can use from their desktops, you can have a Web Service interface other applications can use. Use a Web Service when:

- You will be communicating with another application
- You need to communicate across the Internet
- You need to communicate with code written on another platform (non-.NET)

# In Brief

This chapter presented quite a few new concepts across a range of technologies. Among the important points of the chapter were:

- ASP.NET is the new server-side Web development platform in .NET.

- Web Forms are designed and coded in a very similar manner to Windows Forms.

- XML is a flexible file format for storing structured data, and the System.XML namespace contains many classes for creating and using this format.

- Web Services allow application services to be exposed across a network using a standards-based protocol and format.

# The Upgrade Challenge

For new development projects, there are many reasons to use Visual Basic .NET rather than Visual Basic 6.0. But what if you are charged with maintaining an existing code base that was written in Visual Basic 6.0? Most companies can't afford to spend the time and money required to scrap everything and start over. So, you need to decide what code and components to upgrade, what to maintain in Visual Basic 6.0, and how to do it. There are no easy answers, but there are tools that can help make the task more manageable.

## Deciding Whether to Upgrade

The Common Language Runtime provides a managed execution environment with strong typing and managed memory allocation and deallocation. This imposes certain restrictions that result in improved overall system stability, performance, scalability, and security. In addition, Visual Basic .NET modernizes the Basic programming language by adding first-class object-oriented programming features and strong typing, making it the equal of any modern object-oriented language. However, these dramatic new capabilities also mean that upgrading from Visual Basic 6.0 to Visual Basic .NET is not a trivial undertaking.

Microsoft has redesigned and restructured Visual Basic, resulting in broken compatibility with Visual Basic 6.0. Many of the most compelling new features in .NET could not have been added without breaking compatibility. The following list summarizes some of the new features available in Visual Basic .NET that are not supported in Visual Basic 6.0:

- Inheritance-based object-oriented programming.

- Rich base class libraries, such as those for working with regular expressions, file I/O, and XML.

- Easy publishing and consumption of XML Web services.

- Interoperability with other .NET languages such as C#.

- New language features, including structured exception handling.

- New Windows capabilities, such as control docking and anchoring and GDI+ graphics.

- XCopy deployment; no registration required.

- A familiar model for building Web applications in ASP.NET, using forms, controls, and events.

- Improved data access and data marshaling with ADO.NET.

- A robust security model that includes code access permissions.

The price you pay for all this is that much of your old code won't work as it did before. You need to carefully weigh your options before plowing ahead with a migration plan.

## Some Applications May Not Warrant Upgrading

When considering whether to upgrade your Visual Basic applications, it is important to keep in mind that upgrading to Visual Basic .NET is optional. It is likely that you have at least some applications that you will never upgrade. Some applications won't benefit from the new features in Visual Basic .NET. You'll need to evaluate each application to see whether it's worth the time and money that upgrading will inevitably cost.

If you or your developers had the foresight—and the resources—to create n-tier architectures, with presentation code, business logic, and data access code separated into loosely coupled components, you can consider leaving some components as is. Visual Basic .NET enables you to reference and work with middle tier or data access components that were built using Visual Basic 6.0. In this scenario, you might need to upgrade only the presentation code at first.

## Consider the Cost/Benefit Ratio

Carefully consider the benefits of an upgrade. Clearly, .NET is the future of Windows and Web development on the Microsoft platform. What other potential benefits exist? Scalability? Maintainability? Security? You'll need to weigh these against the costs of the upgrade.

Even if the cost of the upgrade is high, you might still decide to migrate simply to take advantage of the new capabilities in the .NET platform.

There are several cost factors to consider when deciding whether to upgrade.

### Language Differences

Visual Basic .NET expands the language in a significant fashion, building on Visual Basic 6.0 by including new keywords, syntactical elements, conditional statements, modifiers, and attributes. Here are a few examples of language features that have changed in Visual Basic .NET:

- All subroutines require parentheses. For example, `MsgBox "Hello World"` must now be `MsgBox ("Hello World")`.

- Subroutine parameters must be qualified by using the `ByVal` or `ByRef` keywords explicitly.

- The syntax for declaring event handlers has been updated, as has the syntax for event parameters.

- All arrays must have a lower bound of zero. This requirement means that you cannot use Option Base 1.

- Upgrading fixed-length strings can cause problems. In Visual Basic 6.0, values assigned to a fixed-length string in a user-defined type were automatically truncated if they were longer than the fixed length. After upgrading to Visual Basic .NET, strings will no longer be truncated, possibly resulting in incorrect results.

- The `Variant` data type has been eliminated. The closest approximation the .NET Framework offers is the `Object` type, which is the base type for all other types.

- The amount of storage allocated to variables declared as `Integer` or `Long` has doubled in Visual Basic .NET.

- Variables declared in a block of code, such as a loop or an `IF` block, are visible only within that block and any block nested beneath it. In Visual Basic 6.0, a variable declared anywhere in a procedure is scoped to the entire procedure.

You will need to locate and modify sections of code that are affected by these changes to avoid errors or unexpected results.

### Architectural Considerations

Visual Basic .NET does not only present a new language. As part of the .NET development platform, it also presents new architectural options. The OOP features of the .NET Framework and the Common Type System, as well as the loosely coupled nature of Web services—both support a component-oriented, interface-based approach to building applications. Although components and interfaces were supported in Visual Basic 6.0, most programmers build monolithic, tightly coupled applications. The more component-oriented and loosely coupled your application is, the easier it will be to upgrade, and the more choices you will have when phasing in the upgrade over time.

In some cases, your application might rely on features that have changed so drastically in Visual Basic .NET that a complete rewrite is your only option. For example, any of the following elements will need to be redesigned in .NET:

- OLE container controls
- Painting functions
- Clipboard code
- Controls and forms collection code
- Property pages

### Web Applications

Although you can upgrade components of Web applications written in Visual Basic 6.0 using the Upgrade wizard (or the new Upgrade Visual Basic 6 Code option in Visual Studio .NET), there is no tool that will tackle the entire application. The architectural differences between Web applications written with ASP.NET and those that were possible with Visual Basic 6.0 are too extreme to be handled by a wizard or code generator. You will probably want to rewrite Web applications from the ground up to take advantage of the new capabilities in ASP.NET.

### Weighing the Benefits of an Upgrade

To enjoy the benefits from moving a Visual Basic 6.0 application to Visual Basic .NET, you will probably need to re-architect and rewrite most of the application eventually. Choosing to upgrade existing code rather than re-writing it from scratch will almost always be a concession to economic imperatives rather than a pure design choice.

However, those economic imperatives are what keep businesses alive. You will find that parts of your applications can successfully be upgraded using the tools available in Visual Studio .NET, and parts can be kept as is, at least temporarily.

In the end, make your decision considering all of your options. Weigh the benefits and costs and look at the return on investment for your organization.

## Planning Your Upgrade

When upgrading an application to Visual Basic .NET, always begin by clearly defining the goals and objectives for the upgrade. Why are you moving to .NET? What do you hope to achieve? Document your choices and the rationale behind them.

# Creating a Plan

Next, create a plan, even if it's simple one. What steps will you take? What activities are required? How much effort will it take? When it's time to start upgrading, begin your upgrade process by attempting to locate and correct any known incompatibilities in your existing Visual Basic 6.0 application. The Code Advisor (which is discussed in more detail later) is a good tool to handle this task. It is best to resolve as many potential problems as possible in your Visual Basic 6.0 application before attempting the upgrade.

You also must understand the dependencies in your application. Which projects depend on other projects? It is much easier to have a Visual Basic .NET front end interfacing with a COM or ActiveX back end, than the other way around. Always begin your upgrade at the client, and work back to dependent projects in an iterative manner.

# Upgrade Options

There are four basic options to consider when constructing your plan:

- *Leave existing code in Visual Basic 6.0.* This is the do-nothing, easiest option. Although you can't take advantage of the benefits of the .NET Framework, you do have a working application that runs on a supported platform.

- *Perform a partial upgrade.* If your application is composed of two component layers, such as an executable file and one or more ActiveX DLLs, you can perform a partial upgrade by selectively upgrading one or more components at a time. This partial upgrade can be a first step toward a full upgrade. This is the most likely scenario for a large-scale legacy application.

- *Perform a full upgrade.* A full upgrade is going to take the most effort and entails not only upgrading code to Visual Basic .NET, but also upgrading all of the technologies to their .NET equivalents. An application that is fully upgraded has no dependencies on ActiveX or COM objects. This option is likely the most attractive for developers, but is also the most challenging for larger, more complex applications, and it is the most expensive.

- *Perform a partial or full upgrade with interoperability.* This middle-of-the-road option typically entails upgrading major portions of the application, while core technologies remain in COM components. This is frequently a good choice for large-scale n-tier applications where a full upgrade is not cost effective, but where the front-end components can benefit from the move to .NET.

# Preparing to Upgrade

To ensure the success of code migration, there are several changes you should make to the existing code.

### Use Option Explicit Everywhere

If you've been using Option Explicit all along, the task of upgrading will be much easier. If not, it's time to bite the bullet and add the missing variable declarations. Visual Basic .NET is a strongly-typed language, and it requires explicitly defined variables.

### Stop Using Default Methods and Properties

Most form controls have a default property that allows direct assignment of values to the control. Visual Basic .NET does away with the concept of default properties. For example, the following Visual Basic 6.0 code sets the Caption property of a Label control:

```
Label1 = "My caption"
```

You should rewrite this as follows:

```
Label1.Caption = "My caption"
```

### Don't Refer Directly to Controls on an External Form

In Visual Basic 6.0, controls on a form are Public in scope, making it easy to directly refer to controls from outside of the form. To make this work in Visual Basic .NET, you can declare controls as Public, but this is not the default behavior. The best solution is to add property procedures to the form that allow outside code to interact with the form controls.

### Don't Use Implicit Form Loading

If you have a form named frmMain, you can load it implicitly in Visual Basic 6.0 by referring to it, as shown in this line of code that both loads and displays frmMain:

```
frmMain.Show
```

A better way to load the form, which also works in .NET, is to declare a form variable, instantiate it, and then use the Show method to display it:

```
Dim frm As Form
Set frm = New frmMain
frm.Show
```

### Declare Variables on Separate Lines

The following variable declaration works in Visual Basic 6.0, but is not supported in Visual Basic .NET:

```
Dim i As Integer, x as Long
```

Furthermore, the following variable declaration works differently in Visual Basic 6.0 and Visual Basic .NET:

```
Dim i, x As Long
```

In Visual Basic 6.0, the variable i is implicitly declared as a Variant, and x as a Long. In Visual Basic .NET, both i and x are declared as Longs using this syntax. To avoid this kind of confusion, explicitly declare each variable on its own line.

### Don't Use Currency and Variant Data Types

Visual Basic .NET does not support either the Currency or Variant data types. You can replace Currency with a Variant and use the CDec function to convert to the Decimal sub-type of Variant. Visual Basic .NET supports the Decimal data type as a native type. As for variants, use them only when necessary. They must be converted to the Object type in Visual Basic .NET. Database code that uses Variant data types to support Null values will need to be rewritten using ADO.NET types that support DBNull.

### Make All Parameters Explicit

In Visual Basic you don't need to specify ByVal or ByRef when declaring parameters for a procedure. In Visual Basic 6.0, the default is ByRef for intrinsic types and ByVal for other types, whereas in Visual Basic .NET, all parameters are ByVal by default. Making all parameters explicitly ByVal or ByRef before you migrate will short-circuit a slew of hard-to-find bugs in your converted code.

### Provide Default Values for Optional Parameters

The IsMissing keyword in Visual Basic 6.0 enables you to test for missing optional Variant parameters. This is often used to supply a default value for missing parameters in code. In Visual Basic .NET, IsMissing is not supported, and you need to explicitly supply a value for optional parameters, as shown in this code sample where a default value of True is supplied for the optional Boolean parameter blnStatus:

```
Private Function IsCustomer(strName As String, _
   Optional blnStatus as Boolean=True)
```

### Use Intrinsic Constants, Not Magic Numbers

If you've coded your application using the intrinsic constants available in Visual Basic 6.0, the conversion process will be much easier. For example, use vbCrosshair, not the underlying value 2. In addition, use the correct constants in context. Visual Basic 6.0 has no notion of strict constant or enumerated type enforcement—the constants are simply placeholders for integers and constants with identical values can be used interchangeably. Properties in Visual Basic .NET that are typed as enumerations must be assigned values from those enumerations—not integers or equivalent values from other enumerations.

### Watch for Implicit Instantiation

In Visual Basic .NET the As New keywordscause immediate instantiation of objects. This is different behavior from Visual Basic 6.0 where the object is instantiated when it is first accessed. For example, this line in Visual Basic 6.0 does not immediately cause the object to be instantiated:

```
Dim obj As New Widget
```

An instance of the object is created only when the object is first accessed later in the code. In Visual Basic .NET, the previous line becomes equivalent to these two lines:

```
Dim obj As Widget
Set obj = New Widget
```

### Declare Variables at the Top of a Procedure

The scoping rules for variables changed between Visual Basic 6.0 and Visual Basic .NET. The following code sample works fine in Visual Basic 6.0, but gives a syntax error in Visual Basic .NET, because the variable intCount is declared inside of a Do loop, and is therefore visible only in that code block:

```
Do
  Dim intCount as Integer
  intCount = intCount + 1
Loop Until intCount > 10
MsgBox intCount
```

This applies to all loops, If statements, Select Case blocks, and error-handling blocks. Declaring all variables at the top of a procedure ensures that they will be available throughout the procedure when converted to Visual Basic .NET.

### Use ADO for Data Binding

If you use data binding in your application, switch any RDO (Remote Data Objects) or DAO (Data Access Objects) code to ADO (ActiveX Data Objects). ADO data binding is supported in Visual Basic .NET, but RDO and DAO are not.

### Remove Deprecated Legacy Code

Many outdated keywords that were supported in Visual Basic 6.0 for backward compatibility are no longer supported in Visual Basic .NET. Some were removed because they lead to confusing or error-prone coding styles. Others are just no longer meaningful in Visual Basic

.NET. The following are examples of language features that are not supported:

```
GoSub... Return
On x GoTo
Let
LSet (for user-defined types)
VarPtr, ObjPtr, StrPtr
```

Other language constructs are converted by the Upgrade wizard, but are not recommended for use in your applications. In Visual Basic 6.0, constructs such as `DefInt` can be used in the `Declarations` section of a module to define a range of variables of a certain type. The use of the following such constructs should be avoided:

```
DefInt, DefStr, DefObj, DefDbl, DefLng, DefBool
DefCur, DefSng, DefDec, DefByte, DefDate, DefVar
```

`Goto` is another language element that has outlived its usefulness by quite a few years. It is still supported in error-handling code, but you should consider changing such code to use structured exception handling with `Try...Catch...Finally` in Visual Basic .NET.

`Imp` and `Eqv` are also no longer supported in Boolean logic constructs.

# The Code Advisor for Visual Basic 6.0

The Code Advisor for Visual Basic 6.0 is an add-in that assists you in making a successful transition to Visual Basic .NET by ensuring that your Visual Basic 6.0 code complies with predetermined coding standards. These standards are based on best practices determined by Microsoft to produce robust and easy-to-maintain code. The Code Advisor enables you to select which set of standards to apply, and one set is focused on addressing upgrade-related problems. You can also add your own rules.

The Code Advisor scans your Visual Basic 6.0 projects, alerting you when issues are present that could prevent a smooth upgrade. Comments are inserted into your code with links to explanatory help topics. The vast majority of upgrade errors and warnings will be prevented if you run the Code Advisor first and follow its recommendations.

## The FixIt Report

When you run the Code Advisor on a project, it also generates a FixIt report, which contains information about issues found by the Code Advisor. The FixIt report is placed in the project directory and is in an XML format that gets rendered as HTML using an included XSL style sheet. The report has three sections:

- *Issues:* This section contains a list of all issues found, in order of severity. Architectural Issues can be complicated or time consuming; Minor Issues are relatively easy to fix in Visual Basic 6.0.

- *Components:* This section of the report contains a list of all modules in the project (forms, classes, .BAS modules) with a count of issues for each module.

- *Rules:* Contains a list of all rules that were used by the Code Advisor to check the code, with a count of issues for each rule.

When running the Code Advisor in upgrade mode, concentrate on the Architectural issues first. These are the issues that might require you to re-architect or make major changes to your project. For example, if your application uses DAO data binding, this will be reported as an Architectural upgrade issue. Fixing this either means re-implementing the data binding as ADO data binding in Visual Basic 6.0, re-implementing the data binding as ADO.NET data binding in Visual Basic .NET, or removing data binding altogether. This might represent a major change to the project. Architectural issues alert you to upgrade issues that can influence whether you continue with the upgrade.

## Running the Code Advisor

The length of time it takes to scan a project using the Code Advisor depends on the size of the project and the number of issues encountered. If you have a large project, you can scan a single file at a time instead of the whole project. Follow these steps to run the Code Advisor on your Visual Basic 6.0 application, after installing the add-in:

1. Open the project in Visual Basic 6.0.

2. Choose File, Make *<projectname>* where *projectname* is the name of your project. Run the application to make sure there are no errors. Then stop the project.

3. Select the Scope drop-down list on the Code Advisor toolbar, and choose Scope: Active Project to scan the entire project or Scope: Active File to scan only the file currently selected in the Project Explorer.

4. Click the Add FixIts button to have the Code Advisor scan the file, add comments, and generate a FixIt report. A progress bar gives an indication of how long the scan will take, and the Cancel button enables you to abort processing if you become impatient.

5. Click the View Fixit Report button to view the report in your browser.

6. Click the Find Next FixIt button to go to the first FixIt comment in your code. Click the FixIt Help button to open the Help topic associated with that FixIt comment, and modify your code accordingly.

Remember to review Severity 1 (architectural) issues first, because they will prevent your project from upgrading.

Some comments suggest optional fixes or fixes that you might choose to ignore. To ignore a FixIt comment and keep from seeing the comment the next time you run the Code Advisor, you can type No in front of the FixIt remark:

```
' NoFIXIT: Use Option Explicit to avoid ...
```

You can also filter out a rule by clicking the Filter FixIt Rules button and deselecting the rule in the Filter FixIt dialog box. This can be a way of improving performance when scanning large projects—the help file suggests which rules are the most time consuming.

Click the Add FixIts button to re-scan the project. The Code Advisor will remove the comments from any fixed issues, and the new FixIt Report will reflect the lower issue count.

You can run the Code Advisor iteratively, reducing the issue count each time as you fix a set of problems.

## Resolving Architectural Issues

Neither the Code Advisor nor the Upgrade Wizard is equipped to deal with major architectural issues in your application.

You'll need to carefully evaluate the architectural issues involved in migrating to Visual Basic .NET. If there are major issues involved, you might find that simply rewriting the application in .NET is more efficient than attempting an upgrade. This is particularly true for fat Visual Basic 6.0 client applications that have business logic and data access code intermingled with presentation code.

It's easier to migrate independent classes to Visual Basic .NET than it is to migrate forms, because the forms model in Visual Basic .NET uses completely different technology. Encapsulate your logic in classes, even if the classes are compiled into VB executables along with forms rather than segregated in separate ActiveX components.

## Upgrading

The Upgrade wizard is invoked whenever you open a Visual Basic 6.0 project in Visual Studio .NET. The wizard makes as few changes to your code as possible while attempting to alter your existing code so it will work in Visual Basic .NET.

## Upgrading from Earlier Versions than Visual Basic 6.0

Although you might be able to successfully upgrade Visual Basic 5.0 projects using the Upgrade wizard (the file format is similar to that of Visual Basic 6.0), you won't be able to upgrade ActiveX controls in the project. Your best bet with older versions of Visual Basic is to upgrade them to Visual Basic 6.0 first, and then run the Upgrade wizard.

## Upgrading Project Groups

Visual Basic 6.0 enables you to create a project group in which multiple projects are compiled and debugged together. The closest thing to a project group in Visual Basic .NET is a solution, which can contain multiple projects. When converting a project group, you will need to convert one project at a time, starting downstream with the most dependent project, and working your way up the dependency hierarchy.

## Upgrading WebClass Projects

The Upgrade wizard that is included with Visual Studio 2003 can upgrade Visual Basic 6.0 WebClass projects (also known as IIS Application projects). This is a new feature in this version of the wizard. The process for upgrading WebClass projects is essentially the same as for any other project type. In addition, you must have Internet Information Services (IIS) installed and running on the upgrade computer, and have Administrative privileges.

When a WebClass project is upgraded, by default the project is created with a new project name of *projectname*.NET (where *projectname* is the name of the Visual Basic 6.0 project). This name is used when naming a new IIS virtual directory, and the virtual directory is automatically configured as an application in IIS.

If the virtual directory name already exists on the http://localhost server, which is typical in a repeat upgrade scenario, a number is appended to the virtual directory and project names in order to ensure uniqueness.

When a Visual Basic 6.0 WebClass project is upgraded to Visual Basic .NET, the .ASP file for the project is upgraded to an .ASPX file. Any references to the .ASP file within an HTML template file are not automatically changed to .ASPX references. These are not upgraded because a template file might contain references to other .ASP files that were not part of the WebClass project.

In addition, when files are copied to the new project directory during upgrade, only HTML template files are copied. Any other .HTML files or image files are not copied to the new directory.

HTML files are added to a Visual Basic .NET project as content files by default. However, when a WebClass project is upgraded, HTML files are added as embedded resources. If you add HTML files to the project after upgrading, you must set their Build Action property to Embedded Resource in order to make them visible to the application.

## Upgrade Wizard Methodology

The wizard works by converting project types to their .NET equivalents and upgrading the code as best it can. For example, Visual Basic 6.0 forms are converted to .NET Windows Forms, and the properties of controls are converted to equivalent properties of the .NET controls.

### What the Wizard Doesn't Handle

However, there are certain Visual Basic 6.0 elements that either have no direct .NET equivalents or that have equivalents that the wizard doesn't attempt to handle. For example, the following items are not upgraded:

- ActiveX documents
- Collection classes
- DDE
- Designers
- Drag and drop
- Generic objects (form/screen/control)
- Graphics statements and graphical controls
- MDI forms
- Sub Main (or default forms)

If you have any of these elements in your project, you can expect to see them listed as errors, warnings, or issues.

## Errors, Warnings, and Issues

Each time you upgrade a project, the wizard upgrades most of the code and objects to Visual Basic .NET. However, not all items can be upgraded and they require manual modification after the wizard has run. The Upgrade wizard inserts comments in your code for Errors, Warnings, and Issues (EWIs). The Upgrade wizard can insert 50 EWIs, grouped into six categories:

- *Upgrade Issues* are inserted into your code whenever the wizard meets code that will cause a compile error. Upgrade issues mark items that you need to fix before the program will run.

- *Upgrade ToDos* let you know when code has been partially upgraded and needs finishing before it will run. This type of issue commonly arises when you declare a variable of a type that contains a fixed-size array.

- *Run-Time Warnings* alert you to behavioral differences between Visual Basic 6.0 and VB.NET. For example, you might have code that doesn't cause a compile error in .NET, but that might yield unexpected results at runtime.

- *Design Issues* identify differences in the design of a form. Design issues are recorded only in the upgrade report, and do not appear in the task list.

- *Upgrade Notes* are memos that alert you whenever code is substantially changed. Unlike the other types of warnings, these notes don't show up in the Task List or in the upgrade report. You need to manually find them.

- *Global Warnings* are inserted into the upgrade report to alert you to major issues that need attention, such as differences in data binding.

Each comment is associated with a hyperlink (Ctrl-click) that takes you to a Help topic explaining the issue. Bear in mind that the Upgrade wizard isn't infallible. Be prepared to thoroughly review and test your code, even after all errors, warnings, and issues have been addressed. Just because your code compiles in .NET, that doesn't mean that it works the way you intended it to. Allow plenty of time for the upgrade process, and be very careful about deploying upgraded code.

## Upgrading with Command-Line Tools

You can also upgrade using a command-line tool, VBUpgrade.exe. The command-line tool uses the same engine as the wizard and produces the same results, except that no report is generated.

Begin by browsing to the folder where VBUpgrade.exe resides; the default location is:

```
C:\Program Files\Microsoft Visual Studio .NET 2003\Vb7\VBUpgrade\
```

Type **vbupgrade** /**?** at the command prompt to see a list of the available switches and parameters.

The following statement upgrades a Visual Basic 6.0 project named Project1 to .NET:

```
vbupgrade c:\Project1.vbp /Out c:\Project1.NET
```

## Upgrading Script Code

If you use Active Server Pages (ASP) or Windows Scripting Host (WSH) and have your Visual Basic code in scripts rather than VB projects, you can't use the Upgrade wizard to convert the script code to Visual Basic .NET. Follow these steps to use Visual Studio .NET 2003's new "Upgrade Visual Basic 6 Code" option to convert your script code.

1. Open a Visual Basic .NET project and position your cursor in a code window where you want the converted script code to be placed.

2. Open your script code in a text editor and copy it to the Clipboard.

3. Select Tools, Upgrade Visual Basic 6 Code from the menu.

4. In the Upgrade Visual Basic 6 Code dialog box, paste your script code.

5. Click the References tab and click Add Reference to add any needed references to COM objects.

6. Click Upgrade to convert your code, which will appear at the cursor location.

You might find that your upgraded script code is rather heavily laden with upgrade issues that need your attention. You will need to make the decision whether it's worthwhile to upgrade your script code or to rewrite it from scratch in Visual Basic .NET.

## Viewing the Upgrade Report

The Upgrade Wizard will place the upgrade report in the new project folder (unless you upgrade from the command prompt, which only creates comments).

In Visual Studio .NET, double-click the _UpgradeReport.htm node in the Solution Explorer to open the upgrade report.

## The Visual Basic 6.0 Compatibility Library

When you upgrade a Visual Basic 6.0 application to Visual Basic .NET, you will notice that there is a reference to the Visual Basic 6.0 Compatibility library (Microsoft.VisualBasic.Compatibility) in your project. The Upgrade Wizard cannot convert all code because of syntactical or architectural differences. The Wizard uses functions in the Compatibility library so that your Visual Basic 6.0 code can run in Visual Basic .NET without extensive modifications. These functions mimic Visual Basic 6.0 behavior while remaining compliant with the common language specification. You might prefer to replace as many of these calls as possible with code that works directly with the native .NET libraries, although this won't necessarily improve performance. The IL code created by the compatibility classes is probably no less efficient than the IL that would be created by native .NET classes.

## Common Issues to Resolve

The following are some commonly occurring issues that you might need to resolve after you have upgraded your project to Visual Basic .NET.

### Default Properties

Default properties are not supported by the common language runtime (other than indexer properties). If the Upgrade wizard can determine a default property, it will modify your code to state the property explicitly in Visual Basic .NET. If the Upgrade wizard cannot determine the property being referenced, it will leave your code as is and insert a warning highlighting the issue for you to resolve.

### Opening and Closing Forms Issues

In Visual Basic 6.0, you can unload a form and later reload it by calling the form's Show method—without the form ever being flushed from memory. In Visual Basic .NET, the Close method for a form calls the Dispose method under the covers, so that the form is automatically garbage-collected. This can cause subtle behavioral differences that might be hard to detect, if your Visual Basic 6.0 code relied on variables retaining values between calls to show the form.

If the form is shown modally, Dispose is not called automatically in .NET when the Close method is invoked. You might need to destroy the object explicitly to clean up resources.

### Error Number Differences

In some cases, errors returned by Visual Basic .NET might be different from those returned by Visual Basic 6.0. If you have error-handling code in your Visual Basic 6.0 application that relies on values returned by Err.Number, this might cause different behavior in your application.

If you depend on the return values from Err.Number in your code, you should carefully test the results and modify your code as necessary. Or better yet, switch to structured exception handling in your converted procedures.

### DataEnvironment Resource Issues

In Visual Basic 6.0, when you close a DataEnvironment object, any open recordsets and connections are automatically closed. When upgraded to Visual Basic .NET, the DataEnvironment becomes a Public member of the DataEnvironment class; recordsets and connections are not automatically closed.

After upgrading, you need to add code that explicitly closes any open recordsets and connections by calling the Dispose method. Or better yet, use native .NET methods for data binding instead of the DataEnvironment.

### Issues with Data Access Code

DAO, RDO, and ADO code all upgrades easily. However, only ADO data binding is supported. If your application relies heavily on data binding, it is probably best to redo the data binding using ADO.NET.

ADO.NET also makes it much easier to work with stored procedures to perform updates. If you have code that cycles through the rows in a recordset to make parameterized calls to stored procedures, you should consider rewriting the code to make use of an ADO.NET DataAdapter.

# Summary

Visual Basic .NET has caused some controversy in the developer community because of the many ways in which it forces developers to modify their Visual Basic 6.0 code. Microsoft made the choice to sacrifice backwards compatibility in order to take full advantage of .NET features.

The positive effect of this choice is that Visual Basic is a first-class language in .NET. There are very few tasks that can be accomplished more easily or more effectively in another language. The old divisions between VB programmers and C programmers are largely a thing of the past, and it is relatively easy for VB programmers to make use of code samples and utilities written for other C#.

The downside of this new parity, however, is that a great deal of Visual Basic 6.0 code will require work to be upgraded successfully to .NET. Companies with a large investment in a Visual Basic 6.0 code base might justifiably resent the economic burden that has been imposed on them, if they want to keep their code current.

But upgrading is not entirely a lost cause. Tools like the Code Advisor and the Upgrade wizard will allow much of your code to move forward in less time than it would take to rewrite it from scratch. In addition, .NET provides excellent interoperability with COM components (ActiveX DLLs) written in Visual Basic 6.0. ADO data access code is also well supported in .NET.

The hard part is deciding what to upgrade and what to recreate from scratch. For most companies this will require some experimentation and perhaps several iterations. Ultimately, the new capabilities of .NET will justify a complete rewrite for many applications, especially Web applications. However, the return on that investment—and the capital available to fund it—might not be adequate to support an immediate and complete break with the past.

If you have followed Microsoft's advice in recent years to partition your applications across multiple tiers of loosely coupled components, you'll find that you can upgrade some of these components while leaving others intact. However, if you have created a monolithic application with lots of internal dependencies, you might need to choose between keeping it running in the old language or starting over with .NET.

The good news is that once you have ramped up your understanding of the features available in .NET, applications are much easier to build, maintain, and deploy than was the case with the older COM-based technologies.

# Index

## Symbols

## A

*How can we make this index more useful? Email us at indexes@samspublishing.com*

*How can we make this index more useful? Email us at indexes@samspublishing.com*

# G

garbage collection, 182

Get method, 177

GetAddress dialog box

    Address class, 94-95

    calling code, 95-96

    closing, 92

    properties, 91-92

    text boxes, 91

GetAge method, 185-188

GetAgeAtDate method, 187

GetAgeInUnits method, 187

GetCurrentDirectory method, 108

GetDecimal method, 160

GetDirectories method, 108

GetDirectoryName method, 110

GetExtension method, 110

GetFileName method, 110

GetFileNameWithoutExtension method, 110

GetFiles method, 108

GetFullPath method, 110

GetHostByName method, 217

GetHostName method, 217

GetOrdinal method, 160

GetPathRoot method, 110

GetTempFileName method, 110

GetTempPath method, 110

GetUserName method, 203

Global statement, 202

Global Warnings, 276

Global.asax file, 245

Goto keyword, 271

groups, upgrading to Visual Basic .NET, 274

# H

Handles statement, 69-73

HasExtension method, 110

Hello World application

    Visual Basic .NET, 65-66

    Visual Basic 6.0, 63-65

help (/?) option (TLBImp.exe), 231

Help window, 20

hiding windows, 13-14

# I

I/O (input/output)

    streams

        BufferedStream object, 100

        CryptoStream object, 100

        defined, 99

        FileStream object, 100

        MemoryStream object, 100

        NetworkStream object, 100

        properties, 100-101

*How can we make this index more useful? Email us at indexes@samspublishing.com*

# O

*How can we make this index more useful? Email us at indexes@samspublishing.com*

TLBImp.exe

    PIAs (Primary Interop Assemblies), creating, 235-236

    RCWs (Runtime Callable Wrappers), creating, 229-231

Toolbox, 15-17

VBUpgrade.exe, 276

# V

**validating properties, 183-184**

**value, passing parameters by, 54-55**

**variables**

    assigning object types to, 46-47

    declaring

        multiple variables, 39

        object initialization, 39-40

        Option Compare statement, 38

        Option Explicit statement, 34-35

        Option Strict statement, 35-38

        variable initialization, 39

    defining

        Option Explicit, 268

        on separate lines, 268-269

        at top of procedures, 270

    FileName, 104

    initializing, 39

    public variables, 177

    strong typing, 33

**Variant data type, 41-42, 269**

**vbupgrade command, 276**

**VBUpgrade.exe, 276**

**Vehicle class, 190**

**/verbose option (TLBImp.exe), 231**

**View menu commands, Code, 104**

**viewing**

    databases with DataView class, 169

    references, 56

**Visual Basic .NET configuration, 7-9**

**Visual Basic .NET editions, 5-6**

**Visual Basic .NET installation, 6-9**

    EULA (End User License Agreement), 7

    Install Now! link, 8

    Product Documentation, 8

    Service Releases, 9

    WCU (Windows Component Update), 6

**Visual Basic .NET Standard, 5-6**

**Visual Basic .NET, upgrading to.** *See* **upgrading to Visual Basic .NET**

**Visual Basic 5.0, upgrading to Visual Basic .NET, 274**

**Visual Basic 6.0 Compatibility library, 277**

**Visual Basic Developer profile, 9-10**

**Visual Studio .NET, 9**

    files, 24-25

    installation, 6-9

        EULA (End User License Agreement), 7

        Install Now! link, 8

        Product Documentation, 8

        Service Releases, 9

        WCU (Windows Component Update), 6

# Your Guide to Computer Technology

**inform IT**

**www.informit.com**

Sams has partnered with **InformIT.com** to bring technical information to your desktop. Drawing on Sams authors and reviewers to provide additional information on topics you're interested in, **InformIT.com** has free, in-depth information you won't find anywhere else.

## ARTICLES

Keep your edge with thousands of free articles, in-depth features, interviews, and information technology reference recommendations—all written by experts you know and trust.

POWERED BY

**Safari**

## ONLINE BOOKS

Answers in an instant from **InformIT Online Books'** 600+ fully searchable online books. Sign up now and get your first 14 days **free**.

## CATALOG

Review online sample chapters and author biographies to choose exactly the right book from a selection of more than 5,000 titles.

**SAMS**    www.samspublishing.com